Leading with Empathy

for dummies®
A Wiley Brand

Leading with Empathy

by Sharon Steed

for dummies®
A Wiley Brand

Leading with Empathy For Dummies®

Published by: **John Wiley & Sons, Inc.**, 111 River Street, Hoboken, NJ 07030-5774, www.wiley.com

For general information on our other products and services, please contact our Customer Care Department within the U.S. at 877-762-2974, outside the U.S. at 317-572-3993, or fax 317-572-4002. For technical support, please visit https://hub.wiley.com/community/support/dummies.

Wiley publishes in a variety of print and electronic formats and by print-on-demand. Some material included with standard print versions of this book may not be included in e-books or in print-on-demand. If this book refers to media that is not included in the version you purchased, you may download this material at http://booksupport.wiley.com. For more information about Wiley products, visit www.wiley.com.

Library of Congress Control Number is available from the publisher.

ISBN 978-1-394-42079-7 (pbk); ISBN 978-1-394-42081-0 (ebk); ISBN 978-1-394-42080-3 (ebk)

SKY10165101_081026

Contents at a Glance

Table of Contents

Introduction

Everything you've been taught about leadership is incomplete. Not necessarily wrong; there's just always been something missing. The frameworks are real and the strategies definitely matter. The vision, the execution, the accountability — all necessary. But none of it is sufficient. Because all of it depends on the one thing that most leadership development programs spend the least amount of time on: humanity.

The leaders who understand this outperform the ones who don't across industries, cultures, and organizational sizes and types. The research is clear: Empathetic leaders produce higher engagement, better retention, more innovation, stronger psychological safety, and — yes — better financial results.

Yet, empathy remains one of the most underdeveloped, undervalued, and misunderstood competencies in leadership today. It gets dismissed as a personality trait, filed under soft skills, and performed in all-hands meetings but forgotten in one-on-ones. It gets celebrated in mission statements and violated in the decisions that actually shape people's experience of work.

This book is about closing that gap.

It doesn't achieve this by making you a more emotionally expressive leader or asking you to process everyone's feelings or sacrifice accountability in the name of kindness, but by giving you a fundamentally different operating system. This system is built on the radical and evidence-backed premise that genuine understanding of the people you lead is not secondary to your job: It *is* your job. Everything else is just strategy. And strategy only works when the people executing it actually want it to work. Welcome to the work that makes everything else possible.

About This Book

Leading with Empathy For Dummies is not your typical leadership book. I know, you hear this all the time. But this time, it's actually true. I'm a keynote speaker, empathy consultant, and person who stutters. All three of those things — especially stuttering — have shaped how I teach empathy to companies and conferences globally. What makes this book special? And what will you take away from the content within?

- **I take empathy seriously as a discipline, and I'll show you how to do the same.** One of the biggest failures of most empathy-in-leadership books is that they treat empathy in two ways: a personality trait or something that can be turned on and off. These are both incorrect, and this book rejects that framing entirely. I break down empathy as a skill. A practice. A set of learnable, repeatable behaviors that improve with effort. The goal of this is to change how you approach this material; instead of "Do I have this?" you will think "How do I build this?"
- **I address the counterarguments head on, and that helps you avoid the pitfalls.** Most books assume the reader already believes their subject matter (in this case, empathy) already matters and just needs the tools. This book walks straight into the strongest arguments — the bias, the burnout, the weaponization, the efficiency critique — and dismantles them not by dismissing them, but by showing that they are arguing against the wrong thing.
- **I discuss empathy and leadership in groups, so you can grow your practice beyond just one-on-one relationships.** Leading groups with empathy is a tricky dynamic to get a handle on. And the centerpiece of much of this is explaining the science behind why empathy in groups fails, and how to combat those failures in real time.
- **I use myself as the case study, so you can fully embrace leading with empathy.** It's commonplace for books like this to use other people as examples to probe their argument. I decided to go down a different route. Why? Because stuttering is more than just the anecdote that warms up the room before the real content starts; it demonstrates, in lived experience, every principle this book provides. Everything from what it costs to lead without empathy to what it takes to build genuine connection across difference to what happens when people feel seen versus when they don't. In this book, there is no distance between the author and the subject, and I hope you'll feel that intimacy throughout.

Foolish Assumptions

While writing this book, I was thinking about you: my reader. I want to make sure you get exactly what you need from my text so you can be more human in the office and in life. With that in mind, one or more of the following assumptions may resonate with you:

- You have this book in your hands right now because you want to be a better leader not just for your organization but for the specific human beings who show up every day and trust you with a significant portion of their lives.
- You remember the best leader you ever had, and you want to be that for someone else.
- You were promoted because you were exceptional at your job, and not necessarily because anyone taught you how to lead the people doing it.
- You care more about your team than you know how to show and you're looking for the language, the tools, and the permission to close that gap.
- You've confused empathy with softness, and you no longer wish to work with an incomplete definition.

Icons Used in This Book

Throughout this book, icons highlight certain types of valuable information that call out for your attention. Here are the icons you'll encounter and a brief description of each:

REMEMBER

The Remember icon marks the information that's especially important to know. To siphon off the most important information in each chapter, head straight to these icons.

TECHNICAL STUFF

The Technical Stuff icon flags information that's good to know but not essential — you can skip over this detail without missing something vital.

TIP

The Tip icon shows hints and shortcuts you can use to make centering your leadership practice around empathy easier.

WARNING

The Warning icon tells you to watch out! It marks important information that may save you headaches and problems in the workplace.

Beyond the Book

In addition to the information and guidance in this book, you can get access to even more help and information online at `Dummies.com`. Check out this book's online Cheat Sheet by heading to `www.dummies.com` and searching for "Leading with Empathy For Dummies Cheat Sheet."

Where to Go from Here

This book was not written to be a linear read; you can jump in and out as you please, exploring the topic at your own pace and in your own time. If you're really itching to get started with being a better empathetic leader, jump to Chapter 7 — where you will define your goals — and then read straight on through Chapters 8, 9, and 10. Those three chapters are centered on the three Key Empathy Behaviors that are foundational in building your empathy practice.

If you'd prefer to focus more on the leadership side of the equation, head to Chapter 11 and tackle the complicated yet powerful topic of empathy in groups. If you already have an empathetic leadership practice that you feel confident in and maybe just want to direct your attention toward adjusting your current viewpoint, check out Part 4. That's where I discuss identifying your gaps as an empathetic leader, assessing your empathetic leadership style, and measuring your impact without compromising your humanity.

And finally, if you want an overview of empathy — the evolution of the word, a quick history lesson, and what a perfect empath looks like in real life — start from the beginning: Chapter 1. The rest of Part 1 takes you through why empathy matters, why some leaders succeed without it (and how that is a shallow success), and nailing down what your style of empathy is. Lastly, I want to impress upon you that you will fail. I do, and I do it all the time. What matters, though, is that you continue to try to iterate, improve, and show up.

1 Discovering Empathetic Leadership

IN THIS PART . . .

Uncover empathy's origin story.

Understand why and how empathetic leadership matters.

Discover why some leaders succeed without empathy and understand why that success is rarely beneficial for the long-term health of the team.

Create your own empathy map to identify your patterns, not just your assumptions.

IN THIS CHAPTER

» Revealing the history of empathy and how it relates to where we are now

» Thinking of leadership as a relationship, not a role

» Considering empathy as a core value

» Confronting the problems of leading without empathy

Chapter 1

Defining Leadership through the Empathy Lens

Why *not* empathy? Well, it has been argued to be inefficient. Critics say that empathetic leaders get taken advantage of and that empathy can lead to burnout. It can be weaponized. And, of course, there's the bias; it's hard to be empathetic when you don't have some baseline understanding of what another person is experiencing.

And you know what? Those people are not wrong. But they're also missing the point. Because here's the thing: These critics are arguing against feeling everything, *not* against understanding people. And those are not the same thing. Defining leadership through the *empathy lens* is a way of seeing people more accurately. It's a useful tool because having accurate information about people leads to better decisions than assumptions do.

So, instead of arguing the case against it, again ask yourself: Why not *empathy?*

Telling the Story of Empathy

The year is 2026 and everything is about the *vibe*, the *aesthetic.* Instagram feeds are curated to within an inch of their lives, with many influencers using very specific filters, lighting and even high-end camera lenses to get just the right shade of moody. TikTokers sing along to trending sounds with such precision that even I — from a time when you dropped everything when your favorite song came on the radio to press "play" and "record" on your boom box so you could have an actual copy of it — am beyond impressed with their dedication. And empathy? Well, it feels like a lost art.

TECHNICAL STUFF

But aesthetic is actually where empathy as we know it originated. In 1873, German philosopher Robert Vischer coined the term *Einfühlung* in his doctoral thesis *On the Optical Sense of Form: A Contribution to Aesthetics.* In this instance, he was referring to art; more specifically, our ability as humans to project our own feelings, movements, and personality on an inanimate object. He called this *aesthetic theory,* and he was deeply fascinated by our ability as humans to enter into a piece of art and feel the emotions the artist intended. Robert actually got this word from his father — novelist, poet, and playwright Friedrick Theodor Vischer — who used the term *Einfühlen* in explorations of idealism relative to architectural form. A quick look at the etymology of the word brings it all together: The German word *ein* translates to *in/into* while *fühlung* translates to *in feeling.*

In 1909, two British psychologists — Edward Titchener and James Ward — translated the original German word to the English *empathy.* But the meaning? Almost entirely opposite of what it is now. Early theorists used *empathy* to describe the act of a viewer projecting their own bodily feelings and movements into inanimate objects, paintings and nature; basically, exactly how Vischer intended it to be used.

In the 1940s and 1950s, the concept evolved. Psychologists studying social sciences began to focus less on projecting feelings into a painting and more on understanding other human beings. What started as an art-focused aesthetic transformed into an interpersonal skill aimed at grasping another person's feelings; specifically, being able to understand others without damaging their feelings with your own biases.

In a way, empathy has turned back into an aesthetic. Consumers crave the psychological safety in knowing that the brands they invest hard-earned dollars in align with their values. And creators chase emotional connection with their audiences to keep those audiences engaged. That humanity shows itself in digital spaces daily, with the empathy aesthetic impacting things such as color schemes and design choices to make the user experience more inclusive. As a result, online culture has started to reject the curation that once made Instagram the most downloaded app in the world. Now people want rawness, authenticity, and relatability. The empathy aesthetic now shows the messiness of the actual human experience rather than the polished final product.

And then, of course, there's work. Just like empathy, the workplace has drastically changed over the past century and a half, as discussed in Chapter 3. And empathy at work went from non-existent to irrelevant to "maybe a good idea" to a core brand aesthetic for building trust and psychological safety. Organizations now visibly prioritize mental health, work-life balance, and active community engagement projects to project an empathetic image.

REMEMBER

Empathy has gone through many iterations. It's been an aesthetic. A skill. A trait. A feeling. A good idea. A bad idea (toxic empathy, anyone?). A point of contention. A manipulation tactic. And a strategy. But what's always been is a feeling. And not necessarily something you feel inside of yourself, but a feeling used to understand others: their situation, their perspective, and their feelings.

That's what I want you to take with you as you dive into the various chapters of this book. We are all capable of empathy, but your focus needs to be on the desire to pursue it.

Reframing Leadership as a Relationship

The social contract between employer and employee looks fundamentally different to it did even a single generation ago. Gone are the days when command-and-control leadership was the tried-and-true method of functional leadership (see Chapter 3). Workers in today's knowledge economy demand agility and innovation with very little interest in just compliance. Employees now need to feel empowered in their decision-making capabilities. Many of them thrive in creative environments where they can bounce ideas off of each other and explore innovate ways to accomplish their goals. This requires a leader who sees each member of their team as their own person, and not just one part of a larger group.

REMEMBER

Research consistently shows that the majority of employees are disengaged at work, and the primary driver is their relationship with their direct-line manager. It's for this reason that empathy in the workplace isn't a trend, but a response to a real shift in what people need from work and from the people who lead them.

Knowing how empathy fits in with good leadership

Many people believe that empathy is an add-on to solid leadership. They're wrong. What's true is that no other function of leadership works without it because every part or leadership depends on *people*.

REMEMBER

Leadership, at the end of the day, is human. Unfortunately, that's not what we're taught. Most leadership frameworks focus on strategy, vision, execution, and accountability. Those things matter, but none of them function at their highest level without empathy. And people don't follow systems; they follow leaders who make them feel understood. Need proof? Here it is:

- **Empathy makes you a better performer — in your boss's eyes, too.** Leadership development non-profit the Center for Creative Leadership analyzed data from 6,731 mid- to upper-level managers across 38 countries and found that managers who practiced empathetic leadership toward direct reports were viewed as better performers by their own bosses. Empathy doesn't just make your team feel good; it makes you look more effective up the chain (`www.ccl.org/articles/leading-effectively-articles/empathy-in-the-workplace-a-tool-for-effective-leadership`).
- **Empathy drives creativity and engagement.** A 2021 study by global non-profit member organization Catalyst (`www.catalyst.org/en-us/about/newsroom/2021/empathic-leaders-drive-employee-engagement`) of nearly 900 United States employees found that workers with highly empathetic senior leaders reported higher levels of creativity (61 percent) and engagement (76 percent), compared to just 13 percent and 32 percent respectively among those with less empathetic senior leaders.
- **Empathy is a business imperative, not a soft skill.** A 2023 EY (formerly known as Ernst & Young) Empathy in Business Survey of more than 1,000 employed United States workers found that mutual empathy between company leaders and employees leads to increased efficiency (88 percent), creativity (87 percent), job satisfaction (87 percent), idea sharing (86 percent), innovation (85 percent), and even company revenue (83 percent). Chapter 2 discusses why empathy shouldn't be referred to as a "soft skill."
- **Empathy improves team performance and productivity.** Researchers at Durham University and Athens University found that managers who lead with empathy are more likely to increase their team's performance and

productivity (www.durham.ac.uk/business/news-and-events/news/2025/04/empathetic-leaders-get-best-out-of-remote-workers). And that's particularly true for remote and hybrid workers, who felt closer to managers who showed genuine care and clearly communicated their vision.

- **Empathy directly impacts retention.** Catalyst's 2021 research (www.catalyst.org/en-us/about/newsroom/2021/empathic-leaders-drive-employee-engagement) found that senior leader empathy is directly linked to employee retention, and women from marginalized racial and ethnic groups specifically experience less burnout when they have more empathetic senior leaders. Empathy is not just a universal good but also an equity issue.

Realizing why empathy fits in with good leadership

Hundreds of statistics explain why empathy is so impactful for running successful enterprises (and trust me, there will be examples sprinkled through this book), but what about *you*? How would being an empathetic leader directly impact your day-to-day life? And how would that impact affect your team?

TIP

As you go through the following list, consider the specific people on your team or in your organization that you engage with consistently. Because when you lead with empathy — both as a manager of people and as a person yourself — this is your true impact.

Here's what that impact actually looks like, day to day, when you lead the people directly in front of you:

- **Your team feels safe enough to tell you the truth.** Most leaders think they have a pretty good read on their team. What they actually have, however, is a read on what the team wants that leader to see. And usually want they want you to see is what they are most comfortable with sharing. Those two things are rarely aligned. When people don't feel psychologically safe, they struggle to solve problems; instead, they smooth them over until they become crises. When you lead with empathy, people stop performing for you and start being honest with you. And honest teams make better decisions, catch problems earlier, and trust you enough to follow you through hard things. I unpack this more in Chapter 10, which discusses empathetic communication.

» **Your team stops spending energy on self-protection and spends it on the work instead.** Every team has an invisible tax. It's the energy people spend managing their image, hiding their struggles, anticipating your reaction, and figuring out what's safe to say. That tax doesn't show up on any report, but it costs you enormously in creativity, focus, and discretionary effort. Empathetic leadership reduces that tax. When people feel seen and understood, they stop bracing for impact and start bringing their full selves to the work.

» **Your team feels like *they* matter, not just their output.** A profound difference exists between being valued for what you produce and being valued as a person. Most employees have experienced both, and they know the difference immediately. When a leader demonstrates genuine curiosity about someone's experience — not just their performance — it changes how that person shows up. They're more loyal, more committed, and more willing to go beyond what's required. Not because they were told to, but because they actually want to. This is perspective-taking in action, and Chapter 9 dissects the ins and outs of this.

» **Your team gives you the benefit of the doubt.** Every leader makes hard calls. Delivers bad news. Makes decisions that not everyone will like. The difference between a team that trusts you through those moments and one that falls apart is almost entirely relational. When people believe — based on lived experience — that you genuinely understand and care about their experience, they extend you grace when things are hard. They assume good intent, and they are much more likely to stick around for the long haul.

» **Your team becomes more empathetic with each other.** Empathy is contagious. So, when you model genuine curiosity, active listening, and you care for people's experience, your team starts doing it too. They do it with their peers, with other departments, and with your customers. You are building more than just a relationship with your team; you're building your team's culture. And that culture will outlast any single decision, initiative, or difficult quarter. See the nearby sidebar, "The Empathy Impact."

REMEMBER

When your team feels seen, everything shifts. Not just their performance: their relationship to the work, to each other, and to you. That shift doesn't happen because of a policy or a program. It happens because of how you choose to show up. Your team performs at the level of how safe they feel, and how safe they feel is entirely up to you.

THE EMPATHY IMPACT

Empathy doesn't stay where you put it; it's spreads and grows and connects and flourishes. It touches not only the person you are engaging with, but everyone they engage with because everything you do has a broader impact on the world at large. When a leader practices empathy genuinely and consistently, it moves from the individual to the team, from the team to the organization, from the organization to every customer it touches. Here's what that progression actually looks like:

- **On individuals.** Empathy changes how people experience work at the most personal level. Feeling seen by a leader is one of the strongest predictors of engagement, discretionary effort, and well-being.
- **On teams.** Teams with empathetic leaders take more risks, communicate more honestly, and recover from conflict faster. I discuss this in depth in Chapter 11.
- **In organizations.** Empathy at scale becomes culture. Organizations known for empathetic leadership outperform on retention, innovation, and customer satisfaction.
- **For customers.** Leaders who model empathy internally build teams that extend it externally. Customer empathy isn't a marketing strategy; it's a leadership outcome. The organizations that genuinely understand their customers are the ones whose leaders genuinely understand their people.

Establishing Empathy as a Core Value

Most people think of leadership as a position — a title, a level, a set of responsibilities — and, in many ways, it is. Careers advance to leadership when the individual climbing that ladder has achieved something their peers couldn't, and that is a moment of great pride. But the real work of leadership is in the relationships; namely, between the person leading and the people being led. And, like every relationship in life, it is only as strong as the understanding that runs through it.

REMEMBER

The question isn't whether empathy matters in leadership; you're reading this book, so you are very much aware of empathy's value. The question is whether you're willing to hold it as a core value; not a strategy you deploy when it's convenient, but a genuine commitment that shapes how you lead even when it costs you something. For example:

» **As a leader.** A core value isn't something you perform when it's convenient. It's something that guides decisions when it's hard. What does it actually look like to hold empathy as a non-negotiable in your leadership, especially when you're under pressure? When someone is frustrating you? When the business case for the faster, colder decision seems obvious?

For me, empathy became a core value when I saw how the result of not being empathetic impacted my career and — more importantly — my relationships. Your reasons will be your own. But the leaders who hold empathy most consistently are almost always the ones who can trace it back to something personal — a moment where being seen, or not being seen, changed something for them. Chapter 7 breaks down how to define your goals as an empathetic leader, and it's a great place to start if you're itching to change quickly.

- **In the workplace.** Personal commitment is the starting point. But it isn't enough on its own. The goal isn't just to be an empathetic leader — it's to build a workplace where empathy is the shared operating system, where it isn't dependent on any one person's good intentions, and where it doesn't disappear when you're not in the room.

  This is cultural. How do you move empathy from a personal commitment to a shared one? That's the difference between empathy as a personal virtue and empathy as a cultural value. And making that shift is one of the hardest and most important things a leader can do. Empathy that lives only in relationships is fragile.

  Empathy that gets built into how decisions get made, how feedback gets collected, how conflict gets addressed, and how new people get welcomed — that's empathy that lasts. Part 3 of this book discusses the actions involved when leading with empathy, and how to build those structures.

REMEMBER

A culture of empathy — both as an individual and in the workplace — is never an accident. It is intentionally built through goal setting, identifying and closing your gaps, and making it a part of who you are. It's a choice that gets made over and over again, at every level of an organization — as well as at every turn in your own personal journey — until it becomes simply the way things are done here.

Understanding the Loneliness of Leading without Empathy

I never set out to teach empathy. In fact, I never set out to teach anything. I began my career as a writer; as an avid reader in my childhood, I fell in love with storytelling and I wanted to pursue that passion as an adult. Unfortunately, I had an enormous roadblock to getting my writing career to where I wanted it to be: my speech impediment. I'm a person who stutters, and I spent the majority of my life internally struggling with how I sounded. I was both terrified of people but craved the community of others; I avoided talking (to avoid stuttering) but teeming with so many things I wanted to say, and had big goals for my career but not enough gumption to put myself out there to actually grow it. I was trapped in a vicious cycle, and I struggled for close to a decade with how to break free.

It was a speech therapist I was seeing at the time who talked some sense into me. Her name was Stephie, and she was also a stutterer. In our first session, she told me that she could help me make stuttering easier and less noticeable through various techniques. And they would absolutely work, but first I had to be okay with stuttering. I thought she was a quack. How can anyone be comfortable with being different? With struggling to say simple words? With constantly exposing their greatest insecurity?

It didn't seem possible, but I decided to give it a shot anyway. I asked her how to get comfortable with stuttering. She suggested I give public speaking a try. This wasn't a means of developing a new skill, it was exposure therapy. If I spoke and stuttered in front of a large group of people about the thing that made me feel the most vulnerable — stuttering — it would become less scary.

It took a while for me see it — I'm talking about a decade of being a professional speaker — but she was right. I do feel more comfortable stuttering; it doesn't bother me as much and I have come a long way in divorcing my speech from a lot of the negative feelings I attached to it for so long.

Public speaking — and teaching companies, teams, and audiences about empathy — did so much more than just rehab my relationship with my speech; it created an environment for real connection to thrive. As you read this book, I'll share more experiences about stuttering and how it taught me empathy. I hope that, as it has done for many audiences around the world, those stories will help you better understand and embrace empathy in your own right.

TIP

This book focuses on leading with empathy from the leadership — corporate — perspective; but, for a moment, I want you to focus on leading with empathy as individual — not for your team, but for you. In your conversations. In your relationships. In your life in general. Do you lead with empathy? If you aren't sure; that's okay. One of the first things you must do to practice empathy is to be self-aware, so being honest about how you are actually leading is important. What I learned before and during my journey into speaking was that leading without empathy was an incredibly lonely decision. I was leading with fear, pride, and shame around my speech, and I allowed those feelings to guide me away from others and toward a life of isolation. I was so deeply invested in my own insecurities and vulnerabilities that I created an environment where no one felt comfortable connecting. I had no empathy; therefore, I had no community.

WARNING

You may not realize a decline in empathy is happening, because the absence of empathy in leadership rarely announces itself. More often it looks like a leader who is competent, well-intentioned, and genuinely confused about why their team keeps underperforming, disengaging, or leaving. Here's what this looks like in practice:

- **You make the same mistakes repeatedly.** Without empathy, you're working with an incomplete model of the people around you. You don't fully understand what motivates them, what's getting in their way, or how your behavior lands on them. So, you keep pulling the same levers and getting surprised when they don't work. The problem isn't your strategy; it's your data.
- **Your best people leave and you never see it coming.** This is one of the most consistent and costly symptoms of low-empathy leadership. Top performers don't storm out. They quietly disengage first — they stop volunteering ideas, stop going above and beyond, stop investing in the team's success. By the time they hand in their resignation, they've been gone for months. And because no one felt safe enough to tell you what was happening, you never had the chance to fix it.
- **You have authority but not influence.** People do what you ask because they have to, not because they want to. There's an enormous performance gap between those two things. Compliance gets you the minimum. Commitment gets you everything people are capable of. Low-empathy leaders almost always have the first and wonder why they can't seem to get the second. I discuss this in detail in Chapter 12.
- **You confuse busyness with impact.** Low-empathy leaders often work incredibly hard. They're executing, delivering, and hitting numbers. But they're frequently disconnected from the human experience of the work — from what it actually feels like to be on their team. And over time, that disconnection shows up in the metrics that matter most: retention, engagement, innovation, and the kind of sustained performance that only comes from people who genuinely want to be there. Part 4 of this book explains how to measure your capabilities as an empathetic leader and your team's growth.
- **You feel increasingly isolated.** This one's the biggie; I learned it the hard way, and I know how painful it feels. When you operate from authority or distance, you end up surrounded by people but genuinely alone. No one tells you the truth. No one is even comfortable having a real conversation with you. No one pushes back or gives you different ideas. You make decisions in a vacuum and wonder privately why they keep missing the mark. Isolation is the cost of the distance you created because you didn't invest in empathy. Head to Chapter 10 to discover more about forming lasting, sincere connections with others through empathetic communication.

DISRUPTING THE NORM: THE SACRED CLOWN

The highest form of empath is the Heyoka. Originating from the Lakota Sioux culture and tradition, the *Heyoka* — roughly translating as "sacred clown" — was known somewhat as a spiritual fool. They acted as an emotional mirror to the tribes they visited; they reflected people's emotions and hidden dynamics back to them, offering great personal growth along with a big dose of discomfort. Their unorthodox perspective aimed to break people out of their rigid ways so they could view the world differently.

The Heyoka never had the intention of disrupting — of being a contrarian — but their energy shifted the surrounding environment. They forced people to examine their own doubts, fears, hatreds, and weaknesses. And while doing so, they remained both emotionally detached and authentic. The detachment served as an objective catalyst for healing, and their authenticity protected them from being deceived.

The Heyoka's entire function was to help a community see itself more clearly. Their goal was to shake people up when they got too comfortable, too conformist, or too afraid to acknowledge things directly. In a culture with a strong group identify and a hefty social pressure to conform with others (Chapter 11 examines empathy in groups), the Heyoka reveled in their "sacred" role of breaking the patterns. This wasn't out of rebellion but out of service to the community's health and well-being. And they could say what no one else would dare to say because they didn't need permission. Heyoka's were true leaders. Not through authority, strategy, or vision, but through understanding. They were deeply, radically committed to surfacing what the community wasn't capable of seeing on its own. The disruption was the medicine. The discomfort was the point.

I think about the Heyoka a lot when I think about what empathetic leadership actually requires. No, great leaders aren't clowns — though a sense of humor is always a good idea — but because the Heyoka reminds us that genuine empathy has never been the soft option. It has always been the brave one. It takes more courage to stay curious than to stay comfortable, more discipline to listen than to direct, and more strength to make someone feel seen than to simply make them comply. And, maybe most importantly, it takes some levity to question why we have the stances we do about ourselves and about others. Yes, leadership is serious; it's also human. And that's my ultimate goal for you in this book: humanity.

To create conditions where truth-telling is safe; where the quietest voice in the room is on equal footing as the loudest; where it's safe to dissent and invite uncomfortable perspectives; where people feel protected when they say something nobody else is brave enough to; and where teams feel confident enough not just to perform empathy, but to

(continued)

(continued)

build it into their relationships, their structures, and their culture. Because when teams do that, they are doing something ancient. Something that communities have always needed from the people willing to lead them. That's what this book is about. Not leadership that looks good from the outside, but leadership that actually works from the inside out. And it starts, as it always has, with the willingness, the curiosity, and the self-awareness, to genuinely understand the people you're asking to follow you.

REMEMBER

The cost of leading without empathy hardly ever shows up all at once. It's slow and ruminates below the surface. It's quiet, eroding trust over a long period of time. Leaders who operate with empathy gradually start losing access to the truth. By the time the loss of empathy is visible, you've lost your team.

IN THIS CHAPTER

» **Building trust to build empathy**

» **Examining the business case for using empathy in leadership**

» **Reframing empathy from a soft skill to a non-technical skill**

Chapter 2
Understanding Why and How Empathy Matters in Leadership

You already know empathy matters. You probably wouldn't have picked up this book if you didn't. But knowing it matters and understanding why — specifically, mechanically, and in ways you can point to and build on — are two very different things.

That's what this chapter is about. It's going to move empathy out of the realm of "nice to have" and into the realm of "here's exactly how this works and why you can't afford to skip it." It explores how trust is built, and what happens when it doesn't. It discusses what the data says about empathetic leadership and organizational performance, and makes the case that empathy isn't a soft skill and it never was.

By the end of this chapter, you won't just believe empathy matters. You'll be able to explain why — to your team, to your organization, and to the skeptic in the room who still thinks feelings have no place in business.

Building Trust: The Foundation of Influence

Everything in leadership runs on trust. Your authority can get people to show up and your strategy can point them in a direction, but trust is what determines whether they actually bring their best by telling you the truth, taking caveat risks, and staying when things get hard.

REMEMBER

Here's what most leadership development misses: Trust isn't built through competence alone, and it's not built through likability alone. It's built through the consistent experience of feeling safe with someone. Safe enough to be honest. Safe enough to be wrong. Safe enough to not have all the answers. That safety created by empathy and, without it, everything else you're trying to build as a leader is sitting on an unstable foundation.

Differentiating authority from influence

Have you ever been in a room with a leader where you can feel the tension and fear in the air? And you know exactly what happens when those leaders leave the room. The energy shifts. There's a huge relief — a resounding yet silent *whew!* Though the tension may lower, however, the fear persists. As you complete tasks, participate in meetings, and collaborate with your team, you may feel "safe" when the leader causing the issues isn't there, but their presence has a constant negative impact on the team.

On the other end of the spectrum are the leaders who inspire you to do your best just by their presence. They may not be the most verbose or have the much-lauded executive presence, but they lead by building trusted relationships with others. Leaders who prioritize this influence empower the team to take ownership, allowing them to collaborate with each other to reach shared goals. Their influence breeds respect and trust.

REMEMBER

It's for that reason that it is important to know the difference between influence and authority when it comes to empathetic leadership. They are both necessary and impactful when engaging with your team, but in different ways:

» **Authority.** Defined as the legitimate power or right to give orders, make decisions and enforce obedience, *authority* is accepted by those being governed as a just and fair assignment. Late-nineteenth and early-twentieth century German sociologist Max Weber — whose work defined how we understand organizations, culture and the nature of modern society — defined three systems of authority used to maintain social order: traditional, rational-legal, and charismatic.

Traditional authority is based on long-standing customs, traditions, and historical continuity; monarchies and tribal leadership are great examples. *Rational-legal authority* is that defined by rules, regulations, and laws; for example, elected officials and police officers. And *charismatic authority* is legitimized by the personal power of an individual leader: their perceived exceptional gifts, vision, magnetism, or heroic character.

Authority is positional; it comes with a title, a promotion, or badge. People look to you because they know you have the answers as a result of an assignment, something given to you by the organization, institution, or hierarchy. This positional power is also conditional; it can be taken away just as quickly as it was given.

- **Influence.** Defined as the capacity or power to produce an effect on the character, development, behavior, or opinions of others without using direct force or command, *influence* shapes thoughts, behaviors, and decisions. Influence is what drives commitment, and commitment to a cause is the result of genuinely caring about the why.

  Commanding influence is tricky. Because we are inundated with content in our highly digitalized lives, it's harder than ever to break through the noise. That's why a part of influence is people liking you enough to listen to you, achieved by cultivating your personal connections to build a good rapport with your colleagues.

  Beyond how you make people feel, influence requires some level of expertise. This is why it's important as a leader to have a *leadership tenet,* something that grounds you in the type of leader you want to be for your team. I discuss this in more detail in Chapters 6 and 7, but you need to invest in some aspects of leadership — both technical and non-technical skills — that keep you moving toward the influential leader you want to be.

Knowing the distinction between these two elements of power is deeply important to understanding how and why empathy matters in leadership. Authority is positional while influence is relational; empathy is the primary mechanism through which that relational power is built.

To illustrate the difference between — and impact of — authority and influence, view them on a spectrum with authority on one side and influence on the other. With that in mind, let's get into the real difference between them and how those differences look to your team:

- **Authority *tells*, influence *asks*.** Authority-based leaders communicate with directives: here's what we're doing, here's how we're doing it, now go do it.

This one-directional flow of communication tells your team that their input is irrelevant. Influence, on the other hand, approaches conversations from a more diagonal perspective: here's what I'm thinking, what am I missing, and how does this land for you? Asking requires genuine curiosity about the answer; that curiosity — the willingness to be changed by what you hear — is the start of empathy in action. For more about phrases and sentences to use or avoid when communicating with empathy as a leader, head to Chapter 15.

» **Authority *closes*, influence *opens*.** As you climb the corporate ladder, the way you both receive and disseminate information shifts. Generally speaking, you get more and give less information as your power grows. Something you may not be considering, however, is the impact this has on your teams; the way they give you information changes. Leaders with authority may not be aware of that shift, so they are operating on heavily filtered information because their team doesn't feel psychologically safe enough to give the most brutally honest version of events. For that reason, authority cuts off access — or closes — better performance and innovation. Influence, on the other hand, keeps those pathways open. Those teams are being led by leaders who they feel safe enough with to give information that doesn't need to be purified. Such leaders hear about problems as they arise, receive more candid assessments, and get feedback that actually improves their decisions. Strength, stoicism, and openness are discussed in Chapter 12.

» **Authority requires *proximity*, influence works *at a distance*.** Authority-based leaders need to be in the room for their power to function. The issue there is that if there is no oversight, there's less compliance. That's because the leader's values, their way of thinking, their questions, and their standards are not internalized by the people around them. Influence-based leadership, on the other hand, scales no matter the distance. If your team behaves differently when you're not watching, you have authority. If they behave the same, you have influence. To better understand how to intentionally create this kind of environment, head to Chapter 5.

These are not subtle differences. However, if you're viewing authority and influence on a singular spectrum, you can see that both are required. If you are centering empathy in your leadership practice, work on growing your influence after you are given your authority. Happily, as discussed in Chapter 3, leaders who prioritize empathy have a leg up on being influential.

TIP

Leading with empathy while also maintaining authority in depth is discussed in Chapter 12, but here's what I want you to remember: authority is assigned while influence is earned. To make this actionable, replace one directive with a question. Instead of telling your team how something is going to happen, tell them where you're trying to go. And ask how they'd get there. Notice what comes back, who speaks up that usually doesn't, and what you find out that you wouldn't have known if you'd just given the answer. That's influence in its smallest, most repeatable form. And every time you do it, you're building something authority never could: a team that's invested because they were included, not just informed.

WHEN AUTHORITY MASQUERADES AS INFLUENCE

You're reading words that were written on my MacBook Air while using my iPad as a second screen for research. And yes, I did just glance down at my iPhone to check the time. You could say that I'm in the "Cult of Apple" — heavily embedded into their ecosystem with no plans of exiting — and for a while, that was probably an accurate assessment. But these days, it's mostly about the convenience of going to the Apple store when things go wrong. Also, I have no desire to learn a new operating system. So, I stick with what I know because it makes my life easier.

Elsewhere in this chapter, I discussed Max Weber's definitions of authority. One type is charismatic authority. Weber became increasingly fascinated by how social movements are impacted by charismatic leaders. As a result, he developed the *routinization of charisma* theory: the transition of a movement from that of a charismatic leader to a stable institution governed by permanent rules and structures (rational-legal authority).

Weber viewed charisma as revolutionary but non-rational. Yes, charisma is authoritative, but it is neither a reliable nor a trustworthy foundation for longevity. He argued that charisma only existed if it was recognized and legitimized by devoted followers. This brings to my mind companies like Apple and leaders like Steve Jobs.

Jobs (along with Steve Wozniak) built Apple and spearheaded the launch of the Macintosh, revolutionizing the tech industry. His work with Apple is a great example of using charisma to persuade not only a team but large swaths of the public to believe intensely in something. I'm by no means saying that Jobs was an exemplar of empathetic leadership. What he built, however, was so impactful and so game-changing that it was able to survive without him. His and Apple's following is no longer based on personality devotion — which is just a more seductive form of authority — it's based on the products he created and the relationships he built.

It's easy to confuse charismatic authority and genuine influence. Charismatic leaders can look like they have influence because people follow them with great enthusiasm. But it will always eventually collapse. And that's because it was never about the relationship; it was about the image. So, ask yourself what happens to the organization — and your team specifically — if the charismatic leader leaves. And will your leadership survive failure, vulnerability, or the loss of your platform?

Dissecting trust

In 1984, a college junior was picked third in the National Basketball Association annual draft. He spent the first five years of his career as the standout on a team that was in a rebuilding phase; he was Rookie of the Year, set an all-time playoff single-game scoring record, and took that team to consistent 50-win seasons. But they couldn't break through. They were in the same conference as a powerhouse, the Detroit Pistons, and spent the late 1980s losing to them in the Eastern Conference Finals for three consecutive years. It wasn't until the guidance of a new coach — and the implementation of a new philosophy — that this young guard could go from being a great player on an okay team to arguably the greatest athlete and competitor of all time. What was the catalyst of this evolution? Trust.

Of course, I'm talking about Michael Jordan, Phil Jackson, and the Chicago Bulls. When we think of the Bulls, we automatically go to their dominance in the 1990s. But we rarely think about what it took to get there. Jordan, known for his ruthless competitive nature, spent the first five years of his career getting constantly filleted by the media for being a ball hog. It was Jackson and his infamous triangle offense that convinced him that trusting his teammates — passing the ball — would make him even more lethal. The rest, as they say, is history.

Every massively successful enterprise, organization, leader, or superstar you've ever witnessed unearths their rocket fuel after they learned to trust both the process and people involved. It would make sense, then, that you'd always err on the side of trusting the people you work with; because trusting your teammates means that you will, ultimately, be better at your job because you trust them enough to elevate you. Unfortunately, that's not how trust works.

Though trust can be innately built into our biology, it is also actively refined through our experience. Humans are social, and our brains reflect that. We are wired to work together to survive; and when we are bonding socially, our brains release *oxytocin* — affectionately known as the love hormone — that makes us predisposed to trust others.

Rational trust, however, requires a great deal of cognitive evaluation. That's because our conscious mind needs evidence to go "full send" on trusting someone else. What kind of evidence? Here are the four main components required to build trust:

- **Consistency.** You are predictable in your behavior and reliable in following through on promises.
- **Competence.** You demonstrate the ability and skill required to be successful.

- **Integrity.** Your values are aligned with your actions, and you are consistently honest.
- **Compassion.** You show sincere care and concern for others' well-being.

REMEMBER

Trust and empathy are acutely linked. Trust fuels the empathy flame. It lowers defenses, creating psychological safety because the fear of judgment and rejection is no longer in play. Trust fosters vulnerability, making people more willing to express their struggles. It also inspires action and validates experiences; when trust is established, empathetic responses feel genuine. Understanding someone's emotions is only the first step; trust empowers people to offer and accept support without resentment. Empathy also drives trust; it proves that you value someone as a whole human rather than just as a means to an end. Empathy forces you to listen to understand instead of just to speak; and when this is the focus, you have the clarity necessary to both prevent misunderstandings and resolve conflict. This strengthens respect on teams, and that is the core of a relationship that has sincere trust.

TECHNICAL STUFF

Trust isn't just psychological; it's also biological. Neuro-economist Paul Zak's research from a 2005 study published in the journal *Hormones and Behavior* (sbn.org) found that when people feel trusted, their brains release oxytocin, which in turn makes them more likely to extend trust back. It's a biological feedback loop. Trust literally produces more trust at the neurochemical level. Zak found that employees at high-trust companies reported 74 percent less stress, 106 percent more energy, 50 percent higher productivity, and 76 percent more engagement than employees at low-trust companies.

So, what happens when you don't have trust? When you don't feel safe, such as when leadership is unpredictable and the environment feels threatening? Your *cortisol* (your stress hormone, the primary driver for your body's fight-or-flight response) increases. And chronic cortisol elevation impairs memory, suppresses the immune system, disrupts sleep, and literally shrinks the *prefrontal cortex* (the part of the brain responsible for complex thinking and decision-making). A low-trust environment isn't just unpleasant. It is neurologically degrading. The bottom line is that the body works better in a high-trust environment.

REMEMBER

Trust in leadership can only really thrive when there is empathy, and that's because empathy deactivates the threat response. When a leader demonstrates genuine understanding — when people feel seen, heard, and valued not judged — the threat response quiets. Oxytocin rises, cortisol drops, and the brain becomes available for the kind of thinking that actually moves work forward. This is the neurological argument for empathetic leadership in its most direct form: Empathy is the signal that tells the nervous system it's safe, and safety is the precondition for everything else you want from your team.

Justifying Empathy in Leadership

The business case for empathy isn't anecdotal. It's documented, replicated, and increasingly hard to ignore. Decade after decade of research points in the same direction: The leaders and companies that take empathy seriously don't just feel better to work for, they perform better across almost every metric that matters.

REMEMBER

Here's what the data actually says: Empathy prioritizes employee well-being because it centers humanity. And well-being isn't a perk; it's a precondition. People who feel unseen, unheard, or unvalued don't give their best work. They give enough to stay employed. There's a meaningful difference. Research consistently shows that empathetic leadership correlates with higher job satisfaction, greater organizational commitment, and an overall enhanced work environment. This isn't because leaders are being nice, but because employees who feel understood operate from a fundamentally different baseline. Instead of spending cognitive energy managing how they're perceived or bracing for the next bad interaction, their energy is focused on doing the work.

WARNING

The data on what happens in the absence of empathy is equally instructive. In the 2021 EY (formerly known as Ernst & Young) Empathy in Business Survey, 54 percent of respondents reported having left a previous job because their boss wasn't empathetic to their struggles at work while 49 percent left because their boss wasn't empathetic to challenges in their personal lives (`www.ey.com/en_us/newsroom/2021/09/ey-empathy-in-business-survey`). Those go beyond just feelings; those are recruiting costs, onboarding costs, lost institutional knowledge, and disrupted team continuity, every single time.

The mental health dimension is also worth exploring. Businessolver's 2024 State of Workplace Empathy Study (`https://businessolver.com/workplace-empathy`) — surveying over 3,000 employees, HR leaders, and CEOs — found that one in two employees reported experiencing a mental health issue in the past year. And 63 percent of employees who described their workplace as toxic said empathy at their organization needed to evolve. Low empathy and toxic culture travel together.

What empathetic leaders understand is that well-being isn't separate from the work; it's the infrastructure the work runs on. Well-being is arguably the most important business outcome, but there are several others that are immensely impactful:

- **Empathy fuels better decision-making.** Many people think that good decisions require some emotional distance, but research suggests otherwise. That's because empathetic leaders create psychologically safe environments that actually improve team decision-making; when people feel safe enough to speak honestly, leaders are working with better information.

Research from the Center for Creative Leadership, a leadership development non-profit, has noted that empathy is important as a component of leadership due to the increasing use of teams, the rapid pace of globalization, and the growing need to retain talent, and that thoughtfully considering employees' feelings alongside other factors when making intelligent decisions is important (`https://cclinnovation.org/wp-content/uploads/2020/03/empathyintheworkplace.pdf`). This isn't about feelings displacing logic; it's about a fuller picture of reality informing better choices.

But the most overlooked dimension here is that empathy closes the gap between what leaders *think* is happening in their organization and what's *actually* happening. Research conducted by management consulting firm Businessolver (`https://businessolver.com/workplace-empathy`) research found a 23-point gap between how CEOs and employees perceive empathy in their workplace. A leader operating from that kind of disconnect isn't making decisions based on reality; they're making decisions based on a significantly distorted version of it. Practicing empathy is, among other things, a correction mechanism for that distortion.

» **Empathy strengthens culture and connection.** *Culture* is the accumulated experience of what it actually feels like to work somewhere, and that experience is shaped by how leaders treat people. Global consulting firm EY found that 88 percent of employees feel empathetic leadership creates loyalty toward their leaders; 87 percent say it enables trust between employees and leaders; and 88 percent feel it inspires positive change within the workplace. Those aren't marginal effects. Trust and loyalty are the foundational ingredients of a functional culture, and they're both direct outputs of empathetic leadership, according to workers themselves.

  Retention is also impacted. Research conducted by the Society of Human Resources Management in 2024 (`www.shrm.org/topics-tools/employment-law-compliance/global-drivers-of-positive-workplace-culture`) found that workers in positive organizational cultures are almost four times more likely to stay with their current employer. And among employees rating their culture as good or excellent, only 15 percent said they were actively looking for a new job. Culture built on empathy is beyond just pleasant; it's sticky.

  Another thing empathy improves? Engagement. Research shows that 76 percent of employees with highly empathetic senior leaders reported being engaged at work, compared to just 32 percent of those with less empathetic senior leaders. That's the difference between an organization where people are putting in real effort and one where they're going through the motions, and every leader who has managed both kinds of teams knows exactly what that gap feels like in practice.

- **Empathy improves business outcomes.** A 2021 study by research firm Catalyst (www.catalyst.org/insights/2025/empathy-work-strategy-crisis) found that empathetic leaders have more engaged teams and more profitable organizations, and 61 percent of employees with empathetic leaders reported feeling innovative and proactive at work. Compare that to only 13 percent of employees whose leaders were perceived as less empathetic who felt capable of innovation. That's nearly a five-fold difference in the innovation capacity of a team based on a single leadership variable.

  EY's 2023 Empathy in Business Survey (www.ey.com/en_us/consulting/authentic-empathy) found that employees believe mutual empathy between leaders and employees increases efficiency (88 percent), creativity (87 percent), job satisfaction (87 percent), idea sharing (86 percent), and innovation (85 percent). These are more than just isolated benefits; they compound. An organization that's more efficient, more creative, retains its people, and generates better ideas from within is an organization that wins.

  And the cost-avoidance story matters too. Organizations led by empathetic leaders experience a 20 percent increase in customer loyalty, because employees who feel genuinely supported by their leaders bring that quality of engagement into every customer interaction. The empathy doesn't stay inside the organization; it travels outward.

  The bottom line on the bottom line is that 85 percent of surveyed employees reported that empathetic leadership increases productivity. Empathy isn't what you do instead of driving results — it is one of the most reliable ways to drive results.

REMEMBER

Empathy isn't a "values" choice that happens to also be good for business. It is a business strategy, and it's one that operates through people because people are how every business outcome is produced.

Rethinking Empathy as a Non-Technical Skill

Empathy gets dismissed as a soft skill for one reason: most people only see the feeling. They see the warmth, the connection, and the care, and they file it under "nice to have." What they miss is everything happening underneath. Because empathy isn't just something you feel. It's something you do, and something you can get measurably better at.

That's the reframe this section is built on. Empathy is a *non-technical skill:* a distinct, learnable, practicable competency with real inputs, real outputs, and real consequences when it's absent. And once you start seeing it that way, everything about how you develop it changes.

Using emotional and cognitive empathy

For the empathy reframe to have real meaning, look at empathy as beyond just a feeling. Yes, empathy can be a deeply emotional experience, but it is also a thoroughly cognitive one. We use our brains to identify and work through our emotions, but it goes beyond just recognition and consideration — empathy is its own form of data processing. How so? To answer that question, consider what emotional empathy and cognitive empathy are within the context of information processing:

- **Emotional empathy is the resonance system.** When someone tells you they're overwhelmed, something in you responds to that; your body and nervous system register it. This is your brain's mirror neuron system doing exactly what it's designed to do: registering another person's internal state as real information.
- **Cognitive empathy is the interpretive system.** This is the active, analytical work of asking "What is this person actually experiencing?", "What's driving this?" and "What's the gap between what they're saying and what they need?" This is perspective-taking as a deliberate intellectual exercise: closer to analysis than feeling.

WARNING

A leader running on emotional empathy alone drowns in other people's feelings and can't act clearly. The emotional-only leader becomes a mood absorber; their team's anxiety becomes their anxiety, as do their conflicts. Eventually, these leaders either burn out or start avoiding difficult conversations altogether to protect themselves. A leader running on cognitive empathy alone understands people like a chess board, accurately but coldly surveying situations. The cognitive-only leader becomes a problem solver who misses the humanity; they're accurate but they aren't present. And people leave interactions feeling like a case study rather than a human being.

Let's unpack this a bit further with an example. A team member comes to you visibly upset about being passed over for a promotion. If you use just emotional empathy, you feel the weight of their disappointment so acutely that you over-validate, make promises you can't keep, or you avoid the harder truths they need to hear. If you respond using just cognitive empathy, you accurately analyze what they're feeling and why, but your response comes off as clinical and detached. Your teammate walks away not feeling understood, but feeling processed.

Now let's run this back, but with emotional and cognitive empathy working together. You feel the weight of the moment, and you let it register; you don't run past it or manage it away. You acknowledge what this cost them, specifically, without over-explaining or over-apologizing. You give the disappointment the energy that it needs. And then, once they feel like you actually understand what they're carrying, you move into the harder and more useful part of the conversation: the honest assessment, specific feedback, and the clear picture of what the path forward actually looks like.

The emotional channel told you what they needed first. The cognitive channel gave you the tools to actually help them. Together, they produced the only kind of conversation that's both honest and humane. That's the dual system in practice. Not feeling *or* thinking. Feeling *and* thinking, in the right sequence, with enough self-awareness to know which one the moment is calling for.

REMEMBER

Chapter 4 digs into the details the various types of empathy, but the key point to take away is this: You need both cognitive and emotional empathy to properly understand another person's perspective. The reason empathy has been incorrectly labeled as a "soft skill" is that most people only see its emotional surface. They see the feeling of connection, warmth, or care. But empathy is a dual-system process. It operates simultaneously through these two distinct mental channels.

TIP

Emotional empathy generates the signal, while cognitive empathy processes it. Neither is complete without the other. When you think about your default in difficult conversations, which channel do you lean on: feeling or analyzing? Neither answer is wrong, I assure you, but knowing your default is the first step to developing the other.

Practicing empathy, providing data

When you ask someone how they're doing and you actually listen — not just to the words but to the energy, the hesitation, the thing they're not saying — you are gathering intelligence. You're building a richer, more accurate model of that person: what motivates them, what drains them, what they're afraid of, and what they need to be able to perform well.

This is not a soft skill. In fact, it's the same function that market researchers, user experience designers, intelligence analysts, and doctors perform when they're doing their job well. They're gathering signals from human sources that can't be captured in a spreadsheet.

Leaders who practice empathy consistently are, over time, operating with significantly better data than leaders who don't. They make fewer wrong assumptions about their people, they catch problems earlier, and they communicate in ways that actually land. They're not working from a generic model of "employee." Their operating model is regularly updated, accurate and based off of this specific person in this specific season of their work and life.

TIP

Here are a few ways you can start practicing empathy as data collection in your own leadership:

- **Calibrating communication.** Effective leaders don't deliver the same message the same way to every person. They adjust tone, timing, framing, and detail based on who they're talking to. That calibration requires continuous empathetic processing; you're reading feedback signals in real time (Is this landing? Are they shutting down? Are they tracking?) and adjusting. This is why two leaders can give the exact same feedback and produce completely different outcomes. One is processing the room, the other is just talking.
- **Diagnosing what's actually wrong.** When a team member is underperforming, dozens of possible causes exist: personal stress, unclear expectations, skill gap, a dynamic with a peer, a misalignment with the work itself. Empathetic leaders don't default to the most visible explanation. They ask questions, sit with ambiguity, and use what they know about the person to develop a more accurate diagnosis. That's *clinical thinking.* Empathy is what keeps them from over-indexing on the obvious answer.
- **Pattern recognition across people.** Over time, empathetic leaders build a library of human patterns. They notice that one person goes quiet when they're actually very frustrated, while another gets louder when they're scared. They notice that their team's energy shifts in particular ways before burnout hits. This is *data accumulation.* Empathy is the practice that makes you a better reader of that data over time; that's not because you become more emotional, but because you become more observant and more accurate.
- **Perspective modeling.** Before a hard conversation, a high-stakes decision, or a difficult feedback session, empathetic leaders run a mental model. They ask what this current situation is like from where the other person is standing, ask what is it that the other person knows that they don't, and consider what pressures are shaping how this person will receive information. This is *cognitive empathy forecasting* — running a simulation using what's known about another person to anticipate outcomes and calibrate the approach accordingly.
- **Reading subtext.** Most of what people are saying to you isn't in their words; it's in their pauses, what they don't say, and how their body and energy shifts. Empathy is the processing tool that lets you register when someone says they're fine, but something is a bit off. This isn't a feeling; it's *information intake.* You're parsing several data streams simultaneously and holding them against each other to form a more complete picture than the surface conversation provides.

REMEMBER

Empathy isn't the absence of analysis; it's the analysis applied to human beings. That's what moves empathy from a soft skill to a non-technical one. The inputs are human, the processing requires skill and practice, and the outputs — better decisions, better communication, and better teams — are measurable.

Recognizing non-technical skills as survival skills

For much of my childhood, I was a Girl Scout. They say the purpose of Girl Scouts is to build courage, confidence, and character in young girls, so those girls can then go on to make the world a better place. In a lot of ways, I think my participation in Girl Scouts succeeded in those goals. I did so many activities that I would have never even thought of to try if it wasn't for that organization. My troop would put on talent shows where each girl would show off a new skill they'd recently learned. We made leaf rubbings and friendship bracelets. We went to local museums where we learned about the ocean and how to build robots. And, of course, we went camping. I actually went camping several times, where we slept in tents that we had to pitch ourselves and cooked meals over a campfire. For everything we learned, we were awarded a badge. And as I went up the ranks from daisy to brownie to cadette to senior, I racked up quite a few badges. So many, in fact, that I stopped even putting them on my uniform; they are stored safely in a tin container that is still in the basement of my parents' house.

But all these years later, I still remember what I got from those experiences, how I explored new ideas and possibilities, and how I felt a bit better about myself because I got to do something interesting. And all these years later, I now understand that the badge system is a framework for developing competencies that can rarely be graded on a test. It's about trying something new, learning how to solve a problem, growing your skills by potentially being bad at something, and doing it all with other people who are just as interested in learning new skills as you are. It's those skills — the teamwork, the collaboration, and the curiosity — that mattered the most, and those were rarely things I learned in a classroom.

I think much of the confidence, courage, and character that Girl Scouts prides itself in cultivating are because of its focus on non-technical skills: resilience, resourcefulness, collaboration, and leadership under uncertainty. These skills aren't just "nice to haves"; they're what people fall back on when everything else fails. When strategy doesn't work, when the market shifts, when the team is in crisis, or when technology changes everything overnight, you still have your human skills.

The leaders who survive those tricky moments aren't the ones with the best technical credentials; they're the ones who can read a room, hold people together, communicate through uncertainty, and make decisions with incomplete information. That is the empathy skill set.

Survival isn't just about staying employed; it's about staying effective, staying relevant, and staying human in environments that are increasingly pressured and fast-moving. Empathy is the non-technical skill that makes all the other non-technical skills possible. You can't communicate well without it. You can't build trust without it. You can't lead through uncertainty without it. It's not one item on a list of survival skills; it's the foundation they all rest on.

REMEMBER

"Soft skills" implies that the skills considered soft are optional. They're secondary and decorative. You don't really need them to truly climb any ladder or lead a team effectively. "Non-technical skills" says something different; it says these are a distinct category of real skill that requires practice, feedback, and development just like any technical competency. It changes how people invest in themselves and how organizations develop their people. A skill you think of as soft, you tolerate being weak at. A skill you think of as non-technical, you get better at.

IN THIS CHAPTER

» Moving away from old-style leadership to human-centered leadership

» Highlighting indicators that mask low empathy

» Creating depth as an empathy leader

Chapter 3

Recognizing that Some Leaders Succeed without Empathy

Some of the most successful leaders you've ever encountered probably weren't the most empathetic ones. And if you're being honest, you've likely worked for at least one of them. Maybe it was someone who drove results, commanded a room, made fast decisions, or built something genuinely impressive. Someone who, by almost every visible measure, was winning.

This chapter isn't going to pretend that didn't happen. Because it did, and it does all the time. Leaders succeed without empathy every day. So, understanding exactly how that success has a ceiling is one of the most important things you can do as someone who wants to lead differently.

What you'll find in this chapter isn't a takedown of a leadership style. Instead, this chapter takes a clear-eyed look at how old models of leadership got their results, why those models are increasingly mismatched with the world we now work in, and what the indicators of empathy-free success look like. The danger isn't always obvious dysfunction; sometimes the danger looks like a high-performing team, a strong brand, and a leader who hasn't lost anyone. Yet.

By the end of this chapter, you'll understand the difference between success that's actually built to last and success that's built to just appear that way. And once you can see that difference, you can't unsee it.

Exploring the Past and Present of Leadership

TECHNICAL STUFF

Before humans even existed, there was leadership. Alpha male chimpanzees maintained control over their tribes through intimidation, displays of power, and physical strength. For bonobos, matriarchs established leadership through affection, social networking, and conflict resolution rather than aggression. Gorillas tied power to size and physical presence, following the lead of a single dominant silverback. And in non-primate societies, the leader usually was whoever moved first; they capitalized on the need for collective safety. Early human bands relied on a more flexible leadership structure, shifting to the person with the most relevant skill for the specific situation.

As our numbers grew and our societies evolved, the need for more formalized hierarchies became evident. Institutions headed by chiefs, kings and religious leaders sprouted up following the agricultural revolution. Then, in the nineteenth century, the *Great Man Theory* — coined by Scottish historian and philosopher Thomas Carlyle — was introduced. Carlyle stated that "the history of the world is but the biology of great men." This reflected the belief at the time that highly influential and unique individuals — *great men* — were born with natural attributes such as superior intellect, courage, extraordinary leadership, or divine inspiration, and that those individuals shape history.

As we continued to evolve, there was immense pushback on this ideology. The nineteenth and twentieth centuries ushered in a more modern view of leadership that proposed that much leadership is situational and can be learned. That brings us to today, where most people define a good leader as someone with a combination of qualities that center around three key traits: being adaptable, being an effective communicator, and being empathetic.

Because good leadership is situational, those traits look different for every leader on every team in every organization. But the simple fact remains: The central theme of effective leadership is *influence* — empowering others to achieve a shared vision. Multiple ways exist to achieve that, and of course this book discusses the more humane — the more empathetic — way.

But what does success in leadership look like without empathy? And why is that success more fleeting than if you were empathetic? The following sections delve deeper into these questions.

Recognizing that old-style leadership no longer works well

Most of the modern leadership styles developed in the nineteenth and twentieth centuries were forms of a *command-and-control hierarchy* (C&C). This is a traditional top-down organizational structure where decision-making, authority, and communication are centralized at the top. Senior leadership hold ultimate power and that power lessens as you step further down the ladder. As a result, subordinates are expected to execute instructions with no consensus-building.

Command-and-control hierarchy can be implemented in several different ways. While some of these ways can be more easily enforced long term, they're all very limiting when it comes to team success. Here are the main styles:

- **Autocratic leadership.** Where a single person retains ultimate authority, autocratic leaders make all decisions unilaterally. There's no room for team or outside input, and the flow of communication is strictly up-and-down. Employees are given exact instructions and are expected to follow those rules. The focus is placed heavily on productivity, efficiency, and meeting deadlines.

  REMEMBER

  This kind of leadership is beneficial in certain environments where rules cannot be bent; places such as factories, situations where there is a high-risk emergency, or teams that work in strict and standardized compliance are all great examples of this. If you need to make a quick decision or establish a clear direction, autocratic leadership wins the day.

  WARNING

  Unfortunately, employees may feel undervalued, micromanaged, or untrusted and all of these feelings create low morale. Another potential downfall? Stifled creativity. Autocrats are, by nature, discouraging of out-of-the-box thinking and team collaboration. There's also no wiggle room for failure on the leader's part; if you make a bad call, the entire team fails and there is no safety net.

- **Bureaucratic leadership.** This is a highly formalized style of leadership heavily reliant on established rules, policies, and standard operating procedures. Strictly hierarchical with a clear chain of command, bureaucracies prioritize structure, consistency, and compliance over flexibility and innovation. The adherence to established rules and procedures is rigid, but in a lot of cases this is for good reason.

Bureaucracies are highly effective in environments where consistency, precision, and safety are crucial. The two main examples of this are highly regulated industries — government agencies, the military, law enforcement, and healthcare systems — and high-risk environments such as banks, nuclear power plants, manufacturing plants, and settings where deviation from procedure can result in danger.

REMEMBER

The advantages, then, are obvious. Employees know exactly what their responsibilities are and who they report to. There are standardized processes and those guarantee uniform output and operational efficiency. And there's less likely to be favoritism or subjective bias since the rules are the same for everyone. But because of this strict structure, bureaucratic leaders can't offer much flexibility in decision-making and innovation is much more difficult to break through.

WARNING

- **Coercive leadership.** This is fear-based leadership. Coercive leaders demand immediate compliance by relying heavily on threats to keep everyone in line. Psychologist Daniel Goleman, known for his book *Emotional Intelligence* (Bantam Books, 1995), found that coercive leadership destroyed motivation, flexibility, and a team's sense of ownership over their work. People stopped sharing ideas because nothing they said mattered anyway.

  Coercive leadership isn't wholly without application. In genuine crisis — a safety emergency, a turnaround where the organization is days from collapse, a military situation where hesitation costs lives — the decisiveness and clarity of a coercive approach can be necessary in the short term. The problem is that most leaders who use it aren't in those situations. They use crisis framing to justify a default style.

- **Transactional leadership.** A management style based on a system of rewards and consequences, transactional leaders treat employment as just that: a transaction. Leaders set clear expectations — defining goals, tasks, and the exact processes required to complete them — and dole out positive reinforcement or steep consequences based on the results. And those reinforcements can be great: for example, bonuses, promotions, or public praise.

  WARNING

  The penalization of failure, however, discourages deviation from the status quo. That suffocates creativity, kills critical thinking, and makes psychological safety nearly impossible. For the employee working in this system, they really have no reason to do anything beyond what they are told explicitly. And, although this style of leadership does establish a baseline of discipline and structure, it misses the mark motivating and inspiring your team to give you their best.

WARNING

Command-and-control leadership fails over the long term for reasons that are structural, not just cultural. The big issue is that C&C creates dependency, not capability. If every decision flows from the top, people stop developing judgment. They learn to wait for instructions rather than think independently. Over time, your team becomes only as capable as the person at the top — you. And although you are capable, competent, and willing to learn and grow to be better for your team, you have limitations that you have now imprinted onto them. The moment those limitations get the best of you or them — if you're having a bad day or you're overwhelmed — the whole system slows down.

Command and control isn't just less empathetic; it's a strategy that gets results now by depleting the human capital that would have produced results later. Here are a few other reasons why C&C leadership doesn't work in the modern world:

- **It dries up information flow.** In a C&C environment, bad news travels slowly upward, if at all. People learn quickly that surfacing problems is dangerous, so they manage perception instead of managing reality. Leaders end up making increasingly important decisions based on increasingly filtered information, while genuinely believing they have a clear picture. This is one of the most dangerous long-term effects, because you usually don't know it's happening.
- **It burns out the best people first.** High performers, by definition, have options. They also tend to be the people most motivated by autonomy, growth, and meaningful contribution — exactly what C&C withholds. So, the talent most capable of going somewhere else does so. What remains over time is a workforce self-selected for tolerance of control, which is not the profile of a high-performing team.
- **It cannot adapt.** The speed and complexity of modern organizations require distributed decision-making. Problems arise faster than they can be escalated, markets shift before leadership can convene, and the people closest to the work consistently have information that leadership doesn't. Command-and-control structures are too slow and too centralized to respond effectively because they were designed for stability, not change.
- **It accumulates hidden costs.** The disengagement, the turnover, the suppressed innovation, the decisions made on bad data — none of these show up as line items, but they are real costs that accumulate quietly over years. Research consistently finds that disengaged employees cost organizations significantly in lost productivity. The return on investment of C&C looks reasonable in the short term precisely because the damage is deferred.

REMEMBER

Command and control's core problem is that it treats people as inputs to be managed rather than as humans with judgment, motivation, and the capacity to contribute beyond their job description. It works, until it doesn't. And by that time, the failure is visible and the organizational damage is deep; you've lost your team.

Moving toward human-centered leadership

The shift between yesteryear's leadership and the one we crave today began during the 1960s. Douglas McGregor, an MIT technology professor, introduced two key concepts: *Theory X* and *Theory Y*. The former operates under the assumption that people are fundamentally lazy, need to be told what to do, and will avoid responsibility if given the choice. The latter proposes that people are intrinsically motivated, capable of self-direction, and want to contribute meaningfully when the conditions allow.

TECHNICAL STUFF

McGregor was the first to identify the stark change between the management style of those returning to the corporate workforce post-World War 2 and those who were trained from a young age in the knowledge economy of the late 1960s and early 1970s. These younger workers — engineers, designers, researchers, strategists, and the like — didn't need someone hovering over their shoulders, confirming they were doing what they were paid to do. They thrived in a more autonomous environment and, as the economy transformed, it was proof that McGregor's Theory Y was in fact a real thing.

It was in that enhanced engagement, however, that more problems arose as we reached the twenty-first century. Organizations could measure the cost of disengaged workers, and the numbers were alarming. Analytics and advisory giant Gallup found that managers accounted for a 70 percent variance in team-level engagement; the quality of leaders is the single largest controllable variable in whether people are engaged or not. And the cost was steep; in 2024, the global cost of disengagement reached $438 billion in lost productivity.

This brings us to the current reality of leadership and work. Gone are the days when people spend most or all of their careers at one company, capping off their career with a farewell party and a pension. Because of the highly connected environment we inhabit, everyone has options: young workers, high performers, and reliable role players alike. Command-and-control leadership done without caution or empathy will not keep the most coveted members of your team in their cubicles.

Knowledge, creative, and service work can't be controlled in the same way physical labor can because you can't mandate someone's thinking. The workforce has changed, and workers expect more from their leaders. They are less tolerant of bad behavior, and they are more aware of their own value. For that reason, you need to be a human-centered leader.

REMEMBER

The shift toward empathetic leadership isn't a pendulum swing toward feelings; it's the logical response to 60-plus years of evidence that people perform better when they're led as human beings, not managed as variables.

Determining the Success Indicators That Mask Low Empathy

Not everything that looks healthy is actually so. And in low-empathy environments, the most dangerous dynamic isn't always obvious dysfunction; it is the appearance of success. Because when the numbers are good, the brand is strong, and the team looks like it's firing on all cylinders, there's very little pressure to uncover what may be just below the surface. And that's exactly where the problems live.

WARNING

The indicators in this section are worth paying very close attention to precisely because they don't look like warning signs. They look like success, and like you're doing everything right because your team is still highly productive. It looks like you're winning. But each of these indicators has a shadow side; it has a version of success that's been built on compliance, pressure, or performance rather than genuine culture and care. The leaders who can't tell the difference between the two aren't just missing a culture problem, they're sitting on one.

Here's what to watch for:

- **High performance masking fragility.** If I told you a few of the core values of a company were safety, reliability and integrity, would that be a company you wanted to work for? How about if I told you this energy company's corporate vision back in the 1990s was "People, Planet, and Prosperity;" you'd probably want to be a part of a company that centered their work around that kind of esteem — that cared as much about its impact on the environment as it did the people engaging with it.

Well, that company is Pacific Gas and Electric (PG&E), infamous for dumping chromium-tainted wastewater into the spread ponds around Hinkley, California. The result was catastrophic; over 650 residents ended up suffering from severe health issues linked to that chemical. That case, made famous in 2000 by the global hit movie *Erin Brockovich,* was settled, but the damage was done. By all accounts, PG&E is an incredibly successful company. But that high performance and those people-centered core values were just stats and words; they were masking systems that optimized shortcuts at the expense of people's lives. Their high performance was built on a foundation of sand, and it didn't take much digging to uncover the truth surrounding a part of their success.

What lies beneath the surface of your high performing team? For many, it's shaky; Gallup's 2023 research found that only two in 10 employees say they feel strongly connected to their company's culture (`www.gallup.com/workplace/509069/diagnosing-broken-culture.aspx`). In low-empathy environments, high performance is often achieved through pressure rather than investment. Leaders don't care how things are done — if they're done with integrity and safety — so people may hit their numbers, but they're not energized, aligned, or supported.

The warning signs on these teams are clear, and its unusually high turnover. Top performers resign out of nowhere. The department that never misses a target but scores low on every engagement survey. These are the signature of performance built on compliance rather than commitment. High performance doesn't assume health; it only assumes output. And those are not the same thing.

» **Innovative teams masking lack of cohesion.** Contrary to popular belief, innovation can happen in dysfunctional environments. There are, in fact, certain kinds of competitive, high-pressure, ego-driven cultures that can produce bursts of innovative output because incredibly ambitious people are fighting hard to distinguish themselves. The problem is that this kind of innovation is individual, not collective. It's driven by personal ambition, not shared purpose.

These teams may look functional on the surface. But underneath, communication is strained and trust is paper thin. Let's start with the communication breakdown. When cohesion is low, people protect their ideas rather than building on each other's. They innovate around their colleagues, instead of with them. They're reluctant to share their thought processes as they are developing ideas because the environment doesn't feel safe enough for that kind of vulnerability.

And these behaviors lead to a bigger problem: the lack of trust. People view all disagreements as toxic, so they avoid healthy debates. And team members take constructive feedback as a personal attack rather than a tool for improvement. These things can lead to misunderstandings, confusion, and lack of alignment. And because these teams don't have open communication channels, collaboration and teamwork feel threatening.

TIP

How do you know when your innovative team is lacking cohesion? The tell is in the pattern. Do the same two or three people come up with ideas? And are those ideas not fully formed, not bounced off their teammates, and seem to lack any outside influence? That's a team that isn't behaving collaboratively; there's no compounding because everyone is operating in silos. And low empathy is often the reason.

- **Strong brands masking silent culture.** As time moves on and technology evolves, it feels as if all of our content is heavily curated. Especially on social media. Everyone — companies, organizations, influencers, and regular people alike — works their hardest to only put out there what they want the world to see and how they want the world to see it. We do this to find our people, of course, but also because we want to simultaneously grow and protect our reputations. So, we put out content that we hope will drive even stronger loyalty without losing too many dissenters.

  Initially, these entities want to do what's right; but over time, these good intentions can turn performative. And that's when internal culture begins to suffer. Why? Because often, what they express externally is the opposite of what's happening internally. The louder a brand shouts its values externally, the more likely it is that the internal culture is one of compliance rather than shared belief. Those values end up being just another marketing tactic.

  Then there is the weaponization of prestige. You know which brands I'm talking about; the ones that people love to name-drop as their employers to show how smart, accomplished, and "in" they are. And there are great benefits to working at these kinds of organizations, aside from just the cachet. High salaries, trendy perks, and the leg-up on future positions where those things multiply exponentially. The unwritten rule is that — even if the culture is horrific for your mental health — having their name on your resume is compensation enough. And so, it's easy for many employees to accept the brutality of the culture; it's worth it to keep their status.

REMEMBER

Good leaders know that being employed by a prestigious company with high salaries and great perks is a privilege, and they use that to motivate their teams. Great leaders know that they have to create the ideal environment for their teams to succeed, no matter how elite the space is, so they create space for people to voice their opinions while pushing everyone toward the goal. Empathetic leaders know that real leadership is an act of humanity; success happens because of people, not in spite of them.

- **Strong metrics masking weak morale.** The saying "numbers don't lie" is misleading because although a team may be hitting or exceeding quarterly goals, metrics don't measure what's actually happening. That high output can conceal things such as burnout or unhappiness. And then there's the *quiet quitting* phenomenon: Workers may finish their tasks flawlessly, but they refuse to take on extra initiatives, cross-collaborate, or speak up in meetings. Another issue is lack of trust. High performers could feel that their company may only care about their output, not their well-being. That can result in higher turnover.

TIP

The key here is to start gauging real morale. Take pulse surveys by sending short, one-to-three question surveys to get real-time data on workloads or communication clarity. Also, schedule some casual one-on-one time with your top performers and ask them what keeps them at the company and what keeps them motivated to do well.

EMPATHY IS NOT OPTIONAL

It still feels as if most companies are hesitant to really embrace empathy as a viable path toward success. Despite so much evidence proving the value of empathy, so many companies write it off — it's hard to quantify which makes it even harder to justify investing in, and these skills take a long time to really develop, so they don't often offer immediate and easily measurable financial returns.

But there's a big problem here: High performers want to be developed. In fact, research consistently shows that high performers leave roles when their direct-line manager isn't investing in their development, especially when they're micromanaged, constrained, or given no room to grow. Instead of doing the work to develop these skills in their teams, however, it's easier for leaders and organizations to just celebrate and elevate wins without the use of empathy. "See? We don't need that; we're still succeeding!"

Empathy often feels optional because organizations convince themselves that they don't need it. They'll find the numbers that align with their beliefs, and then they'll reward the teams that function "successfully" without it.

So, what is the answer here? How do you convince people that empathy isn't optional; that it's necessary for team and organizational success? The way forward is to understand a few reasons why success without empathy gets rewarded, so you can move past this roadblock:

- **Confidence reads as competence.** When someone walks into a room with certainty, the brain registers it as capability. It's a cognitive shortcut, and it's difficult to override even when you know it's happening. Leaders who project confidence get promoted, get listened to, and get the benefit of the doubt in ambiguous situations. Confidence and competence, however, are not the same thing, and confidence without empathy produces a leader who is certain about things they haven't fully understood yet consistently surprised when their assured read of a situation turns out to be wrong.

  Confident leaders who lack empathy tend to make decisions that look right on paper and feel wrong to the people living them. And because their confidence reads as competence, the people around them are often reluctant to say so. The leader keeps operating on a version of reality that no one is correcting, and the team keeps absorbing the consequences of decisions made without their full picture.

- **Empathy is invisible.** Organizations measure what they can see; they can point to the decision, track the timeline, and celebrate the outcome. Empathy is almost entirely invisible. You can't see the moment a leader chose to stay in a hard conversation instead of redirecting it; the follow-up question that unlocked the real answer; or the repair that kept a high performer from quietly deciding to leave.

  This is one of the biggest reasons empathy gets overlooked as a driver of success. It doesn't show up in the metrics that organizations use to evaluate and reward leadership. What shows up instead is the output — the decision made, the target hit, the project closed. And because the empathy that made those outcomes possible is invisible, the credit goes entirely to the visible element. And so, the organization keeps rewarding and promoting the visible element and keeps wondering why the teams led by its most decisive leaders have the highest turnover.

- **Fear only works for a while.** Fear is an extraordinarily effectively short-term motivator. It activates the nervous system, drives compliance, and produces output. Leaders who lead through fear often produce impressive short-term results because the people around them are working hard to avoid a bad outcome. And in sprint moments — a product launch, a quarterly push, or a crisis — fear-based leadership can look like exactly the kind of drive and urgency the situation requires. The problem is that fear is metabolically expensive. You cannot sustain heightened threat response indefinitely without breaking down.

Choosing the Long Game: Creating Depth with Empathy

Something that's difficult for me to come to terms with is how much better my relationships are now that I'm "out" as a stutterer. Like many people who stutter, I spent a very long time trying to hide it. I would avoid words and sounds that I wasn't confident I could say with fluency, and I lived in a world of negative "what if's."

> *What if* people didn't understand me and I had to repeat myself?
>
> *What if* I told a joke but stuttered in the middle of it so it didn't land?
>
> *What if* people heard me speak and decided what I had to say wasn't worth it because it took me too long to just spit it out?

Unfortunately, because I spent so much time thinking only of myself — *my* feelings, *my* voice, *my* insecurity — all of my relationships suffered. I felt an incredible amount shame around speaking up. I was so deeply concerned about how I would sound that I didn't show up at all. I was swimming in shallow waters, confident with the decision I was making in the moment but with no real plan for venturing out into the deep or what would happen if I tried. *Creating depth* means venturing out into that deep because you won't know what is possible until you challenge yourself. It's taking a risk to broaden your view. That's what creates empathy.

REMEMBER

Depth defines direction; the more depth you have, the more options are available to you. The more you learn — the more you read and explore and converse with those who are different to you — the more varied your path forward can become. That's why creating depth with empathy is so important; because without empathy, you aren't ever going to be open enough (or self-aware enough) to even casually engage with the idea that you are missing out on something.

So, how do you create depth with empathy? Here are a few things to keep in mind about different types of depth:

- **Depth through staying when it gets uncomfortable.** Most empathetic exchanges stay surface level because one person exits the moment it gets hard. Real depth happens when you don't leave, or when you show up even if it's scary. Real depth happens when someone says something vulnerable, difficult, ugly, or possibly incorrect and you stay present instead of changing the subject, offering a solution, or making it about you.

Leaders who don't do this may win in the short term. They can issue directives, hit targets, and never once sit in the discomfort of a hard human moment. And for a while, the results will look fine. The team performs because they have to, not because they want to. But the moment there's a crisis, a choice, or a better offer somewhere else, the people who were never truly met will leave the second they get the chance. Shallow success is loud until it is suddenly silent.

» **Depth through asking a follow-up question.** The first question gets the official answer. The second question — asked after a pause, after you've absorbed what they've actually said — is what gets the real one. Depth in empathy is often just wondering if the first answer was the whole truth.

  Leaders who don't ask the second question operate on the official version of reality. And the official version is almost always optimistic, sanitized, and just outside of what's really and actually happening. They succeed because most of the time, the official version is close enough. But they're always the last to know when something is actually breaking. And that's because they never built the kind of relationship where someone would tell them the truth.

» **Depth through being wrong about someone.** Some of the deepest empathetic connections come from a moment where you realized you had someone completely figured out and then something happened that showed you how wrong you were. That recalibration creates a kind of intimacy that agreement never could.

  Some leaders are skilled-enough readers of people to get a workable read without real empathy. They categorize quickly, manage to type, and it mostly works. The problem is that managing a category is not the same as leading a person. And when someone doesn't fit the box — when they're struggling in a way that doesn't match the model or growing in an unanticipated direction — that leader has nothing. They mistake their read for the relationship, and when the read is wrong, there's no relationship to fall back on.

» **Depth through repair.** Leaders who succeed without empathy never really go back. They move on, they manage forward, and expect everyone else to do the same. There's no accountability for the cracks they leave behind because the results cover for them. But unrepaired relationships accumulate like debt: invisible on the balance sheet until the moment of reckoning, and then suddenly they are everywhere at once.

  Depth through repair means you have to go back and course-correct the mistakes you made in the past as you go forward. As a leader, this requires self-awareness of what you did, where you went wrong, and the impact it had on the team.

You may have read these last several paragraphs and recognized yourself; not in the depth, but in the absence of it. You may have not asked a follow-up question, instead taking the "official" answer as *the* answer. Maybe you categorized someone in a certain way and never considered that you could be wrong (until now). I'm sure you've thought about the times you ran away from discomfort instead of sitting in it. And you also might recognize that it worked. Your team hit their numbers; your project closed; and nobody quit. Well, at least not yet.

That's the thing about shallow success, the kind that has no empathy. It doesn't announce itself as shallow. It looks like leadership because it produces results and it can go on for surprisingly long time before it hits the fan. But it always does.

REMEMBER

Depth is what makes success durable. It's what makes a team stay when they have other options, tell the truth when it's easier not to, and show up fully when the stakes are real. Leaders who never built it don't lose everything at once — they just slowly lose the people who had the most to give. And by the time they notice, those people are already gone.

IN THIS CHAPTER

» Understanding the four types of empathy

» Defining your empathy spectrum

» Mapping your strengths and weaknesses

Chapter 4
Identifying Where You Are on the Empathy Spectrum

Before you can develop your empathy practice as a leader, you need an honest picture of where you're starting from. That means understanding what empathy actually looks like in its different forms, getting comfortable with the emotions underneath it, and taking a clear-eyed look at both where you show up and where you check out. The question is not whether you have empathy — because you already do — the question is where you are on the spectrum of it, what form it tends to take for you, and what happens under pressure.

By the end of this chapter, you'll have the beginning of your own empathy map, one that's actually true to you, your strengths, and your weaknesses. And that's the only map worth building from.

Understanding the Different Types of Empathy

WARNING

Most people use the word "empathy" as if it is just one thing, as if empathy is simply the ability to understand and share the feelings of another person and that is it. But that definition flattens something that is actually layered, complex, and worth understanding in its distinct parts because how you empathize matters as much as whether you choose to do so in the first place. And to truly identify where you are on the *empathy spectrum* (the range across which your empathy operates — from the specific type of empathy you default to, to how it holds up under stress), you need to know what exactly that spectrum looks like. So, the first step is defining what empathy really is in every form and type.

REMEMBER

Four types of empathy exist, and each one operates in its own way. *Cognitive empathy* works through understanding; *intuitive empathy* works through perception; *emotional empathy* works through feeling; and *compassionate empathy* is what happens when all of those three types of empathy convert into action. Figure 4-1 shows all four types, moving across the empathy spectrum. You probably already use all four, you just may not have names for them yet. Each type has its strengths. Each has its failure modes. The most effective empathetic leaders don't rely on just one of these types; they develop fluency across all four, learning when to think, when to feel, when to trust their gut, and when to move. The following sections explore the four types of empathy.

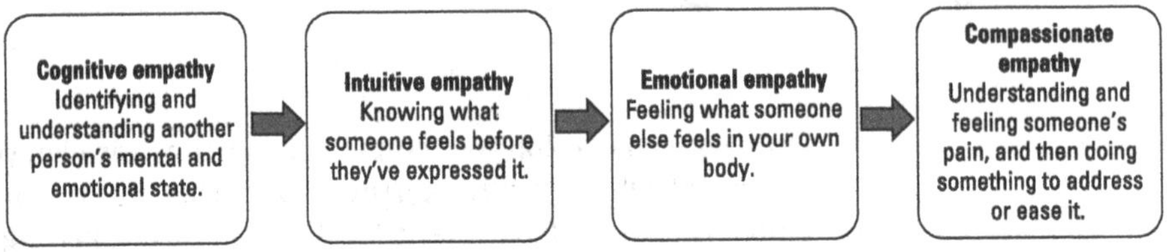

FIGURE 4-1: The four types of empathy.

Cognitive empathy

With deep roots in developmental psychology, philosophy of mind, and neuroscience, cognitive empathy is by far the most studied of the empathy types. It's the capacity to understand another person's mental state — their thoughts, beliefs, intentions, and perspective — through mental modeling rather than feeling. When you think of empathy, you are most likely thinking of cognitive empathy. It is trying to see or understand another person's perspective. A few of the core components of cognitive empathy are:

- **Narrative imagination.** Many philosophers have argued that one of the deepest forms of cognitive empathy comes through *narrative*. By that, they mean the capacity to imaginatively inhabit another person's life story, understanding how their history, circumstances, and meaning making shape their present experience.

  TIP

  What does this look like in real time? It is understanding someone's life as a coherent story with origins and trajectory. It's grasping how their particular circumstances constrain and shape their choices. And it is recognizing that their behavior that seems strange or wrong makes sense from within their world. Narrative is a central part to the pursuit of understanding others. And it is in that love of story that I think empathy can really show itself.

- **Perspective-taking.** This is the deliberate act of stepping into another person's point of view; it's seeing the situation through their eyes, from their history, with their values, and their concern. It's distinct from theory of mind by being more active and effortful. Perspective-taking is not just knowing that others have perspectives but actively inhabiting them.

  TECHNICAL STUFF

  American psychologist Adam Galinsky's research on social psychology has found that perspective-taking is extremely beneficial. It reduces stereotyping and prejudice, improves negotiation outcomes, and increases creative thinking by exposing you to different framings.

- **Theory of mind.** This is the ability to understand that other people have minds, with their own beliefs, desires, intentions, and knowledge states that are different from yours. Is this obvious? Yes. However, theory of mind is one of the most significant cognitive developments in childhood, and it happens around ages three to five. It unlocks the entire social world; lying, persuasion, cooperation, storytelling, human and moral reasoning all depend on theory of mind.

  TECHNICAL STUFF

  Theory of mind in action is called *mentalizing*; the ongoing, dynamic process of reading and modeling other minds in real social situations. Developed by psychoanalyst and clinical psychologist Peter Fonagy, mentalizing is simultaneously holding various ideas in your mind such as what the person knows and doesn't know, what they want and fear, what they believe about you, what they believe about themselves, and how history is shaping their current state.

Intuitive empathy

Though not an established technical term the way that the other types of empathy are, intuitive empathy is real and important; it is the capacity to know what someone is feeling or needing before conscious reasoning catches up. There's some overlap with emotional empathy, but it is quite distinct; it's less about feeling what another person feels and more about knowing their inner state through perception. Let's break it down further:

- **Pattern recognition.** Research psychologist Gary Klein is known for his work on naturalistic decision-making. He found that experienced ER nurses and firefighters don't make fast and accurate decisions by analyzing options; they make them through pattern recognition built from thousands of prior encounters. Intuitive empathy works the same way.

  REMEMBER

  Pattern recognition can be distorted by history just as much as it is sharpened by it. You see what you know; so, if your early environment was that of unpredictability or constant threat, your pattern recognition may be calibrated toward that threat, and you'll read a situation as hostile even if it is not. This is why self-awareness is such a key component of empathy. You have to know your own *patterns* — your own tendencies, weaknesses, and blind spots — well enough to catch when you're reading a situation with bias.

- **Somatic knowing and limbic resonance.** *Somatic knowing* is a felt sense; its experienced knowledge rooted in physical sensation, bodily movements, and the nervous system. The body knows before the mind does. This is because the nervous system is processing social information constantly but we don't know this is happening because it's going on below the threshold of conscious awareness. Our body, however, takes note of the micro-changes in someone's breathing, the subtle shifts in someone's tone of voice or vocal rhythm, and the tiny postural adjustments. And, although we don't realize it, we are reacting; we just view that reaction as a "gut feeling" or a vague sense of something being off. *Limbic resonance* takes this a step further. Coined in Fari Amini, Richard Lannon, and Thomas Lewis' *A General Theory of Love* (Random House, 2000), the three University of California at San Francisco psychiatry professors claim that the limbic brain functions as a channel of connection between people. Two people in genuine emotional contact will, over time, begin to physiologically regulate each other; their heart rates, cortisol, and even their brainwaves start to sync. When people say they feel *seen*, this is what they're talking about.

  What all this means is that if you are physically distracted, emotionally closed off, or just waiting for your turn to speak, you are not fully available to the person sitting across from you. And that person knows it, even if no one can articulate exactly what's wrong with the interaction.

REMEMBER

Your body is always reading the room, but are you listening to it? As a leader, you've been trained to trust data, analytics, and logic. But intuitive empathy asks you to trust something that can't really be measured: your gut.

Emotional empathy

Emotional empathy, also known as *affective empathy*, is the ability to physically and emotionally experience what another person is feeling. This form of empathy goes a step further from just understanding the other person; it is feeling what they feel. Here are a few of the core components:

- **Affective resonance.** Psychology defines *affective resonance* as the psychological and sociological dynamic where an individual shares, mirrors, or experiences a corresponding emotional state in response to another person's emotions or shared environment. Now this probably sounds very similar to emotional contagion; you see someone else crying, so you become verklempt. But while emotional contagion is a one-way reaction to another person, affective resonance is a shared experience between people, when they are moving and being moved together.
- **Emotional contagion.** This is primitive and automatic. You unconsciously catch others' emotions through mimicry of facial expressions, posture, and vocal tone. And that feeds back into actually feeling what they feel. It operates below conscious awareness and precedes any deliberate response.

  TIP

  When it comes to empathy, use emotional contagion as a point of data; if you feel something intense when you see another person experiencing that same intense emotion, remind yourself that this feeling is helping you better understand the other person.
- **Emotional recognition.** To feel with someone, you first have to accurately read what they're feeling. And this is more challenging that it seems on its face. You have to read facial micro-expressions, body language and posture, vocal tone and rhythm, and figure out what you would feel in this exact situation. Most of us don't have the time, energy, or capacity to see and think of all of these things during conversations, especially difficult ones.

  WARNING

  You cannot resonate with an emotion that you haven't identified. You can't "feel into" someone's experience if you have misread what they're experience. Think of it this way: If someone is feeling shame but you read it as anger, you'll respond to anger. Your empathy may be genuine, but it will be misdirected.

REMEMBER

Emotional contagion generally happens automatically, but *accurate* emotional empathy — the kind that actually serves the people you interact with — requires that your perception of their state is correct.

Compassionate empathy

Compassionate empathy is the most action-oriented type of empathy. It is the ability to understand someone's feelings and share their experience, while using those feelings to take action to help them. It's a combination of cognitive understanding (someone is upset), emotional resonance (knowing what it feels like to be upset), and a desire to support them through this process without being overcome by that same emotion. Here are a few core components of compassionate empathy:

- **Action calibration.** Not all compassionate responses look the same. Sometimes the most compassionate action is listening without offering solutions. Other times, it's direct intervention. And occasionally, it's giving someone space and time to work through the issue in their own capacity. *Action calibration* is the judgment to know which response actually serves the person. Remember that what one person needs to see and feel from you in regard to empathy is going to be different to what another person needs.
- **Affective concern.** The emotional engine behind compassionate empathy, *affective concern* is a genuine feeling of care and concern for another person's well-being. And it goes beyond simply recognizing or resonating with their pain. It's the difference between feeling what someone feels (emotional empathy) and caring about what happens to them. Affective concern is what motivates you to act rather than just witness.

REMEMBER

- **Perspective integration.** Compassionate empathy draws on both emotional and cognitive empathy simultaneously: both on your feeling and understanding. This integration is what allows you to respond usefully rather than just reactively. Pure emotional empathy without cognitive understanding can lead to overwhelm or misdirected action. Perspective integration is what keeps compassionate empathy grounded and accurate.

Preparing to Discover Your Empathy Spectrum

Empathy isn't one size fits all. Empathy exists on a spectrum: You will experience empathy differently both unconsciously and consciously depending on the situation you find yourself. It's important to identify where you are currently on the empathy spectrum and to develop an empathy practice that becomes almost second-nature.

Before exploring the spectrum, however, you need to understand why we *feel* in the first place. Because if we unpack empathy fully — if we uncover it slowly and deliberately as if we were peeling an onion — you'd see that at its core, empathy is *feeling:* identifying what others feel and attempting to better understand why they feel what they are feeling in the first place.

TIP

The goal of this section is for you to uncover your own core; you need to understand why you feel and how your feelings relate to the world at large because the only way you can truly discover your own empathy spectrum is by being comfortable with the inner workings of both your mind and your emotions.

Understanding why we "feel"

TECHNICAL STUFF

In 1859, Charles Darwin published his most famous work, *On the Origin of the Species*, which transformed modern science and shaped the modern understanding of humanity's place in the natural world. His theory of evolution stated that all life evolves through natural selection; organisms inherit traits that better help them both survive and reproduce, and those traits become more common over generations. But Darwin's lesser-known work published 13 years later focused on the internal qualities — the emotional expressions — that drive species forward. It was Darwin who, in his 1872 work *The Expression of the Emotions in Man and Animals*, argued that people feel as a means of survival. He proposed that emotional expressions are innate, heritable, and evolved because they offer a survival or communicative advantage. Fast forward 150-plus years, and scientists all agree that feelings are an efficient system for navigating a world full of danger, opportunity and, of course, other people.

Emotions are invaluable to our experience as humans. They can, however, be intimidating and uncomfortable sometimes. So, before you combine empathy with emotions, consider what emotions are actually doing for us in the first place:

» **Emotions are genetic.** According to several studies on twins (both identical and fraternal), genetics counts for about half of our emotional traits. Genes, however, aren't responsible for specific emotions; they shape the machinery underneath.

WARNING

It's worth noting here that, though you may have inherited some emotional tendencies from those that came before you, it's crucial to keep in mind that it is never just genetics. Genes set tendencies, not destinies. A genetic risk for depression might not manifest in you if you have a strong emotional support system, low stress, and good sleep. Another factor? Life experiences. Trauma and nurturing can literally change how your DNA expresses itself, sometimes across generations.

REMEMBER

You inherit an emotional range and style. But your experience — your culture, relationships, and choices — shape where within the range you actually land.

» **Emotions are information.** For a very long time, I tried to dampen my emotions. As a naturally sensitive person, I've always been deeply aware of the feelings in the room. If someone was uncomfortable, angry, or upset, I would feel it immediately. And I allowed how they felt to impact how I felt.

Unfortunately, I would allow their feelings to cloud my judgment and my ability to communicate effectively. Basically, I would internalize others' emotions in a way that was harmful and unproductive; I was looking at others' emotions as a threat, not as an opportunity to learn.

What I should have focused on was using their emotions as a data point, as information. Because feelings aren't just a byproduct of thinking; they are a form of thinking. Fear signals danger and prepares your body to flee. Disgust steers you away from things that could make you sick. And love and attachment bond you to people worth protecting and being protected by.

REMEMBER

Emotions are guidance systems; they are fast and automatic when you compare them to deliberate reasoning. And we have them because they solve urgent problems quickly, or — in the case of identifying emotions in others — they can give us a clue into what the problem at hand is.

TECHNICAL STUFF

- **Emotions are useful.** Portuguese neuroscientist Antonio Damasio is renowned for pioneering the somatic marker hypothesis; this theory posits that human emotion and rationality are intertwined, and that emotions are biological mechanisms essential for survival, decision-making, and conscious awareness. He found that patients who had damage to the part of the brain linking rational thought to emotional and bodily signals made terrible decisions. And they did so because they had no felt sense of which options were good or bad.

  When we feel something, those emotions trigger our bodies. It generates subtle signals — a faster heartbeat, tightening of the gut, muscle tension — that we identify as positive or negative. These somatic markers, according to Damasio, act as a rapid pre-screening system that narrows your choices before conscious reasoning kicks in. Your emotions, therefore, aren't just giving you data; they are integral in not only helping you survive but also navigating the complexities of life.

- **Emotions are relational.** Emotions pre-date language; children don't speak fluently until they are two or three years old, but they are very effective at expressing their emotions as early as one to two months. We share our emotions through our facial expressions, tone of voice, and through physical actions such as crying or laughing. Emotions are also contagious; this is why one person with a bad mood can impact the entire office, family, or crowd. This emotional contagion is deeply related to empathy.

Each of these emotions shapes which type of empathy comes easiest for you and which takes more effort. Someone whose emotions run hot and relational may default to emotional empathy; someone who processes feelings more analytically may lean to cognitive empathy. Keep this in mind as you move toward mapping your own spectrum.

Exploring basic and social emotions

Psychologists agree that we have six *basic emotions:* joy, anger, sadness, fear, disgust, and surprise. These basic emotions are innate and universally shared across all cultures, regardless of ethnic, linguistic, or regional differences. But there are other emotions — *social emotions* — that exist almost entirely in relation to others. Let's look at a few of these social emotions before we move forward to how they shape your empathy spectrum:

- **Awe** is characterized by a deep sense of wonder, admiration, and respect often mixed with fear or reverence. Research suggests awe diminishes the ego and increases *prosocial behavior* (any voluntary action intended to help or benefit another person or society as a whole), making people feel a part of something larger than themselves.
- **Contempt** is the feeling or attitude of regarding someone or something as inferior, vile, or worthless; it is usually paired with a strong feeling of disrespect or superiority. Contempt communicates that someone has violated the moral order and is beneath consideration, and it is considered by researchers to be the single strongest predictor of relationship breakdown.
- **Embarrassment** is an uncomfortable emotion triggered by the fear of being negatively evaluated by others. It signals that you've violated a social norm; you are aware of that violation; and you often end up feeling exposed, awkward, or have a sudden urge to hide or run away.
- **Gratitude** is the feeling of appreciation, thankfulness, and recognition of the good things in one's life. It strengthens bonds and signals reciprocity, the foundation of cooperation.
- **Guilt** is a self-conscious emotion characterized by regret and remorse, which arises when you believe you have caused harm or failed to meet expectations. Guilt motivates people to repair relationships and make amends; it is a social maintenance emotion.
- **Pride** is a deep satisfaction with one's own achievements, qualities, or associations. It signals status and achievement, and it invites others to recognize your contribution to the group.
- **Shame** is a painful emotion driven by a negative evaluation of yourself. This is the feeling that you are fundamentally defective in others' eyes.

All of these social emotions come from the basic emotions noted at the start of this section. Shame and guilt can be rooted from fear, sadness, or anger. Contempt could be traced back anger or disgust. Pride could stem from sadness, anger, or even joy. Gratitude and awe can come from joy, surprise, and, in awe's case, fear. And embarrassment could be anger, sadness, fear, or surprise. So these social emotions are secondary. They are the emotions you feel in response to both the situation in combination with your basic emotion.

It took me years to understand this process, especially as I was unpacking my relationship with my speech. As a person who stutters, I felt embarrassment and shame constantly; me sounding different to everyone else meant, in my mind, I was violating a social norm that I had very little control over, and I felt that others viewed me as fundamentally defective because of it. Of course, this wasn't true. But what I didn't understand until later was why this was false. My shame and embarrassment came from fear, anger and — this one is difficult for me to admit — some disgust. I was constantly afraid of talking — of how much I would stutter, angry that I couldn't speak like everyone else, and disgusted at how I sounded when I did speak. Once I was able to identify what I was actually feeling — by divorcing my basic emotions from the ones I conjured up — I was able to work through those emotions more productively.

What, then, about empathy? Well, there was another side effect of better understanding my own emotions; I was able to more easily identify the basic emotions people were feeling and not just focus on the social ones. We get lost in the social emotions, and that happens because we allow our emotions to get clouded by what others think. You lose your ability to empathize with others when you invest too much capital in those social emotions. Those are the emotions that keep you in the comparison trap, and they prevent you from seeing what is real and true.

But there is good news here; these social emotions can also help you better understand others. Empathy is in many ways the foundation that makes social emotions possible. Guilt, shame, and gratitude require you to model other minds. And empathy is truly shaped by who you identify with, who you care about, and what you consider important.

REMEMBER

Understanding what social emotions are and the basic emotions they come from means that you can more easily follow along on any emotional journey someone may invite you on. It's in those journeys that you also experience real empathy, and that's how you form the basis of your empathy spectrum. This is the basis because your spectrum isn't just about the four empathy types you use; it's about how well you can separate what you're actually sensing in someone else from what your own social emotions project onto the moment. Someone with strong emotional or intuitive empathy but poor basic-emotion awareness will often *feel* like they're empathizing when they're actually reacting to their own shame, guilt, or comparison. The clearer you get about your own emotional wiring, the more accurately you can place yourself on the spectrum — and the more reliably your empathy will land on other people's actual experience rather than your projection of it. Emotional self-awareness isn't a separate skill from the spectrum; it's the lens you're using to read it.

Mapping Your Position on the Empathy Spectrum

This chapter acts as a guide for laying out your empathy spectrum. In the earlier sections, you've discovered what the various types of empathy are, you know what a few of their core components are, and you understand how they work together — or on their own — to get you closer to understanding other people. You've also figured out how to decipher your basic emotions from the ones that happen when you attach your own feelings to what you think others feel about you.

REMEMBER

Empathy isn't binary; it's not something you just turn on and off nor is it something that is going to be the same in every situation you find yourself in. And, as touched on throughout this chapter, your emotions aren't binary either. How you feel at any given moment, on any given day will determine what you are capable of empathetically.

TIP

Your empathetic responses, therefore, will not always align with your overall intentions. They will, however, fall on a spectrum based off of your natural inclinations and what you've committed to improving. It's your job to make sure that your spectrum doesn't extend too far in either direction. Lean too far into over-identification and you burn out; lean too far into detachment and your team stops feeling seen. Know your natural range, and catch yourself before either edge costs you.

What are those bookends, and what's in the middle? You determine that by answering these three questions:

- **What are you already doing that is empathetic?** This includes everything. Every emotion you are able to identify in others. Every gut feeling you get in specific situations. Every time you felt like your emotions got caught up in another person's, causing you to behave more or less emotionally, rationally, happily, or excitedly.

  After you figure that out, put your behaviors into the various categories of empathy described earlier in this chapter: cognitive, intuitive, emotional, and compassionate. Once you've sorted your behaviors this way, you'll likely notice you lean heavily on one or two types and rarely touch others. That's your natural *empathy signature* (your default pattern of empathy types under normal conditions). It tells you which type to keep leaning on, and which type you'll need to consciously build if you want fluency across the full spectrum instead of relying on the one or two moves that come easiest to you.

- **What are you doing that is apathetic?** Identify the situations where you experience apathy and, since this is about leadership, put more of your focus on apathy at work. Is it when you're doing repetitive tasks? Or when you feel invisible after something you've done goes unacknowledged? How about when you feel burned out or overloaded? Then identify the behaviors you engage in during those moments of apathy. Do you isolate yourself? Do you become more emotionally blunt, where you speak in a monotone voice or show limited facial expressions? Do you stop caring about or responding to others?

  This is important to know because it tells you what happens when your empathy doesn't have anywhere to land or nothing left to run on. You see, you never stop being empathetic. And that's the key. The opposite of empathy isn't apathy; it's indifference, the fundamental lack of concern for others' lives that isn't rooted in depletion but disposition. Indifference doesn't care and never did. Apathy cared and ran out. You need to not only know what happens when you run out but also what you are feeling — both your basic emotions and your social ones — when that moment happens. Identifying your apathetic behaviors lets you know where in that spectrum you get kicked off.

- **Where are you succeeding and where are you losing steam?** Succeeding doesn't mean perfection; it means consistent. Where are you regularly showing up emotionally? And not just when it's easy, not just with people you like, and not when you're well rested and the stakes are low. These moments of showing up regularly — rather than only when it is easy — are your strengths, and they're a worthy foundation to build from.

  Losing steam is equally important to identify, and it's worth being specific about this. Most leaders aren't losing empathy all at once; they lose it in particular conditions, with particular people, and around particular types of conflict or pressure. Maybe you're strong in one-on-one conversations but check out in group settings. Maybe you lead with compassionate empathy in a crisis but go cold when someone is underperforming. Maybe your cognitive empathy is sharp, but your emotional empathy shuts down when you're overwhelmed. The pattern is the data. And the data is what lets you lead with intention rather than just instinct.

By answering these three questions, you're not just gathering observations. You're plotting actual points on your spectrum: which types you default to, where your capacity runs out, and under what conditions. Put those points together, and you have your map.

REMEMBER

Your map is your position on the spectrum, made specific and personal. The spectrum is the range that exists for everyone; the map is where you, specifically, currently sit on it — including your defaults, your blind spots, and your breaking points.

TIP

Your map is also the starting point for concepts throughout this book. If your map shows that you default to cognitive empathy but go cold emotionally under pressure, that's exactly the pattern the 3C Method in Chapter 13 is built to help you interrupt. If your map shows strong intragroup empathy but weak intergroup empathy, Chapter 11's work on bridging group divides will matter more to you than it might to someone else. And if your map shows a fatigue gap that shows up specifically in one-on-ones, the recovery work in Chapter 14 gives you a direct next step. You'll get the most out of every chapter by knowing, specifically, which parts of your own map they're speaking to.

2

Becoming an Empathetic Leader

IN THIS PART . . .

Build an empathetic mindset to identify when your brain centers you instead of other people.

Define empathy in real-life and real-world terms and understand how it relates to leadership.

Identify your goals as an empathetic leader.

Develop a patience practice to transform your empathetic leadership.

Discover the impact of perspective-taking as a leader and create systems to better understand the views of your team.

IN THIS CHAPTER

» Applying empathy to leadership and knowing what good leadership looks like

» Understanding the value of being an empathetic leader

» Establishing the type of leader you want to be

Chapter 5

Exploring the Mindset of Empathetic Leadership

Human brains are incredible synthesizers of information, working constantly to get us through our work and personal lives. They are prediction machines storing every bit of information we possess and recalling it with ease when we need it most. Unfortunately, our brains are often wrong, especially about other's intentions.

Consider this: You get a three-word email at 4:48 p.m. from one of your coworkers. It's direct and to the point, but it could also be interpreted as terse. You assume the worst, that this person is frustrated with you and therefore is expressing that negative emotion through their text. You aren't sure how to phrase your response. Should you just address the issue at hand, or should you ask if you've done something to offend them? Their actual reason for the email's tone? They were rushing for the train and trying to send their response to you before the end of day.

Your brain isn't as helpful as it thinks it is. That's because it places you at the center: *your* feelings, *your* concerns, and *your* needs. You, after all, are the main character in your own life, so it makes sense that your brain centers you and your story. It's for this reason that your mindset is so valuable. Empathetic leadership starts with recognizing that your first interpretation is usually about *you*, not *them*. You must shift your thinking from assumption to awareness; that's the heart of the empathetic mindset. This chapter walks you through unpacking the mindset of how empathetic leaders think, feel, and approach leading their teams.

Approaching Leadership with Empathy

Think about your best experience working on a team. One where you felt consistently motivated to do well; felt encouraged by both your teammates and leadership, even when you failed; and always felt confident in your voice, your impact, and your value. This experience is heavily influenced by a leader that centers empathy in everything that they do.

At the top of the organization are the culture creators, but the middle — the managers and leaders working directly with individual contributors — are the culture carriers. That is why it's so important for those heading teams to work in a way that will best reflect both the company's values and their own abilities. And empathy should always be the centerpiece.

REMEMBER

Approaching leadership with empathy means being an *open leader*. To be so, you must be:

- Open to conversations even if, in your mind, they don't feel necessary
- Willing to identify and understand your biases when you can't see past an issue
- Ready to acknowledge your gaps and be committed to learn why you are lacking in those areas

Your mindset matters, and it's a key component in building your empathetic leadership practice.

Identifying Good Leadership

Good leadership is rooted in empathy. Need proof? Consider this: If you could describe the best manager you've ever had, what would you say? You'll probably start with broader terms such as how much you respected them, how they were great communicators, and how they treated people fairly. Eventually you'd start naming specific details that stuck with you, and how those experiences were better than those you had with other managers. You'd talk about moments where they helped you work through a difficult problem with patience and precision. You'd reflect on how they gave feedback and the way you were able to walk away from that conversation with tangible next steps.

REMEMBER

This section focuses on helping you better see yourself as an empathetic leader. The biggest thing to remember as you read through is content is that your greatest asset is your self-awareness. To be an empathetic leader, you need to know who you are: your thoughts, your behaviors, how those thoughts and behaviors impact your team, and how to shift those thoughts and behaviors toward empathy.

Empathetic leadership traits, skills, and gaps

When you talk about good leaders, you are describing two things: the natural traits they possess that work well in leadership and the skills they've honed over their career through trial and error. Those innate traits and earned skills combined can create a positive experience and team culture or an environment that is toxic, unsafe, and ultimately negatively impactful for your team's success.

REMEMBER

When preparing your mindset for leading with empathy, you need to know what comes to you naturally (your traits); what you've seen, learned, and experienced throughout your career as both an individual contributor and a manager (your skills); and what you lack in those areas that would make you a more empathetic leader (your gaps).

How you approach leading with empathy will have a lot to do with a very specific personality trait: where you lay on the introvert/extrovert spectrum:

- ***Introverts* gain energy from solitude.** They thrive in the inner world of their thoughts and ideas, preferring silent reflection to that of social interaction. They may seem reserved and quiet, especially in large groups, but that does not mean they are shy or nervous.
- ***Extroverts* gain energy from social interaction.** They thrive on the hustle and bustle of a large group setting. They love being around people and engaging in more social activities (such as meetings). Extroverts are often more talkative, assertive, and are considered outgoing.

- ***Ambiverts* have a mix of both traits and can balance between introversion and extroversion.** They lay somewhere in the middle, which is why there's a spectrum. Ambiverts are adaptable; they can find a way to thrive in both large groups and individually, finding energy in both social situations and alone time. Most of us are ambiverts who lean slightly one way or the other.

I swing more toward introversion on this spectrum, which means I do my best work alone. As a keynote speaker, most of my day-to-day work involves writing content or having one-on-one conversations; both of these tasks really lend themselves toward introversion. The act of speaking itself is also a more introverted task where I speak nonstop for an hour or more: no interruptions, no back-and-forth dialogue. Post-talk, when I have to speak to a lot of people, I know that I have to approach the large group as singular conversations. This is how I can maintain the same energy through every interaction.

TIP

Think about where you lay on this spectrum. How can you use that personality trait to your advantage in your career?

WARNING

Empathy is both a skill and a trait. Unfortunately, it can also be a gap. This is why leading with empathy can be incredibly difficult for people, because not all of us possess the natural abilities to lead well. Luckily, we can become empathetic and be a good empathetic leader by defining our empathetic traits, identifying our leadership skills, and knowing where we need to fill the gaps.

Traits are innate and natural. Like our eye and hair color, our IQ, and our height, we are born with specific traits that — barring science — cannot be adjusted. One specific trait that shapes how you approach empathetic leadership is where you lay on the introvert/extrovert spectrum detailed earlier in this section. *Skills*, on the other hand, are introduced, honed, and optimized over time. Things such as public speaking, writing, and leadership are things that we pick up along our career journey.

Then there is a gray area. This gray area includes both the traits you have a natural ability toward and skills that you have a propensity to be better at than others. But these are also the things that are necessary when you're aiming to lead with empathy. The three most valuable in this category include:

- **Communication.** Effective communicators are considered eloquent and articulate, but most importantly they understand the importance of listening and the impact of their delivery (listening in detail is discussed in Chapter 8 and empathetic communication features in Chapter 10). Good communicators know that people leave every conversation with two things: a message and a feeling. The message is a directive that determines next steps, and the feeling is sets the stage for the next interaction. This is where relationship building comes into play (see the later bullet on this).

» **Decision-making.** Good leaders know that their decisions make or break their team's success; empathetic leaders know that their decisions create and carry the overall culture of their team. Great managers make decisions based on productivity, not politics. And this is important because true empathetic leadership doesn't always result in you making the most popular choice. It will, however, be the choice that is best for a positive team culture and overall team success.

» **Relationship building.** Empathetic leaders know that every person on their team needs something different from them — the leader — in order to be successful. They treat each person as an individual, and they focus on building their relationships based on who that person is and what that person needs.

REFLECTING ON A LEADER'S IMPACT

My junior-year high-school religion teacher gave me my first lesson in both empathy and leadership. I went to Catholic school for 12 years. Though I am not Catholic, the quality of education was the best available in my area; you had to take an entrance exam, and the acceptance rate was under 40 percent. My parents valued education above all else, so this was a great decision for our priorities and values.

When you go to Catholic school, whether you are even a Christian or not, you take religious-education classes. When you're younger those classes are about the sacraments and scripture. When you get older, however, those classes turn into discussions about how to live your life. As a student, I viewed religion as kind of a blow-off class. Yes, you had exams and papers, but it wasn't nearly as challenging as the other coursework. Until my junior year. That was the first year that the teachers began to really treat us children like adults, and you could really feel that in the religion classes. We got to talk about what we thought, how we felt, and consequences in a way that didn't feel judgmental.

I don't remember much about the content of the work, but I will never forget my religion teacher that year. She encouraged conversations, even if they had nothing to do with what was in the book. She wanted us to feel comfortable giving our actual opinions, not just what we were supposed to say according to the church or the nuns. And she asked follow-up questions in a way that made us think about our decisions from a place of curiosity and not shame. She was the first teacher I had that validated my feelings; I had a voice and ideas, and they were just as a relevant as the adults' voices and ideas.

My high-school religion teacher taught me what empathetic leadership looks like in real time, and I didn't even know it was happening. And that's what an empathetic leader does; they lead you to where you need go but make it feel like a team effort. That's ultimately the impact that you want to have on your own team.

TIP

This gray area — where your gaps reside — is where you need to work on reframing your traits as skills. You need to view every single thing that makes leaders effective and empathetic as a system, not a foregone conclusion. This is important because you'll be less likely to chalk up your mistakes as personal failures but instead view them as an opportunity to improve.

How good leaders support their teams

At 30,000 feet, the world below gradually weaves from green flatlands to wooded areas to industrial hubs to urban cityscapes to hills and mountains. You can see the city grid slowly morph into suburban sprawl, and then a few moments later into rural farmland. The variability may be fast, but it makes sense. It fits together because you understand how the landscape shifts.

At ground level, however, everything is more intricate. You see the nuanced chaos of the city, the miles of highway surrounded by corn stalks, or traffic lights and storefronts for blocks into the horizon. It can be overwhelming at times. And other times there's so little variation in the landscape that you lose yourself in the enormity of it. But if you have a guide — someone who can tell you where to go, to point out landmarks, to be there with you when things get confusing and you get lost — navigating these differences on the ground is easier. And you feel empowered in your independence.

This is what good leaders do for teams. Anything can look successful from the outside. It all blends together seamlessly because of the space between the observer and the daily grit behind the work. And it blurs the imperfections. When good leaders come to the helm, they know that to enjoy the view from 30,000 feet they have to be a good partner for you at ground level.

TECHNICAL STUFF

A 2018 University of Munich study published in *The Leadership Quarterly* in 2025 (`www.sciencedirect.com/science/article/pii/S1048984325000086`) found that teams that identified and followed a leader were 19 percent more successful at completing tasks than teams without leadership. Other teams were told not to choose a leader but were offered monetary incentives to complete the same tasks. Those teams had a 12.5 percent higher probability of completing tasks successfully, but they more often than not ended up inadvertently picking a leader as the task was being completed.

Why did this happen? It comes down to intent versus impact. This is discussed further in Chapter 11 when exploring empathy in groups, but here's what I want you to remember right now: Team members may *intend* to operate as equals, but the *impact* of that structure is confusion, duplication, and stalled progress.

A leader steps in — often without meaning to — simply by starting to narrate what's happening, asking clarifying questions, or redirecting energy. Their *intent* might just be to help. The *impact* is that they become the leader.

That's what good leaders do for teams: they organize. A good leader collects what everyone knows, synthesizes that data, and directs how it gets applied. Leaders emerge not because they are good at assigning tasks, but because someone makes others feel both seen and heard.

REMEMBER

Good leadership is intentional partnership. It offers direction and support with curiosity but without judgment.

Empathy and leadership: A perfect match

REMEMBER

The trait that all good leaders have in common is empathy. It is more than just the tie that binds; it's the thread that weaves among us all, connecting every single one of us no matter how different we may seem. Empathy, at its core, is a great equalizer. When done correctly, empathy levels the playing field by opening our minds to experiences different to our own. Which is why empathy is consistently listed as one of — if not *the* — top skills every good leader needs.

Leadership is a 360-degree job. Yes, you must excel at the technical aspects of the role. But you also have to do be highly adept at the softer skills that many of us don't necessarily invest much in during our earlier careers. The good news is that empathy, like leadership, is a skill that can be improved over time with practice and focus. And luckily to be a good leader, you need to err on the side of empathy.

REMEMBER

What does leadership look like when it's rooted in empathy?

- **It revels in self-awareness.** One of your most valuable assets as a leader — and person — is your capacity for introspection. You need to be able to look at yourself with as little bias and judgment as possible; view both your good and bad habits as data points; and be aggressively honest with who you are and how you are coming across to your team. Leadership rooted in empathy means critiquing yourself just as much as you do your direct reports.
- **It prioritizes transparency.** People need to feel included in order to give you their best efforts; you make people feel included by treating them as a collaborator, not just a "worker bee." And that's why empathetic leaders prioritize transparency, within reason of course. They understand that, when things get really challenging in the workflow, their teams need to understand how their work plays into the bigger picture.

- **It practices patience.** A foundational principle of understanding, patience is a skill that goes far beyond leadership. It is the motor fueling resilience. It drives focus, combats stressful situations, and builds stronger relationships. And it leads to better problem-solving while creating a more positive team culture. Good leaders know that patience walks so empathy can run. Point blank, there is no empathy without patience.
- **It listens without judgment.** Problem-solving is a fundamental part of leadership. And not just problems with work; interpersonal tiffs, mental health struggles, and helping direct reports balance work with life are all job requirements. People leaders need to know how tap into their humanity because a lot of their job is people focused. Listening without judgment means your team can feel more psychologically safe receiving feedback and having uncomfortable conversations.
- **It centers communication around understanding.** Nine times out of ten, your goal when speaking in a conversation is to be understood. Yes, you want to be heard and given the space to share and to be influential; but ultimately, you want to know that you are sharing something that is going to be received in the intended way. Empathetic leaders know the impact of both their words and silences. And they know that interaction is a jumping off point. So, they communicate with empathy to make sure that everyone is understood.

Reaping the Rewards of Empathetic Leadership

Sometimes, the best way to succeed is to begin with the end in mind. When in you're in the trenches of leadership, dealing with the tedious day-to-day of emails and personalities and deadlines and spats, it can be difficult to remember the reason why you are prioritizing empathetic leadership. Besides, isn't your job to just get stuff done? Yes, of course. And that's the advantage of empathy.

REMEMBER

Let's delve deeper into the benefits of empathetic leadership:

- **Teams display more innovative behaviors.** A 2023 MIT Sloan Management Review (`https://sloanreview.mit.edu/article/why-innovation-depends-on-intellectual-honesty`) asserted, "Innovation flourishes when people on a team can openly debate and disagree." This is possible because of leadership. Empathetic leaders are modeling to their direct reports how to communicate effectively; how to be direct yet respectful; and the importance of being open to hearing varying opinions. This is how innovation — which is so valuable to team success — has a chance of happening.

- **The work environment is more supportive.** When we know what our role is, when we are granted independence and space, when we are allowed to solve our own problems, all while being outwardly appreciated and valued by both our teammates and our managers, the environment is considered supported. That autonomy is a direct result of an empathetic leader.
- **There is a positive emotional culture.** Empathetic leaders use language that is motivating, clear, and honest, and connects new information to old experiences. Empathetic communication is discussed in detail in Chapter 11, but for now remember that the result of this kind of language is an organizational culture characterized by joy, pride, and gratitude.
- **Greater acceptance of feedback.** Studies have found that leaders showing a high level of empathic concern can provide negative feedback to their teams while still maintaining a positive, supportive, and productive environment. Teams that are led well by managers that center empathy can receive positive feedback with steadiness. And negative feedback? It will be received as a data point; it's a necessary course correct that may be difficult to hear now but will be beneficial in the grander scheme.

TIP

Leadership is responsibility. The way you approach those responsibilities — your behaviors, your thoughts, your words, your emotions, your intentions — deeply impacts those you are responsible for. When you're in that position, empathy matters more than ever. Your mindset as an empathetic leader needs to be rock solid. Keep these pointers in mind:

- **Remember your own experiences.** Empathy at its heart is understanding where another person is coming from. A part of that is remembering your good and bad experiences with your own managers.
- **Name your traits, skills, and gaps.** Knowing who and where you are right now is the best starting point for being an empathetic leader.
- **Make it a team effort.** Empathetic leadership isn't just giving directives; most of the time, it's having a discussion.
- **Align your current habits with future results.** Your team is a product of your leadership. There's no better reason to center empathy in your leadership practice.

The mindset of an empathetic leader is one of understanding: the pursuit of it, the encouragement of it, and the recall of your own experiences.

Becoming a Better Leader through Empathy

We live in a world of extremes. Superlatives. We drive by signs that say things like "the best biscuit in Tennessee" or "the world's largest all-vegan grocery store." We scroll through any number of online feeds and see influencers strolling along the most stunning beaches; professional cleaners working on — in their words — the dirtiest house they've ever seen; or a Make-A-Wish child meeting a world-class athlete.

Most of our life, however, is not extremes. It's going to our very regular yet reliable grocery store where we always get a warm smile from the cashier. It's doing eight reps at a medium weight while listening to a song we kind of like at our local gym. It's having the same "How was your weekend?" conversation with your cubicle mate.

Sure, there is comfort in the routine. Our routines form our habits and set us up for success in every area of our lives. But the humdrum of the sameness can get a bit boring and, if we're not careful, grating. It's why so many studies suggest doing something just a little bit different every once in a while. Wearing the expensive cologne on a non-special occasion or taking the long way home after work on a random Tuesday is not only good for our brain, but also our sanity. And it makes that day more memorable.

It's because of those routines, though, that we have the structure and stability required to be able to enjoy an extreme every once in a while. When we do have an exceptional experience, we can use it as motivation. And if we have a really horrible experience, it's much easier to identify what went wrong, why it happened, and where to go from here.

And herein lies the benefit of empathetic leadership. You never hear memorable stories about "okay" leaders: Those managers that showed up, did exactly what they were supposed to do, engaged with their teams in an appropriate yet average manner, and then went home. You do, however, hear stories of either great managers or horrible ones. The difference between those two is that great managers have a structured, stable routine seeded with empathy principles. The standard of how they treat people is high. That way when they are able to go above the norm — to be "exceptional" — they create memorable moments for their direct reports.

REMEMBER

Greatness doesn't happen by chance; it's intentional. It's focused. And it's habitual. Identifying that you wish to be this kind of leader is more than just an idea; it's rooted in a commitment to your team and yourself. You choose every day who you will be for your team. By making that specific choice, you are also choosing the "you" who will show up for yourself: your intentions, your focus, and your habits.

So, what's your "*why*"? By which I mean your optimistic, hopeful reason for being an empathetic leader. Do you want to more influential? Build better relationships? Do you want your team to be more open with you? How about being more resilient? Or do you want to put the humanity of work at the center?

TIP

Any time you feel uncertain about the path ahead, remember your "why." Understanding your "why" shapes your "how." If you don't have a driver in your empathetic leadership practice, it is difficult to maintain it.

IN THIS CHAPTER

» Identifying what empathy really means

» Leading well through human-centered management

» Understanding empathetic leadership

» Exploring how empathy impacts leadership

Chapter 6 Characterizing Empathetic Leadership

Everyone has a dream house. You know what you want it to look like with your chosen architectural style, color palette, and type of lot imprinted on your brain. You want to move through your house with joy and ease, knowing that each room is exactly how you envisioned it. And it's more than just the physical building; it's your lifestyle. It's your favorite coffee shop that you can get to in under five minutes. It's the neighborhood's appeal, school districts, and proximity to your favorite local spots.

A big part of that dream is creating it, earning it with hard work and focus and dedication. It's saving money for years, scrolling through listings, talking to contractors, and being handed the keys. It truly is more than just your home; it's the place where you'll cook dinner with your partner, have a lazy Sunday watching movies with your best friend, and stay up late helping your kid with their science fair project at the kitchen table. You're sourcing a house, yes, but you're creating a home and building a dream life.

This same approach should be taken when establishing an empathetic leadership practice. You need to break it down into parts (the same way you do when you're planning, saving for, buying, and building a home). You need to be aware of where you are; define where you want to be; and identify the steps it will take to get there. Empathetic leadership is a skill and — just like investing in real estate — you need to know the process.

This chapter nails down the basics of empathy and leadership; then, it marries those two ideas into one concept to start your journey as an empathetic leader.

Defining Empathy

For a while, empathy was Beyoncé. It was the darling of soft skills. You couldn't walk past a breakout at a conference center without someone talking about empathy. The idea of it was unparallel in the business world. Everyone from *Fortune* 500 CEOs to researchers to celebrities were talking about how impactful and valuable empathy was in their lives.

But there was always a part of the conversation missing: the *how*. How do you engage empathy? How do you approach conversations with empathy? And how do you define empathy in a way that feels significant and realistic to you? This section answers those questions.

Understanding what empathy really is (with a walk in the park)

Empathy, in dictionary terms, is defined as being aware of, understanding, being sensitive to, or indirectly experiencing the feelings, thoughts, and experience of another being. I've always found this definition to be quite broad and, honestly, not very helpful. It describes empathy but it doesn't give us any guidance into how to be actionably empathetic. It also doesn't break down the various types of empathy and how empathy is a layered experience.

So, let's go for a walk. Metaphorically, of course! Over the next couple of pages, I break down the various types and traits of empathy and *empaths* (people with a heightened capacity to feel, absorb, and internalize the emotions, physical sensations, and energy of others as they were their own). And as I do, I want you think about empathy as a walk through a park to a coffee shop. Are these two concepts pound-for-pound comparable? Somewhat, yes. They can be done in several different ways with ultimately the same outcome, but what changes is the experience.

REMEMBER

Let's begin with the three types of empathy broadly recognized by researchers.

- **Cognitive empathy.** According to a 2022 editorial in research journal *Frontiers Psychiatry* (`www.frontiersin.org/journals/psychiatry`), cognitive empathy is the intellectual ability to identify and understand another person's mental state, perspective, or emotions without necessarily sharing those feelings. This is when you see that someone is feeling a certain way; they explain to you why they are feeling that way; and you understand the why behind their emotion.

  Cognitive empathy allows you to see another person's perspective without absorbing or experiencing their emotions. In conversations, it sounds like "I see how you got there" or "I get why you think that way." Put a different way, cognitive empathy is that walk to the coffee shop. It's to the point; you know where you are going, how to get there and why you are going there in the first place. Cognitive empathy — in this walking metaphor — is the destination.

- **Emotional empathy.** What we typically think of when we hear the word "empathy," emotional empathy is feeling *with* another person. Have you ever teared up at the sight of someone else crying? That's emotional empathy. Also known as *affective empathy,* emotional empathy goes beyond just understanding how someone feels. It's recognizing an intense emotion in another person; connecting their expression of those emotions with your own experiences; and feeling deeply right along with them.

  Let's go back to our walking metaphor. A step above just going to get coffee, emotional empathy is taking a second to say hi to your neighbors' kids as they rush off to school. It's feeling extra grateful to be outside and breathe in the fresh air. It's snapping a few photos of the leaves along the way because they're slowly filling up the trees after a long winter. It's letting your dog sniff a little bit longer instead of pulling her leash to quicken her pace. Emotional empathy is enjoying the journey.

- **Compassionate empathy.** Also known as *empathic concern,* compassionate empathy is when you take those deep feelings you experience during emotional empathy and spring into action to help or assist. Natalia Piszczek, a licensed counselor for the online mental health provider Thriveworks (`Thriveworks.com`), describes it as feeling motivated to act communally, share, and care. One of the hallmarks of compassionate empathy is that you do not insert your own feelings or experiences into the situation. It's being in the moment, acting with care for the individual, and not being judgmental as you are doing all of this.

  Compassionate empathy is a walk and talk. You of course want to get coffee (your destination) and enjoy being unplugged and outdoors (your journey). But you want to experience this with someone else while having a conversation. You want to hear about their new role at work; their aging parent's illness; how they feel about the state of the world; and what happened on their last vacation. Compassionate empathy is being a part of the community.

REMEMBER

Empathy is like a walk in the park; the destination is the same, but the experience can vary depending on the energy you put into it.

Identifying the qualities of empaths

When I first started speaking at events, it became clear that people needed something tangible to really embrace empathy. Because we all know it exists, and we kind of know it when we see it. But no one really knew how to actively be empathetic. I'm a person who stutters, and my stutter became a great tool at teaching empathy because it forced people to be empathetic. The audience had to focus intently on listening because sometimes it took me a moment to just get a word out. They were confronted with a person being vulnerable in public, and that simple act forced them to examine their own vulnerabilities. They were also curious because I am so different to any other speaker they'd seen at events.

REMEMBER

Talking about empathy should include behaviors behind it and the qualities that drive it. Because, if you view empathy as an idea, it isn't tangible. How can you take a concept with you throughout your life if you don't know the *how* behind the *what?* That's what my goal is in every talk I give: to put listeners in the position to walk the walk of an empath by engaging in the actual qualities required to be one.

So, what are those qualities? This list defines them:

- **Accountability.** Empaths understand that most mistakes that happen on teams are indicative of a larger systemic failure. As a result, they are ruthless in finding the root of the issue, making them slow to place blame. They are also quick to hold up a mirror and dissect their part in failure.
- **Active listening.** Empaths know that listening is just as active as part of every conversation as speaking. They listen with the intent to understand not to judge. Empaths give people their full attention; let people finish their thoughts without interrupting; are aware of nonverbal language and queues; ask clarifying questions before jumping in with their response; and use silence as a way to encourage dialogue. Active listening is explored further in Chapters 10 and 11.
- **Curiosity.** True empaths know the value of being life-long learners. They know that their experiences are theirs alone. That's why they view every person they meet as an opportunity to expand their own world view. Being curious and genuinely interested in what others have to say, have gone through, think, and feel is a hallmark of empathy.
- **Emotional intelligence.** Being *emotionally intelligent* means not only understanding your own emotions but also your capacity to perceive and understand someone else's internal states as well. Empaths are able to take stock of

situations from an emotionally intelligent viewpoint because of their ability to tap into the meaning behind emotions.

- **Patience.** Patience is a foundational trait. If people want to be good at anything, they need to be patient. It makes resilience possible; keeps everyone focused; and is a push toward productivity when the motivation slows down. Patience is especially valuable when communicating with others. Patient people are able to listen more intently and with less judgment, and are more open to sincerely understanding how people feel. And they have better *emotional regulation* (the ability to manage identify, understand, and manage your emotions in real time, especially under pressure).
- **Self-awareness.** People need to know who they are, what they are capable of, and how they impact others. Those who are self-aware are very comfortable holding a mirror to themselves and addressing those issues. This is an empathy trait because in order to truly understand others and their experiences, we need to be honest with ourselves about us and our experiences.
- **Understanding.** The baseline meaning of empathy, empaths are always seeking to understand what others are experiencing. They know that there is a lot that they *don't know*, so they don't take things too personally since they don't have full context on why people are behaving a certain way. Their goal is to always get the full picture of a situation before they move forward. This is discussed further in Chapter 9, which details all things perspective-taking.

Knowing what empathy is not

Life is a series of lessons. If you're aware enough — and accountable enough — you can find the learning experience in everything you experience. Even the most shameful parts of yourself, like your embarrassing moments or your deepest vulnerabilities, can be opportunities for self-reflection. For me, that was stuttering. For a very long time, I looked at stuttering as something that I should be greatly ashamed by. I tried to hide it; get around it; and ignore it.

I spent countless moments — ones that I should have been engaged in great conversations with friends or adding to a group discussion in class — internally struggling with how I was going to approaching speaking. I could never lose myself for hours in discourse with those around me because I was too busy in my own head, worried about what I'd say and how I'd sound. Everything was about me and coming across as normal.

And herein lies the problem. I never really listened to others. I wasn't ever really *in* a moment. And I was a bit incapable of truly feeling *with* someone else. Because I couldn't get past *me*: my fears, my insecurities, and my feelings. Stuttering did, in the long run, teach me the tools to be actively empathetic. But before it did that, it showed me the internal thought processes and mindset that make empathy impossible.

REMEMBER

It's important to know what makes someone empathetic — the traits and qualities that drive empathy — so that you know what behaviors to focus on. In that same vein, knowing what empathy is *not* is equally as valuable. Because knowing what to do is only half the battle; being able to identify what behaviors aren't inherently empathetic will show you the path toward a successful empathy practice.

WARNING

I hear a lot of people define what empathy is, and many of the things they describe are not empathetic. Let's remove the veil. Here are some behaviors you are doing that you may think are empathetic behaviors but actually are not:

- **Agreement.** Have you ever agreed with someone just to keep the conversation moving? Or because you knew it was the only way to get out of an argument? Or maybe because you were just tired in that moment and had no interest in investing energy into that person and their opinions? You were not being empathetic; you were being dismissive.
- **Being nice.** As huge of a proponent as I am of being nice, it is often times not an empathetic behavior. Niceness is flat, rarely going beyond the headline to get to the meat of the article. The purpose of empathy is to go deeper and learn more.
- **Blame.** Blame comes from a place of self-protection. You see something went wrong, you feel unsafe because the impact may land directly onto you, and so you point the finger elsewhere as to avoid any part of the collision. But blame flies in the face of accountability which impedes your ability to learn, to understand, and to be empathetic.
- **Passive.** Empathy is an active exercise. It requires that you ask follow-up questions; seek clarity; pursue perspective; and prioritize patience. All of these are behaviors that require your energy and attention. Being passive is not an option.
- **Projecting.** Your experiences are yours alone; even if you were with several people, their perspective of what happened will be different to yours. Do you know what else will vary? The emotions attached to that experience. Just because something made you feel a certain way — uncomfortable, confident, seen, uneasy, happy — it doesn't mean that everyone else will emotionally experience the situation in the same way. Projecting your emotions onto another person centers your feelings, and it is not empathetic.

I want to take a moment to talk more about being nice. Being nice is always a good idea; however, it isn't always empathetic. When you are being nice to people, it is often in the form of surface-level politeness and maintaining social norms. It's agreeable, pleasant, and satisfactory. In the best case, niceness is a way to maintain civility in a difficult situation. The worst case? It's pacifying and dismissive. It's putting a bandage on a problem that actually needs a stitch. Kindness, on the other hand, involves actual empathy.

TECHNICAL STUFF

Neuroscientist Dr. Marcia Goddard researches the impact (and difference) of "nice" and "kind" behaviors in high-performance individuals. She highlights that often the nice thing to do in most situations is going to be beneficial to one or two people, while the kind thing usually involves the best interests of the group as a whole. In many cases, being *nice* is an ambiguous behavior that leaves a lot of wiggle room for interpretation. *Kindness*, on the other hand, is direct, transparent, and thorough. Being nice often flies in the face of empathy; being kind drives it.

Figuring out what empaths need from others to thrive

Just as one person can change a culture for the better, it only takes one person to destroy it. For empathy to be truly successful, the environment needs to be one where it can be cultivated with somewhat ease. Everyone truly needs to be on the same team for empathy to have any shot of working.

REMEMBER

To create a culture where empathy can thrive, these five things need to be present:

- **Direct and honest communication.** There needs to be a level of transparency for empathy to blossom. Yes, we all need to be honest and open and willing to share our stories. But we also need to be diligent in how we speak to one another; we need to be aware of our tone and the emotion behind our words. Empathy is truly driven by communication, and that requires us to be intentional speakers and active listeners (see Chapter 10 for more on speaking with intent and active listening).
- **Freedom.** The freedom to feel and express emotion is a true catalyst for empathetic behavior. People also need to be free to embrace their past, their history, and what they've been through as a form of connection to the humanity in others. Environments need to have some level of freedom for empaths to do that work of connection, especially when it feels uncomfortable.
- **Respect.** Being an empath in part means being a bit vulnerable. Empaths are opening themselves up to being wrong; to knowing less; and to learning more by humbling themselves. And it is much easier to do this when all people

involved are respectful not only of that process but also of how far empaths are willing to go emotionally to understand others.

- **Sincerity.** When someone wants to share something with you — whether it be a quick chat in the office kitchen or their life story — you should consider that a privilege. Because every moment a person gives to you is an investment of two of the greatest resources: their time and their energy. Being sincere — taking their investment in you seriously and graciously — is required for empathy to be present.
- **Trust.** In order to harvest trust in any situation, there needs to be a seed. That's because growing anything requires there to be roots, water, sunlight, and the appropriate environment for growth. Empathy is no different; empaths need to have at least a little trust in the people around them — and their environment as a whole — to bloom.

Comparing sympathy, empathy, and compassion

Remember our walk in the park earlier in this chapter? People experience that same walk in several different ways but the result is the same. Let's broaden the scope of this experience a bit by reviewing some often-confused concepts:

- **Sympathy.** *Sympathy* is feeling sorry for someone: having pity for their circumstance.
- **Empathy.** *Empathy* is feeling with someone: sharing their emotion.
- **Compassion.** *Compassion* is feeling for so someone so deeply that you are compelled to act.

The main culprit of confusion is sympathy. Empathy is often confused with sympathy because they both require an emotional response to the plight of another person. The key difference in these two is how you experience those feelings. Sympathy is distant and rational; you see someone is sad and you understand that they do indeed feel sad. Empathy, on the other hand, is a more emotional experience. You *share* the other person's feelings and embrace them as your own.

Going back to our walk, sympathy is the physical act of taking one step after another. You have a goal and you are doing exactly what it takes to get there. Empathy a step above; it's enjoying the walk, taking in the sights and being grateful for the experience of being outside. Sympathy is passively engaging in the activity; empathy is being immersed in the experience.

And then there's compassion. Compassion is being so deeply invested in what another person is going through that you are motivated to help. Where empathy is somewhat of an emotional mirror, compassion pushes past *feeling* to taking supportive *action*. This is a "walk and talk," where the walk is the destination.

REMEMBER

Sympathy, empathy, and compassion are three steps on the same staircase. With each step you take, you get emotionally closer to experiencing the feelings of another human being. Sympathy is passive; empathy is active; and compassion is action.

Characterizing empathy on your own terms

Very early on in my speaking career, I discovered that people need something really tangible to relate to empathy. Everyone knew it was a good idea, but no one really knew how to engage with the concept. Everyone knew what empathy was, what it looked like, and how it felt, but so few people knew how to recreate it in their own life. After hundreds of conversations, I realized that engaging empathy was similar to the concept of being in love.

Brand new love is exciting; it's so blissfully effortless that it flows out of you like a waterfall. You see "your person" and you just know what to do. You give them all of your time and energy and attention, and they do the same. You both feel seen, heard, and valued, and it takes little to no effort. Why? Because you're love. And the world just makes sense.

Eventually, however, the high of the newness wears off. The heart flutters you felt slow to a soft wave, and you settle into the routine of an actual relationship. The mundanity of life creeps in slowly, then all at once. And you are confronted with the idea that a loving relationship is a life partnership, and you have to figure out the terms. Your partner needs specific things from you to feel loved, and you the same from them. You have serious conversations about what the relationship looks like and feels like, and how both parties can stay happy and fulfilled in it.

TECHNICAL STUFF

Love turns from an incredible, joyous, euphoric *idea* to an intentional, strategic, well-thought-out *choice* that you have to make every single day. Empathy is the same. Every person in your life is going to need something a bit different from you to feel seen, heard, and valued. Empathy is the walk get there, but *how* you get there varies based on who you are, what you value, and what the person you are engaging with needs.

Empathy truly is defined by you: the relationship you are trying to develop; what you are; the goals you've set for yourself; and how you want to present to the world.

REMEMBER

Being an *empath* — being empathetic — is a choice. And you have to choose it before every single interaction every single day. You define what empathy looks and feels like for you based on your strengths and the situation.

Defining Human-Centered Management

One of the most heavily researched soft skills is leadership. We are all leaders. We are all capable of shifting someone else's thoughts and behaviors simply by walking into a room and sharing our perspective or showing others a different way to do something. We can lead quietly with hushed tones and few words. We can lead colorfully with interesting stories and a sense of whimsy. And we can lead stoically with fortitude and precision.

We are also all managers. We manage ourselves, our time, and our to-do lists. We manage our homes and our schedules. Many of us manage the schedule of children and partners and pets. And we are always managing how we interact with the world: our words, our intentions, and our expectations.

To lead well, you have to pin down managing people. And great first step is being a *human-centered manager*. This is a kind of management that prioritizes organizational results by viewing people — you and your direct reports — as not just resources but as the primary driver of company success. It also, however, centers employee well-being, dignity, and personal growth.

It's easy to forget that we are all always managing and leading — and we always have been — when we first get promoted into a leadership position. That makes sense, because it's easy to manage ourselves. We have a lifetime of experience, trial and error, and success in what works for us. Throwing others into the mix makes managing — and, as a result, leading — more challenging.

REMEMBER

Management is a title; leadership is a job. Management is tactical, while leadership is emotional. And that's why you need to root your leadership practice in empathy.

Managing and leading teams successfully

Sometimes, it feels as if we are living in a constant state of change and evolution. The moment we get comfortable with one technology, here comes the next iteration. There always seems to be something better just over the horizon; if we wait long enough, it feels like everything will eventually be replaced by the next version.

TECHNICAL STUFF

This extends to science. Researchers are constantly learning new things about the human body; developing new cures for old diseases; and creating products and processes that enable athletes to continue to set world records. It's easy to think that because humans, technology, and industry keep evolving, so will how we approach things such as communication, leadership, and relationships. That's not the case. Because at our core, we want the same things in the current day as we did 15, 100, 300, or 3,000 years ago.

We want to be included. We want a sense of community. We want to know that there are people in our corner. We want to be wanted and needed, helpful and helped. We want to be valued and to add value. And we want to be a part of a team — both at home and out in the world — working toward something that is bigger than us alone.

TIP

When you are considering what a good manager and good leader is, keep in mind who you are at your core. Yes, there will always be new ways to communicate and create and organize. As long as you are living, you will probably come to a point where you will need to learn a new technology. And that new thing may change the *how* of being human — how you speak or listen, how you make cool things, how you work with others . . . but it won't change the *what.*

That's what leaders need to always keep in the back of their minds. Your job is a people-first enterprise; always keep humanity at the center. How do you do that? Check out the nearby sidebar, "Timeless Leadership Skills" to examine some key leader abilities.

TIMELESS LEADERSHIP SKILLS

Here are six key leadership skills that are truly timeless:

- **Agility.** No two of anything are the same: projects, days, people. Great leaders know this; they invest in being nimble so each and every person or situation gets what it needs to be successful.
- **Clear communication.** Being a clear communicator means communicating with clarity; creating an environment that encourages autonomy; and providing context.
- **Critical thinking.** Being open-minded; having a learning mindset; pursuing perspective; and a willingness to evaluate the opinions, judgments and decisions of others are all critical-thinking traits that great leaders embody.

(continued)

(continued)

- **Discernment.** A combination of your intuition, instinct, and pattern recognition, discernment is about having acute judgment resulting from years of life and work experience along with the ability to process situations in a non-linear capacity.
- **Integrity.** Integrity is consistency, accountability, honesty, and ethical decision-making. These combined create a culture of trust, and the best leaders lead teams that trust them.
- **Resilience.** Great leaders show up every day with a can-do attitude. They face turmoil, discomfort, curveballs, and unexpected pivots with grace; and they know there is a solution to every problem.

Knowing what to avoid as a manager and leader

Culture isn't what you say: it's what you do and what you tolerate. Your habits are your priorities. And what your team sees you consistently do is what they will associate with you as a manager, leader, and human being. Just as it important to know what to do to lead and manage well, you need to know what not to do.

WARNING

Most managers don't fail because they lack intelligence or drive — they fail because of blind spots they never knew they had. The following pitfalls are common, correctable, and worth examining honestly, even if some of them feel uncomfortably familiar:

» **Being boundary-less.** Boundaries are necessary for order and to maintain respect. When there are no boundaries, the line between leader and friend can become blurred. This can look like favoritism and loss of objectivity. If you want to erode authority quickly, don't establish boundaries.

» **Being inconsistent.** One of your goals as a people manager is to maintain a good enough morale that your team is successful. If morale sinks, then there goes trust. The culture will suffer next. And, as moods take a downturn, so does productivity. You can avoid this domino effect by being consistent: in your behaviors, in your messaging, and — as much as you can — in your own moods. Consistency breeds stability and ensures fairness. So much work now is fluid: how and where we work, the constant threat of change, and the potential for layoffs means that managers need to have a steady hand as often as possible.

» **Being rigid.** Being rigid means being unwilling to learn, grow, and evolve as you are exposed to unfamiliar ideas and pathways. As a people manager, this rigidity can externalize itself as perfectionism, closed-mindedness, and fear.

- **Being unaware.** One of the best skills you can develop is being sincerely, unbiasedly aware both of yourself and of the world around you. Not knowing the full picture could result in poor decision-making which means you could be operating at full speed with significant blind spots. This doesn't even consider how not being aware of your own limitations can cause you to overestimate or underestimate your capabilities; ignore vital feedback; or misread critical situations. A lack of awareness is potentially lethal to team dynamics; avoid it at all costs.
- **Centering yourself.** When a child is well-behaved, polite, bright, and pleasant to be around, we immediately think two things: good genes and great parenting. What we are seeing is the result of a lot of hard work behind the scenes: loving discipline, long talks, answering seemingly endless questions, and a true investment of time into that child. Parent is selfless, and children are a direct reflection of that. Being a people leader is quite similar. When your team looks good, you look good. Why? Because your team is a direct reflection of your selflessness: your guidance, mentorship, your extra time, and your energy. It is for this reason that centering yourself is in no one's interest.
- **Not taking responsibility for mistakes.** Or even worse: blaming. And as the Indigenous proverb goes, pointing the finger at someone else means there are three fingers pointing back at you. Ownership truly does go both ways: own your wins and be accountable for your part in your losses. Not taking responsibility can foster a culture of blame which leads to toxicity, disengagement, and — ultimately — higher turnover.

Defining Empathetic Leadership

In life, one thing that is for sure is change. If you're lucky, you'll experience eight, nine, maybe even 10 decades of learning, growing, and evolving. Sometimes, those lessons will be small or insignificant beyond a few months or years. But other times, you'll look back on an experience, a day, or a choice and see just how deeply and thoroughly it changed you physically, emotionally, and mentally.

There are two choices in my life that I know will stay with me until the end. One of those is fitness. I'd always been fascinated by it but also terrified of going to a gym and picking up a barbell. But one day I decided that my desire was greater than my fear, and that choice alone has made me physically strong but also mentally tough. I can face so much more of life because of my commitment to fitness.

The other choice was deciding to pursue public speaking. Of course, it changed my career and my life drastically just by putting me in rooms and spaces where

I would not have been otherwise. But the bigger impact was the people I met along the way. The woman who came up to me after a talk and said she was struggling with bipolar, and how much my session helped her put more work-appropriate words to her feelings so she could talk more freely about what she was going through with her manager. The fellow speakers I met along the way who encouraged me to keep going, even when I felt like an imposter and wondered if I belonged. The woman who came up to me crying while I was eating lunch and started telling me about her life struggles, thankful she felt like she could actually talk to someone without judgment.

Speaking at events taught me to be a better communicator. I discovered how to put a story together and attach it to actionable takeaways so everyone in the audience could go along on that journey with me and continue it on their own after the talk finished. It also forced me to really practice what I preach. Yes, leading with empathy means creating a space where people can express themselves to you without judgment. But it also means sitting in that moment with another person, allowing them to process their feelings, and learning to stay present even when you feel like you're out of your depth.

Sometimes things enter your life, and it feels like their presence changes your DNA. And it's not because they or it have done anything specific. It's just who or what they are that impacts you so deeply that you see the world a from a fresh, optimistic perspective.

REMEMBER

This is what I mean when I talk about the essence of empathetic leadership. Your goal when leading with empathy is to of course pursue varying perspectives so you can better understand others. In doing that, you are also creating a space for another person feel seen, be heard, and experience real value.

By making your world bigger with your pursuit of understanding, you are also making their world better because they feel that they have a real place in it. That is leading with empathy.

Leading with empathy

TIP

Leading with empathy means just that: walking into every situation being an empath first. You should be listening to understand, not to judge; communicating with clarity, not to speak over someone's head; being emotionally regulated and self-aware, not being intimidated by strong emotions; and approaching difficult situations with compassion, not indifference.

Leadership on its own is an art and a science. Good leaders uncover what's beneath the surface in others, helping them discover their strengths and encourage growth through both compassion and pressure. If you define empathetic leadership in those terms, it's pursuing each of your team members' perspectives to help them better achieve success. Empathetic leadership is not only a mindset, but also a skillset.

WHAT TEAMS WITH EMPATHETIC LEADERS LOOK LIKE

It's one thing to talk about empathetic leadership in abstract — it's another to see what it actually produces. And the results are hard to argue with. Teams led by empathetic leaders don't just feel better at work; they perform better, stay longer, and show up more fully. The data backs this up, but so does common sense: When people feel genuinely cared for, they give more of themselves. Here's what that looks like in practice:

- **Higher retention.** Studies have been screaming this for years: people don't leave companies, they leave managers. Keeping the best talent in the building is largely due their day-to-day experience, and nothing impacts that more than their direct-line manager. According to the Society of Human Resources Management (`shrm.org`), 92 percent of employees prefer to stay on teams with empathetic leaders longer than without.
- **Highly engaged.** Teams with empathetic leaders feel seen, heard, and valued. One of the most impactful results of that is engagement. According to research, individuals on teams helmed by empathetic leaders feel more empathic concern for not just their leaders, but also their fellow teammates.
- **Lower levels of stress and burnout.** When anxiety in teams is high, so is stress and burnout. That means that turnover is right over the horizon. When teams are led by empathetic leaders, their nervous systems are more relaxed. They don't rush immediately into fight or flight which means they are much slower to panic. Less panic equals less stress because they know their manager isn't one mistake away from a blowup. Having an empathetic leader means workers don't have to fight for their metaphorical lives at their cubicle.
- **More psychologically safe.** The research is clear: higher empathy on teams equals higher well-being of all involved. Soongsil University academic researcher and professor Sang-Woo Hahm confirmed in a 2017 study published in the *Journal of Internet Computing and Services* (`www.jics.or.kr`) that empathetic communication is a key factor in reducing burnout and the symptoms of exhaustion. Teams with empathetic leaders report feeling better both mentally and physically, which is a direct result of feeling supported by their leader.

Identifying the elements of leading with empathy

Empathy isn't a personality trait that you either have or don't — it's a practice, and like any practice, it's made up of specific, learnable skills. The elements shown in this section form the foundation of what it actually looks like to lead with empathy in the real world: not in theory, not in ideal conditions, but in the daily moments of managing people, navigating conflict, and building a culture where everyone feels seen.

REMEMBER

Understanding these elements is an essential step in learning to lead with empathy:

- **Cultivating trust: Being honest, reliable, and competent.** Empathetic leadership starts with trust. Everyone on your team needs to trust their teammates' willingness to listen without judgment. Your team needs to trust that you will create and maintain an environment where empathy can thrive. You as the leader need to push that culture of trust throughout the entire system. And you do that through your own vulnerability, because trust grows where vulnerability is planted.
- **Learning mindset: Asking the "why?" and "how?" questions.** It is nearly impossible to lead with empathy if you do not have the full picture of what's happening. Empathy thrives in transparency because everyone is open to sharing their experiences, ideas, and opinions no matter how unpopular or outside of the box they are. Empaths are lifelong learners; their empathy drives their passion for knowledge. Good leaders know that learning is growth and evolution, and they are constantly reminding themselves that some of the best bits of information come from conversations they have with teams. Leading with empathy drives those learning-based conversations. It's asking the *why* and *how* questions. Why do you feel this way? How are you feeling? Why isn't this working? How can I help?
- **Self-awareness: Reflecting, understanding, and acknowledging biases.** *Self-awareness* is the capacity to impartially acknowledge and comprehend one's own emotions, strengths, weaknesses, and values. About 95 percent of people think possess true self-awareness. Unfortunately, according to research, only about 10 to 15 percent of people actually do. And, according to Harvard Business Publishing Corporate Learning (`harvardbusiness.org`), self-awareness is a foundational component of emotional intelligence and a cornerstone of human-centered leadership. Both of those things are integral in being empathetic leaders. They address this awareness gap by constantly being reflective. What does this look like? First, it is accepting that we are all biased and understanding that it is completely normal and okay to be so. The problems with bias start when you use that bias against other people. Second, it's

identifying what you could be potentially be biased for or against. Biases come from the part of your brain that relies on fast, automatic thinking to keep you moving forward. This is why biases are based on early life experiences, race, culture, gender, societal messaging, family, media, and education. Finally, it's unpacking how those biases could be impacting your leadership ability. Everything from the way you speak; your tone of voice; your body language; how you listen; what you hear; how quickly you respond to others; your decision-making; and how you approach conflict are all a result of your biases.

» **Activated communication: Using active listening and agile speech.** Many of us approach conversations incorrectly. We go into them wanting to get our point across, so we prioritize speaking: the words, the message, and the impact. Then we wait for our turn to speak again, already armed and ready with a response. That waiting period? It's when we're supposed to be listening. But we're not; we're planning our next move. Empathetic leaders know that every part of the conversation is active. They approach conversations the same way that tennis players approach a match. They know that how their opponent hits the ball back to them will determine what they will do in response. When they aren't paying attention or they assume what their opponent will do is when they fall behind. Leading with empathy is especially prevalent in communication because so much of how you show empathy comes out in your words: both the ones you speak unprompted and the ones you say in response to what someone says to you. Activated communication shows empathetic leadership because you are practicing active listening and agile speaking.

Realizing the Impact of Leading with Empathy

As an empathy consultant, I spend much of my time facilitating workshops on how to be actively empathetic in companies and at conferences. The goal is simple: reframe empathy from a great idea to a behavior. I guide my audiences in how to be empathetic, and then we create a system to more easily engage with empathy in every situation. For some people, this exercise is an outside of the box way to better connect with their teammates. But for others? It's a necessary conversation.

In one of my earliest experiences facilitating, I hosted a workshop at a tech conference in Colorado. This was very new content for me, and — if I'm being entirely honest — speaking so directly to people in a very small room made me uncomfortable. I still wasn't confident as a speaker because I was so green, and I am a stutterer. I still experienced concern around people being able understand me well. So, conducting a workshop with a small group (around 15 people) in a small room made me very unsettled. But I persisted. And we had a great conversation around how to be empathetic; why vulnerability is such a key part of empathy; and how we take these principles into our offices.

After the session, one of the participants approached me in the hallway. He'd been quiet throughout the session. I actually thought he was mostly uninterested in the content, and I wondered if he was getting anything out of it. When he walked up to me afterwards as I was going to my car, I was a bit confused. It took him a moment to speak, and I was a little hesitant but obviously curious as to what he had to say.

He told me — between looking away and a lot of nervous filler words — that he was *very* grateful for the work I was doing. That it was needed. That I should keep going. Because I was helping people.

Then, before I could respond or ask a follow-up question, he scurried away. And I was left completely stunned. I truly thought he'd been unimpacted. But I could not have been more wrong. The simple act of talking about empathy moved him — someone clearly uncomfortable with having a conversation of this nature — to say that it was important.

I've mentioned several times that we are all leaders. We all have influence, and our behaviors — big or small — can change people's lives. Seriously. A sincere smile. Asking how someone's day is going and staying to listen to the answer. Lingering after a meeting to tell someone you really appreciated what they had to say. Leading with empathy means establishing the relationship and setting the stage for the future.

REMEMBER

You have the power to design how your life looks: what you say, how you feel, and how you approach others. In doing so, you also have a huge impact on those around you. Leading with empathy gives you a greater opportunity to make that impact positive. And empathetic leadership means that you'll create an environment where you'll make everyone's life around you better.

IN THIS CHAPTER

» Figuring out your empathetic leadership style

» Digging deep into what motivates your leadership

» Reflecting on who you are now and who you want to be

Chapter 7 Defining Your Goals

Before you can lead others with empathy, you need to know yourself first. That means being honest about who you are as a communicator, how you show up as a leader, and — most importantly — who you want to become. This chapter helps you define the goals that will anchor your empathetic leadership practice. From identifying your communication and leadership styles to understanding the cultural footprint you leave behind, this is a deeply personal review. It's not about changing who you are, it's about building on it. The most effective empathetic leaders aren't born; they're intentional. And intention starts with setting goals for your empathy practice. Let's begin!

Identifying Your Empathetic Leadership Style

Who are you as a leader now? Who do you want to be as a leader in a month? In a year? In a decade? At the end of your career? Most people find themselves in leadership positions because they are great individual contributors, and you are probably no different. You excelled at the technical skills delegated to you in your previous roles so well that you were promoted to do the assigning yourself.

Unfortunately, managing people isn't a role that is extensively taught at any level. Most of us have to learn on the job.

You've probably taken your good and bad experiences with your previous managers, cobbled together an approach that feels like it could be successful, and moved within your management journey with those loose parameters as your guidelines. But you may be at the point where you need a bit more. You may have developed your own idea of how you manage well. You could be a seasoned middle-manager looking to hone your tried-and-true management practices. Or you might be ready to make the leap to upper-level management and need to get a solid framework in place to really optimize both your own and your team's success.

REMEMBER

Wherever you are in your management career, empathy needs to be deeply woven into your approach to leading others. You must move past thinking of yourself as just a people manager; you are an empathetic leader. Defining your goals in this sense means breaking down your personality, your communication, and your leadership style to see how exactly you can root everything you do in empathy. A lot of how we approach the world comes from where we lay on the introvert/extrovert spectrum (discussed in greater detail in Chapter 5). It's important to know where your personality sits on this spectrum because that determines what settings you are most powerful and influential in, making it easier to identify and operationalize the empathetic leadership style that's best for you.

Categorizing your communication

Communication is a highly studied, dissected, and debated soft skill. And that makes sense; our communication is so deeply intertwined with our identity. How you speak — your vocabulary, quickness and wit, eloquence and articulation — is a defining characteristic. As a person who stutters, my negative relationship with my speech made me also feel bad about myself. And I didn't really develop a positive view of who I was a person until I dealt with my speech struggles.

This sentiment is true for so many of us. As a keynote speaker and an empathy consultant, one of the tenets of my work is positive and effective communication. My research and work with companies have shown me that the better we feel about our communication, the better we feel about ourselves. So much of what you do, who you are and your impact on others is a result of your relationship with communication.

REMEMBER

A good first step when defining your goals is to categorize your communication from being a destination with the end in mind, to being a journey with the emphasis on the experience of all involved. The following list shows four communication styles, and — although the majority of lists in this book are alphabetical — these are ordered in a different way. See if you can figure out how they are listed before I spill the beans:

- **Direct.** Direct communication is exactly that: direct and to the point. It's clear, concise, and honest; it prioritizes efficiency and facts over subtlety, eschewing ambiguity and hidden meanings. It's characterized by clarity, conciseness, and being straight forward. Those who speak directly prioritize efficiency and facts over softening their language or reading between the lines.
- **Analytical.** Analytical communicators ground everything in logic, data, and precision. This approach prioritizes facts over emotion or abstract concepts; these communicators validate every assumption by first asking "what's the evidence?" before asking "how does that feel?" Analytical communicators want to be sure they are correct before they chime in with their opinion.
- **Expressive.** This emotionally driven style of communication is built around storytelling and a big-picture vision. Expressive communicators prioritize connection and inspiration over precision. This approach rallies the team, and people leave remembering how the person speaking made them feel.
- **Collaborative.** Collaborative communicators believe in shared decision-making and joint problem-solving. They encourage this by actively seeking out other people's perspectives because they know that when people help to build the answer, they become invested in the team's success. Their default is always "we" over "I."

If you read this list and thought that it was ordered from least empathetic style to most, you'd be correct. Direct communication eliminates emotions entirely; analytical communicators are searching for truth; expressive communicators rely on connection (at the occasional expense of precision); and collaborative communicators are naturally curious about others.

REMEMBER

All of these approaches have a place in empathetic leadership — every moment you experience as a leader will require something different to the last. Knowing your default communication style isn't necessarily about the style itself; it's about exposing the gap between how you intend to lead and how you're actually landing with people. I discuss this more later on in this chapter when you crystalize your goals.

Determining your leadership style

If how you speak impacts how you feel about yourself (see the previous section), then how we lead impacts how others feel about us. To lead with empathy, you need to first know how you lead in general. Depending on who you ask, there are an infinite number of leadership styles, but let's work from these six widely accepted styles:

- **Authoritative.** Do you prefer a hands-on approach to leadership? Do you prefer to act more as a mentor or coach as opposed to just a manager? Do you value a clear, highly defined direction for your team? Do you prioritize open communication with each individual on your team? If these are appealing to you, you are an authoritative leader.

  Authoritative leaders generally have strong bonds with their direct reports because they greatly invest in their team trusting them. They prefer personalized feedback, making decisions quickly and confidently, and providing clarity within the system. Empathy, therefore, is a foregone conclusion as transparency is prioritized.

- **Delegative.** Do you trust your team to succeed without extensive direction from you? Do you know exactly who to give certain tasks to, who can handle a few extra assignments, and who maybe needs a break from extra work? Are you an expert at identifying potential in people who only you know how to tap into it? If any of this resonates with you, then you are a delegative leader.

  Delegative leaders have a "let them do" attitude; they don't micromanage or get too involved and are generally considered less intrusive because they put power into their teams' hands. This style of leadership requires an incredibly high level of trust from all sides. Because of that trust, delegative leadership strengthens creativity, encourages employee growth, and maintains employee satisfaction at a higher level. That trust also helps empathy thrive.

- **Participative.** Do you thrive in open, candid communication with your team? Do you prefer to have a more transparent communication style with most solutions coming from a collaborative standpoint? Do you encourage constant feedback from your team? Is inclusion one of your core leadership values? If this resonates with you, then you are a participative leader.

  Engagement is a hallmark of *participative leaders.* Everyone is involved in making significant decisions, and that encourages collaboration among the team and organization. Because of this, creativity thrives under participative leadership. It's in that creativity that empathy really shows itself; everyone feels empowered to contribute and their teams are excited to learn various — sometimes opposing — ideas.

- **Servant.** Do you consider yourself a "giver"? Are you committed to building a strong sense of community, belonging, and shared purpose? Do you prefer to influence with rational and consensual approaches? Is your primary purpose of being a leader serving your team as a way to motivate them? You may therefore be a servant leader.

Servant leadership was coined by leadership expert and former corporate executive Robert Greenleaf in 1970. It centers on the needs of others above oneself. Greenleaf believed that prioritizing growth, well-being, and empowerment of team members increased engagement, improved innovation, boosted collaboration, and reduced turnover. Deeply tied to empathy, servant leadership is about understanding and supporting people's unique circumstances.

» **Transactional.** Do you prefer to rely on structure over motivation? Are you more interested in following established routines over a more creative approach? Do you use a rewards-based system to keep your team successful? Do you prefer a more practical leadership approach that focuses on tasks and goals over everything else? If so, then transactional leadership most aligns with your style.

  Transactional leaders are very much managers first; they are straightforward, specific, and singular in their approach to team success. The result of this style of leadership is that everyone knows exactly what needs to be done to be successful, and they know what their role and work is doing to push the entire system in the right direction. Empathy, in this case, is in the reliance on a static structure.

» **Transformational.** Are you charismatic? Do you inspire people with compelling stories of grit and perseverance? Do you articulate your vision so eloquently that everyone enthusiastically sprints to fall in line? Do you hold such positive expectations that you truly believe everyone on your team can do their best, and you are constantly communicating that to them? If so, you are considered a transformational leader.

  Transformational leaders drive teams through constant change with a sense of purpose and passion. They motivate everyone on their team to surpass what they think is possible for themselves. Transformational leaders show empathy in the pursuit of knowledge; they want to know exactly how to speak to each person on the team so they can be properly seen, heard, and motivated.

TIP

Where do you see yourself most in these styles? Determining which one is most aligned with who you are naturally is vastly important because your leadership style is the core operating system your goals run on. If you set empathetic goals without knowing your style, you're essentially writing software for hardware you haven't checked. Most notably, though, knowing your style reveals whether you're operating from positional authority or from earned influence (this is discussed in depth in Chapter 12).

MORE THAN WORDS: YOUR COMMUNICATION MEDIUMS

When determining your communication and leadership styles, don't forget that you participate in both of these behaviors in various ways. Translation: Your communication medium matters. Here's a quick overview of those mediums to keep in mind:

- **Listening.** How you listen when other people are speaking leaves an imprint that never goes away. The way you listen is often read by others as the way you communicate. Invest in listening.
- **Nonverbal.** Much of your communication falls in this category. This includes your body language and posture, facial expressions, eye movements, *haptics* (the use of touch in communication), and tone of voice.
- **Verbal.** This is what everyone thinks of when they think of communication: speaking face to face with others both in person and via technology. This includes one-on-ones, small groups, meetings, and talks you give in front of large groups.
- **Visual.** This is a two-parter and it includes your *visual approaching,* as in your grooming and clothing choices, as well as any *visual aids* you create in presentations. Human beings are deeply visual, so everything you create without words has a massive impact.
- **Written.** Keep in mind how you communicate through words. Here's a hack: How you're feeling when you're composing communication will probably come across in the words on the screen.

Fleshing Out Your "Why"

Here's an off-the-wall fact that always blows my mind: Humans have explored less than 10 percent of the ocean! Being 70 percent of the earth's surface, much of it is pitch black with crushing water pressure and extreme cold which makes it very unsafe for human exploration. Yet we persist because much of what goes on in the deep sea helps us better understand ecosystems that regulate climate and could even uncover biomedical breakthroughs such as pain treatment or cures for cancers.

I've always been fascinated by deep-sea divers. Partially because I'm terrified of the ocean; its vastness feels suffocating and not knowing what lies beneath gives me nightmares. But I have a deep respect for those who face the fear of the unknown so they can learn more and make the world better as a result. I understand a deep-sea diver's "why"; the passion behind their work — especially when it gets scary — is what keeps them pushing through when they want to turn around.

REMEMBER

Your *why* is what keeps you going when the *how* seems impossible.

Knowing who you are as both a leader and a communicator (as outlined earlier in this chapter) is an excellent exercise in both goal setting and self-awareness. You need to be honest about who and where you are now so you can put the proper systems in place to become who you want to be in the near future.

WARNING

An overlooked step between transforming the current you into the future you is to get extremely specific about your *why*. Unfortunately, many people miss or gloss over this step because many people can work toward a goal with little to no emotional attachment to the outcome. But for a lot of us, including myself, we need a reason to keep going when things get messy, uncomfortable, or difficult. Fleshing out your *why* is like deep-sea diving; the further you go, the more you understand the underpinnings of the ecosystem (or in our case, the underpinnings of empathetic leadership). You need to know what lies beneath — its substance, its makeup, its impact — to make the surface more livable.

Defining success through human-centered outcomes

All leadership is human-centered leadership. Your goal as a leader is to lead people — *humans* — through their endeavors with the ultimate result being team success. As a leader, however, you have to consider more than just the destination; the journey — the experience every member of your team has with you and one another — is equally, if not more, important. Hence why empathetic leadership is so invaluable; it centers the humanity in all of us, so we never forget *why* we are working so hard together.

Our *outcomes*, the goals that we define in our empathetic leadership practice, need to be human centered as well. They need to be defined not only as what we envision ourselves to be, but also what we want the people most impacted by our behaviors to feel. When we think about our dream house, we're not thinking just about the physical space. Of course, we want the perfect location, ideal layout and true-to-us finishes. In reality, our dream house creates the ideal setting for our dream *experiences*. We think about our kids working on a science project as we pick the perfect table for the breakfast nook or the family dinners we'll have in the dining room as we're looking for just the right color for the walls. Every little decision matters not necessarily because of how it will look to us (though that is extremely important) but how it will function in the life we've built with the people we love.

REMEMBER

This same "dream house" approach should be utilized when defining your goals as an empathetic leader. It is absolutely understandable that you want to come across in a certain way, but your true success is going to be in the experience your team has on that journey. And when it comes to empathy, everything needs to be about the people. Where do you begin? You need to define what you want your results to be and how you want your team — and the individuals in it — to feel.

Your behavioral impact: How you want your team to feel

Impact trumps intent, yet you perhaps find yourself apologizing by saying something to the effect of "That's not what I meant." What's probably happened is that you've spoken freely with little thought, let your emotions lead the way, or haven't taken time to consider what you are saying before it comes out of your mouth. Being human-centered means knowing exactly what your impact is on others.

REMEMBER

Designing your *behavioral impact* means knowing exactly what you want the experience of others to be when they are with you. For example, you may strive to be:

- **Empowered and powerful.** Cooperation, encouragement, positivity, and showing sincere appreciation are all easy cues to make the people you are talking to feel empowered.
- **Interested in their work and them as people.** Investing in your people goes beyond opportunities for career growth; it's about investing time and energy into who they are and what they do. Teams who feel their company cares about their well-being are more productive, more profitable, experience higher customer engagement, and have fewer safety incidents.
- **Respected, heard, and understood.** These three are grouped together because you can't have one of these without the other two. You are open to conversations and feedback, and you listen to your team with the intention of learning not judging. Your team feeling respected by you is one of the most influential tools in your arsenal.
- **Trusted.** Employees who received daily feedback from their managers are more likely to trust the overall organizational leadership. Trust is built two ways: everyday interactions and consistent behaviors. You do this by showing that you are listening; maintaining eye contact, positioning your body so it is facing theirs, and paraphrasing what was said to you back to them before responding are all great starting points. I discuss listening in Chapter 11.

» **Valued.** Employees who feel valued by their managers are more motivated to do their best work. You value people in your conversations by recognizing and celebrating their achievements, you remember the things they say to you and bring them up later, you're genuinely curious, and validate and reflect on their perspective.

REMEMBER

Knowing your behavioral impact matters because it's the moment your goals stop being internal diagnoses and start becoming outward-facing accountability. Naming this impact closes the loop between your intent and your execution; in other words, you turn "this is the impact I want" into a concrete practice.

Your cultural footprint: What you want your results to be

A simple smile can brighten someone's spirit. They might smile at someone else and ask them how their day is going. That person may in turn go above and beyond to help a coworker who seems particularly stressed. That coworker will then speak a little more positively throughout their day. One of the people those positive words fall on might go home that much happier because of it.

TIP

Think of your intentions as seeds. You plant them in one tiny plot of land, in that singular moment, and they grow not just above, but below. They turn into stems, blades, branches, petals, and leaves. They are functional, increasing oxygen and absorbing pollutants. They're beautiful, with their vibrant colors and refreshing smells. They're also constantly growing, shifting, and spreading; they sway in the wind, becoming a part of the atmosphere and pollenating new plants in new places. But their roots remain, continuing to seep deeper into the earth, expanding their firm foundation. Seeds are planted in one spot, but their impact goes far beyond just their one place.

REMEMBER

Your *cultural footprint* is your intentions plus your impact. What you do lives far beyond the moment. Your words, tone, and behaviors continue on through those you interact with. So, who you are has a deep impact on those around you. When defining your goals as an empathetic leader, identify what you want your cultural impact to look like after you leave the room:

» **If you want a cultural footprint of trust, be transparent.** Don't shy away from giving your team information about strategy, performance, and sales. A very quick and direct way to be transparent is to admit when you've dropped the ball. Global leadership consulting firm DDI's 2023 Global Leadership Forecast report (`www.ddi.com/global-leadership-forecast-2023`) revealed that leaders who acknowledge their failures (more on this in Chapter 13) are 7.5 times more likely to maintain trust than those who do not.

- **If you want a cultural footprint of support, be an open leader.** That same DDI report found that people are over five times more likely to trust leaders who show vulnerability. Prioritize it. In many cases, that means allowing your teams to be transparent with you as well. People need to feel comfortable bringing problems to you, especially when things are not going as planned. Being open to feedback prevents those problems from completely breaking down. I talk about vulnerability as an empathetic leader in Chapter 10.
- **If you want your teams' success to be enabled, focus on inclusive collaboration.** Everyone's perspective matters because everyone's experience is different. No two people — no matter how similar, how aligned — will view the world in the same way (Chapter 9 dives deep into perspective-taking).
- **If you want to give your team room to run, give them autonomy.** For many people, the best way to learn is to do. Autonomy is self-governance; it increases your team's intrinsic motivation because they have more control over how they complete their tasks. Chapter 12 discusses leading with transparency to build emotional clarity; this relates directly back to autonomy.
- **If you want to give your team clarity of purpose, prioritize planning.** In order for everyone to know how to succeed, they need to know what success looks like on at ground level as well as 30,000 feet (in Chapter 15, I break down how to balance planning and accountability with empathy). Why? Because people do not perform well if they don't know the difference between "good enough" and "great." Set clear, measurable goals as well as timelines to get to those goals.

REMEMBER

Your cultural footprint outlives you; it's what you leave behind when you walk out of a room. Focus on the behaviors that drive the culture you want to create for right now as well as in the future.

Anchoring your goals in understanding

Your goals work better when they fit into your world as a whole. When you are *anchoring your goals* in understanding, you are putting them in the context of your actual life and not your idealized one. Here's an example of what not to do: You are an analytical-communication introvert working in a remote company that eschews hierarchical structure for a more participative environment, but your goal is to be a transformational leader with daily in-person standups and total transparency from your team. Do you see the disconnect? Where you currently are does not align with where you want to be in your career.

TIP

View your goals as a roadmap. You can always get to your destination; it just might not look like what you thought it would when you left your point of origin. When you define and anchor your goals, keep in mind:

- Yourself (what you are capable of and what you want).
- Each member of your team individually (the competency, skill, and talent of each individual).
- Your team as a whole (what your team can actually achieve within the system).
- Company goals and values (where the company wants you to go and how they want you to go about getting there).
- Your career goals long term (where you want to be in 1, 5, 10, 20 years, and beyond).

Crystalizing Your Goals

Who do you want to be? We have very specific ideas of what we are capable of based on what the world perceives as valuable. Early on, an adult in your life — usually a teacher or a parent — sees a specific strength in you, and they begin to encourage you to pursue that strength. They put you in situations where you can explore it more, where you can really shine. It makes you feel confident and capable and special. It's exactly what a child needs to care a little bit more about school. And you take that same energy into adulthood: you try something, you're good at it, and you keep going back to it.

WARNING

Unfortunately, the opposite can be true as well. When you're bad at something, especially as an adult, you tend to avoid it. And that makes sense; your time is sacred, so why would you spend it doing something that drains you? But something that is lost on most people is that much of what you do is a muscle; the more you do it, the better you get. Sometimes, the "being better" you seek is actually just confidence. You may never be the best at something, but the self-assurance you get from working really hard at it and seeing improvement is well worth the effort. Eventually, this activity becomes a part of you not by chance but by choice. You choose who you want to be.

I spent most of my life almost positive that I could never be a good speaker because I was a stutterer. Because good speakers are fluent, easy to understand, and relatable. I wasn't any of those things, so I could never be a good speaker. I wasn't fluent when it mattered: in front of people. And when I get really nervous, I stutter a lot. But then I realized the stories I told myself about what I was capable of were incorrect. As a result of that, my goals changed and so did my habits. I formed much of my life and my habits around achieving my newfound goal.

REMEMBER

Your habits define you in many ways. And for empathy to be a defining characteristic, you must identify the habits of empaths that you can insert into your own life. Your job is to establish the habits that align with who you want to be as an empathetic leader. For help with assigning habits to goals, see the sidebar at the end of this chapter.

Empathetic leadership isn't something you arrive at by accident; it's something you build with focus, precision, and intention. That starts with two uncomfortable questions: who are you right now, and who do you to become? This isn't about reinventing yourself overnight — though I jumped into speaking head-first, it still took me years to get comfortable on stages and with stuttering — it's about taking an honest inventory of where you stand today. The goal isn't perfection; the goal is intention. And intention only works when it's backed by a plan you can actually follow through on.

Knowing who you are now

Where are you right now? And where do you want to end up? When defining your goals, the first step is identifying your starting part and establishing your destination. Earlier in this chapter, I outlined the various communication and leadership styles. Now is the time to determine what both of those are for you:

- **Communication style.** How do you communicate right now? Your communication style is a result of where you lay on the introvert/extrovert spectrum; what nets you the best results in conversation and which style do you feel most confident embodying?
- **Leadership style.** What kind of leader do you want to be? To figure out your leadership style, determine what your behavioral impact and cultural footprint are currently. If you're not sure, pull aside a few teammates and trusted advisors to get their take on how others view you.

REMEMBER

Who you are right now is more than enough to continue being exactly who currently are; and there is absolutely nothing wrong with that! Because where you are right now is a combination of a lifetime of interpersonal exchanges, relationship building, professional development, and countless hours of conversation with people from many walks of life. Becoming the empathetic leader you want to be means taking what you've learned and adding to or eliminating from it: not necessarily changing it.

Knowing who you want to be

Determining who you want to become can be intimidating. You may feel that there are so many things you could be and so many versions of yourself that you could highlight or sunset. Ultimately, however, there's only two things you need to focus on when making this choice:

- **Define your core orientation.** This is your *internal why.* How do you want to feel going into, during, and leaving conversations with your direct reports? How do you want to speak to your team in meetings? What do you want your internal thought process to be as you navigate work as a leader? Your internal why is the mindset — the mantras, affirmations, and thought processes — that define you. Remember, your behaviors and habits are a direct result of how you think consistently.
- **Design your outcomes.** This is your *external why,* a combination of your behavioral impact and your cultural footprint. How do you want your team to feel when they are in a meeting with you? How about when they email, text, or talk to you on the phone? What do you want people to say about you as a leader when you have left the room? Your external why defines those pieces of you that you leave behind.

TIP

To make this easier, create an analog avatar. This is the representation of who you want to be to your team. Get as creative as you want with this exercise: write in a journal, make a vision board, or even create social media accounts with this version of you in mind. What is the kind of content that this version of you is engaging with? What kind of books do they read? How does this you make people feel? When does this you wake up, and what exactly do they do to get ready for their day? How do they wind down? What are they thinking before a meeting? The deeper you go into who you want to be, the more real and tangible this new you is to achieve.

ASSIGNING HABITS TO GOALS

About 50 percent of Americans make a New Year's resolution. After 30 days, about 25 percent of them are still committed to them. By the years' end, anywhere from 10 to 16 percent of people have accomplished their goal. The moral here isn't that people lack character or drive or passion; it's to remind you that change is incredibly difficult. Our minds and our bodies fight us when we go against what we normally do. And eventually we revert back to factory settings.

You are what you do. You are also what you value. Sometimes, what you do and what you value just don't align. This isn't entirely your fault', because willpower can get fatigued as well as strengthened. Research shows that decision-making requires the same mental energy as resisting temptation.

So how do you fight against the urge to go back to who you were before?

- **Audit your current habits.** You are already doing tons of things throughout the day that require little to no energy. What can you add to what you already do that will help you achieve your goals? Maybe it's getting to work five minutes earlier to have a longer catch-up with someone on your team. Or it's taking the last five minutes of a video call to ask how the person is doing.
- **Make it easy.** For everything that isn't an easy add to your routine, figure out a way to make it impossible to skip. A great way to do this is tell someone else what your goal is and have them check in with you to see if you actually did it that day.
- **Set a timeline.** How do you best keep yourself accountable for your goals? For many people, it's blocking the time off of the calendar or writing a physical to-do list and then experiencing the accomplishment of crossing an item off when completed. Whatever way that is for you, I strongly suggest putting a time cap on it. Add one new habit a week and devote some time to it multiple days in that week. That way it truly becomes a habit and not just an exercise.

IN THIS CHAPTER

- Understanding and exploring the role of patience in leadership
- Knowing the pros and cons of being a patient leader
- Mapping your impatience before it maps you
- Turning patience into a behavior, not just a belief

Chapter 8
Practicing Patience

You have almost certainly been told at some point in your life to be patient — as if patience were simply a decision you could make on the spot, like choosing what to order for lunch. But patience isn't a switch you flip. It's a skill you build, a practice you return to, and — when you get it right — one of the most powerful tools in your leadership arsenal.

This chapter is about understanding patience from the inside out: where it comes from, why you lose it, what it costs when you do, and how to get it back. Whether you are naturally calm under pressure or someone who has to fight for every moment of stillness, this chapter meets you exactly where you are — because patience starts not with other people, but with you.

Defining Patience

Learning how to cope with difficulties in a healthy, sustainable way is a true cornerstone of being patient. Because so many people prefer to defer or completely avoid suffering, the art of being genuinely patient is waning. When we don't like what we see or experience, we often choose avoidance rather than patience. But avoiding situations essentially means hitting pause on them. Practicing patience means being more measured and intentional, whereas avoidance — which is what happens when patience feels too much like hard work — means nothing gets done.

REMEMBER

With that in mind, here's a definition of patience that encompasses its true value in leading with empathy. *Patience*, in this sense, is slowing down to remain productive. It's moving forward — albeit at a slower pace — with measure and motive so as to not leave anyone or anything behind. Empathy tells you what someone needs. Patience is how you actually give it to them. One is the awareness; the other is the act. You can't sustainably have one without the other, which is exactly why patience belongs at the center of any honest conversation about empathetic leadership. Patience is the delivery mechanism for empathy.

Patience is the foundational key empathy behavior; it's a load-bearing pillar of empathetic leadership. And for so many good reasons:

- **Patience is what makes listening *active*.** Time and attention are patience in action. You can't teach active listening without first teaching someone to slow down — they are the same skill wearing different names.
- **Patience is how empathy becomes *consistent*.** One singular empathetic moment won't build trust. A pattern does. Steady listening is what turns problems into lasting progress. Patience is a mindset; consistency is the method.
- **Patience protects empathy from burning out.** Patience acts as a buffer; it slows the emotional intake down to a manageable pace. Both empathy and patience work hand-in-hand to give leaders the freedom to fail forward while learning from mistakes, inspiring positivity to tackle challenges, while also teaching timing and tact when working with other people.
- **Patience is what closes the empathy *perception gap*.** According to the 2019 Businessolver State of Workplace Empathy Study (`https://businessolver.com/news/businessolver-study-reveals-leadership-experienced-key-shifts-in-perception-of-workplace-empathy`), 55 percent of CEOs believe they lead with empathy but only 28 percent of employees agreed. The gap doesn't exist because leaders don't care; it's there because caring without slowing down is invisible to the people around you. Patience is the proof of empathy; it's the part the other person can actually see and feel.

Exploring the Skills of Patience

To really get to the bottom of what patience looks like for you as an empathetic leader, you need know it looks like in action. Patience is a skill, a muscle that can be developed with precision and consistency. Here are the three main skills that contribute to being patient:

- **Cognitive reframing.** Your brain isn't wired for patience; it's wired for survival. And this survival wiring is magnificently unhelpful when your goal is to be an empathetic leader. Instead of erring on the side of caution, you catastrophize. Need proof? Think about the last time someone pushed back on one of your ideas. You probably took offense and immediately thought they were challenging you. Now imagine if you instead thought that they were critically engaging with your work. Do you see how that small reframe can change the whole feel of the conversation? This is *cognitive reframing*, and it is a crucial skill to developing your patience.

  TECHNICAL STUFF

  Research published in the *Journal of Consulting and Clinical Psychology* (www.apa.org/pubs/journals/ccp) found that people trained in cognitive reframing techniques showed significant reductions in emotional reactivity, improvements in interpersonal functioning, and measurably greater capacity for tolerating frustration.

  WARNING

  I want to pause here and address something directly, because it comes up every time I talk about this in my keynotes. Someone always asks: "Isn't this just making excuses for people?" The answer is no. Cognitive reframing is not convincing yourself that everything is fine when it isn't. The leader who reframes isn't the one who lets everything slide. They're the one who can look at a situation clearly enough to know what it actually requires and respond directly to that, rather than to the negative version their brain generated immediately.

- **Emotional regulation.** Let's say the quiet part out loud: Most of us are terrible at emotional regulation. It's not because you're weak or immature or not trying hard enough; it's because you were never taught how to regulate your emotions. You were taught how to identify them and then, most likely, told to calm down. To be the bigger person. Or told that some feelings were too much for the moment, too unprofessional, or inappropriate. So instead of learning to be measured, you were forced to be muted.

  TECHNICAL STUFF

  Emotional regulation is not suppressing your feelings; it's influencing them. The American Psychological Association (www.apa.org) defines emotional regulation as the ability to monitor, evaluate, and modify emotional reactions — both positively and negatively — to achieve personal goals, align with values, and respond rather than react impulsively. You are a feeling person leading other feeling people through genuinely challenging situations. It's not a question of *if* the feelings are going to come, it's what you do with them *when* they arrive.

Impatience is an emotional response before it's a behavioral one. This means that if you want to actually practice patience as a skill, you have to intervene at the emotional level first. You catch the feeling before it becomes an action; you emotionally regulate.

- **Mindfulness.** If emotional regulation is the *what* of patience, then mindfulness is the *how*. When you become impatient, you're quicker to jump to conclusions, react with anger, and experience frustration. This happens because your attention switches from what is happening right now to what could potentially happen next. Impatience is a future-focused state; your mind is already at the outcome while your body is still in the conversation. *Mindfulness* does the opposite; it anchors you here, in this moment, with this person, in this exchange.

TECHNICAL STUFF

Jon Kabat-Zinn, a pioneer in Western mindfulness, defines mindfulness exactly in this way: as paying attention, on purpose, in the present moment, and non-judgmentally. The science backs up this claim. Research from 2025 published in the journal *BMC Psychiatry* (`https://pmc.ncbi.nlm.nih.gov/articles/PMC12121785`) found that mindfulness training directly increased participants' ability to tolerate delay and resist impulsive responding; and those are two core components of patience.

REMEMBER

Chapter 7 explores setting your goals as an empathetic leader. A big result of those goals is that you will build better relationships with each individual on your team. Those relationships are built on your ability to persist in discomfort; that's possible as a result of building your patience muscle.

Identifying the Benefits and Drawbacks of Being Patient

We rarely talk about this aspect of management, but one of your most important jobs as a leader is to care about people. You of course have to assign, oversee, explain, circle back, and all of the other task-oriented responsibilities involved in making team successful. But your team is made up of people, and they need to be guided; and no one wants to follow someone that they don't think cares about them.

This is likely a part of the reason you are reading this chapter of this book, to discover how to better show that you care. Patience is obviously a profound way to do that. Think about it: The people who are most patient with you in your life are the ones that care for you the most.

It's easy to see why patience is so beneficial in your personal life, but what about at work? Why should you invest the time and effort into being more patient; what happens if you take it too far; and how do you find that perfect balance that allows you to reap the benefits without harming your other professional relationships? These are excellent questions! Let's find the answers.

Highlighting the benefits of being patient

In empathetic leadership, patience is a strategy. When leaders slow down long enough to truly see and hear the people around them, something remarkable happens — teams become braver, smarter, and more resilient.

REMEMBER

The benefits of patient, empathetic leadership aren't soft or abstract; they show up directly in how your team performs, grows, and sticks together under pressure:

- **Better coaching and development.** We are all operating at our own pace. Great leaders have a knack of identifying the speed at which someone can pick something up and the distance they can take it. They can see this because they take the time to truly listen to what their teams are saying and notice how they are behaving. Leaders who prioritize patience ask probing questions and seek to understand individual employee perspectives.
- **Enhanced decision-making.** Good leaders feel confident that some degree of success is inevitable when things are moving forward with momentum and intention. Great leaders take this a step further; they know that an even greater success is achievable when they allow time for analysis and critical thinking. Patient leaders have seen what decisions look like when people are rushed, reactive, or motivated by fear. They give their teams the space to develop solutions based on the root cause not the symptoms.
- **Improved team morale and trust.** Leaders who practice patience create psychologically safe environments for their teams. These leaders actively listen to their teams, which allows space for both learning and sharing new ideas. As a result, individuals feel safe asking for help and admitting mistakes without fear of punishment. A high team morale and an environment ripe with trust are both hallmarks of good leadership.
- **Stronger resilience.** You know what is really effective at killing momentum? Anxiety. It's a fight-or-flight response that overwhelms the brain and sends you from productivity to survival. Survival mode leads to paralysis and fatigue. Patient leaders know this, so they prioritize calm during setbacks and sustainable growth over quick fixes. Resilience thrives in an environment that encourages patience.

Spotting the dangers of being too patient

Patience is a virtue — until it isn't. I've seen a simple misunderstanding derail an otherwise well-intentioned leader. Patience is the foundational key empathy behavior but not because you are tasked with taking anything and everything thrown at you. The idea behind patience is to get you in the correct mindset to have empathy — to create the internal conditions that make genuine connection and understanding possible — not to enable bad behavior. Patience is also not an excuse to let problems fester while you wait for them to resolve themselves.

WARNING

Here's what no one tells you about being too patient: it feels like a virtue while it's happening. It feels like grace and compassion and giving people the benefit of the doubt. It feels like leadership. And then one day you look up and your best people are quietly furious, your underperformers have gotten comfortable, and your team has concluded — correctly — that nothing you say actually means anything. That is avoidance wearing empathy's clothes. And it is one of the most common and costly mistakes I see leaders make. If you're concerned that you as a leader are perhaps being too patient, to the point of detriment, these are the things you should look out for:

» **Breeding resentment in high performers.** The tricky thing about resentment is that it builds slowly, quietly, and often times completely undetected by the ones who care the most. By the time you notice what's happening, it has already done significant damage. When a leader is too patient with underperformance, the people who are not underperforming notice. They *always* notice. And it's not just that there are people who are lagging behind; they notice that it doesn't seem to matter.

TECHNICAL STUFF

Research on employee engagement by consulting giant Gallup in 2025 (`www.gallup.com/workplace/659279/global-engagement-falls-second-time-2009.aspx`) found that one of the most consistent predictors of disengagement among high performers is the perception that poor performance is tolerated by leadership. That alone drives more voluntary turnover among top talent than compensation, workload, or even the relationship with their direct manager.

» **Indifference.** Silence often speaks louder than any word or action. Because when people get angry about something, that means they still care. Once they become despondent — once they stop saying anything all — that's a dangerous position. This indifference can also impact your behavior as the leader, because your extreme patience can actually come across as indifference. There is a concept in psychology called *benign neglect;* it's the idea that inaction, when it comes from a place of good intention, is still neglect.

TECHNICAL STUFF

In 1983, founding researchers of leadership derailment Morgan McCall and Michael Lombardo published groundbreaking work (`https://lmu-munich.academia.edu/Departments/LMU_Center_for_Leadership_and_People_Management/Documents`) that found that one of the most common patterns in leaders who fail is not aggression or poor decision-making; it is consistent avoidance of timely action. Leaders who wait too long to address problems; or who give too many chances; or who mistake inaction for compassion until the situation has deteriorated past the point of easy repair.

» **Underperformance.** There is a version of patience where a leader gives their team room to grow because that leader believes deeply in their people. But empathetic leaders know that patience with a person's progress is not the same as patience with a pattern of underperformance. You can be endlessly patient with how long it takes someone to learn, to grow, to find their footing in a new role — and you can simultaneously be unwilling to let a damaging pattern continue without naming it clearly and directly.

The clearest expression of patience as empathy is the willingness to have the hard conversation when someone isn't performing at the capacity you need them to; empathy in this case is caring enough about the individual and your team to tell that person the truth.

Finding the right balance

So where exactly is the line between the patience that builds empathetic leadership and the patience that undermines it? Here is the most honest answer I can give you: It lives in your intention.

Patient leadership that comes from genuine curiosity —wanting to understand what's happening for someone before you respond to what they're doing — is what this entire chapter is built on. It creates safety. It produces trust. It gives people the conditions they need to do their best work and to grow through their struggles.

Excessive patience that comes from conflict avoidance —not wanting to have the uncomfortable conversation, or prioritizing your own emotional comfort over the other person's genuine need for honest feedback — is something else. It feels like kindness, but it functions like neglect.

TIP

The question to ask yourself when you notice you've been patient with someone for a long time isn't if you are being too hard on this person. It's if you are being honest with this person. Because the most empathetic thing you can do for someone who is struggling, underperforming, or behaving in ways that damage the team is to tell them the truth — clearly, compassionately, and early enough that they can actually do something about it.

That is not the absence of patience. That is patience fully realized — patience that trusts people enough to tell them hard things, that believes in their capacity to grow through discomfort, and that refuses to protect them from the information they need to become who they're capable of being.

REMEMBER

Patience is a virtue. And so is honesty. The best empathetic leaders know that you cannot truly have one without the other.

Understanding Why You Experience Impatience

You are in constant motion, even when you are sitting still. Your brain is always working: contemplating the past, examining the present, and preparing for the future. And your body is right there with it, maintaining your current state while gearing up for whatever future state may come.

Patience is often times a mirror. It's an exercise in sitting in dormancy. For a lot of us, it is a distressing feeling because being that stillness is where our reflection lies. And we don't always like what we see. This section breaks down why we feel so triggered and examines how we get so impatient in the first place.

Uncovering the roots of losing your patience

A 2024 study conducted by psychology researcher Kate Sweeny found that impatience is the emotion people feel when they face a delay that seems unfair, unreasonable, or inappropriate. Specifically, the study results published in the journal *Personality and Social Psychology Bulletin* (`https://journals.sagepub.com/doi/10.1177/01461672241284028`) identified three scenarios that create a perfect storm for impatience: when the stakes are relatively high, when the state of waiting is unpleasant, and when someone is clearly to blame for the delay.

Impatience may be the symptom of your frustration, but it's most likely not the cause. Usually, your impatience roots from something misaligned internally. Let's take a look at a what it could be for you:

- **Lack of control.** Control and impatience are inseparable; if you lift the veil of every feeling of impatience and frustration you experience, you'll likely find that you are actually grasping for control. That's because your brain treats loss of control like physical danger. When impatience turns to frustration, you begin switching off the part of your brain most responsible for high-level thinking while activating the area associated with the fight-or-flight response.

  Consider how you respond to being stuck in traffic on a casual Sunday afternoon versus a Tuesday morning while heading to a meeting. It's the same traffic, but it's a completely different experience. And the difference isn't the delay; it's how much control you feel over the outcome. That stripping of autonomy is exactly how your team feels when they are being micromanaged or their decisions are second-guessed. Your need for control — causing you to be impatient — creates a chemical stress response in the people you lead.

- **Self-centeredness.** When the world revolves around you, everything that doesn't move at your pace feels like an obstacle. Other people's timelines, processes, emotions, and needs become inconveniences rather than realities worth respecting. And inconveniences, by definition, make us impatient.

  TECHNICAL STUFF

  This isn't entirely your fault; you suffer from *egocentric bias,* a term coined in 1980 by psychologist Anthony Greenwald to describe how the brain naturally puts you at the center of every story. This bias causes you to be more self-centered than you realize, which prevents you from empathizing with others. That leads you to either assume that others share your feelings or viewpoints or ignore how others feel or think altogether.

- **Shielding anxiety.** We all behave differently when we experience anxiety. You may be someone that addresses it head on, admitting that you feel uncomfortable and a bit scattered. Or you could be someone that laughs, lashes out, or shuts down during moments of discomfort. Whatever you do to avoid anxiety, there's usually a bit of impatience wrapped up in your feelings as well. That's because anxiety leads to impatience because the anxious brain perceives waiting as a threat. You struggle to tolerate not knowing the outcome of a situation, and that leads to the need for immediate closure and speed.

  I'm generally a pretty calm person, but this is painfully true for me. I absolutely despise waiting; and any time I know I'm going to be in a situation where waiting is the norm — such as going to the airport, being put on hold, or engaging with any government agency — my body starts to go haywire. My heart rate speeds up, my breathing quickens, and I am immediately aware of just how long everything is taking.

TIP

If you struggle with impatience, physically slow down. I know that seems like very remedial advice, but it's true and it's proven by science. Slowing down literally rewires your brain. One of the most cited pieces of neuroscience on slowing down comes from Harvard University. The study, led by psychiatrist and researcher Dr. Sara Lazar, found that mindfulness increases grey matter in areas of the brain related to self-awareness, compassion and emotional regulation. As little as ten minutes a day of focused breathing can begin to rewire your nervous system. Find out more here: `https://sara-lazar.mgh.harvard.edu/publications`.

TECHNICAL STUFF

If you need even more reason to pause, consider this: Slowing down reduces the cortisol that makes impatience worse. Impatience fuels stress. When we rush or dwell in frustration, our bodies flood with cortisol. Research shows that chronic high cortisol is linked to reduced cognitive function, and repeated stress impairs the area of the brain most critical for memory and learning.

Slowing down is not just a passive act; it is one of the most neurologically sound things you as a leader can do.

Identifying your personal path to impatience

Some people are naturally patient. They approach every situation with grace and calm, navigating discomfort from a place of *equanimity* (the psychological ability to stay mentally and emotionally calm, balanced and composed during periods of high stress, pressure, or difficulty). And they are truly remarkable specimens. But for the other 99.9 percent of us, we need to learn to confidently operate in the chaos that is impatience.

TIP

You can do so by knowing exactly how you got there in the first place, by considering your *four M's* in the following order: identify your mood, survey the moment, examine your material, and define your meaning. Here goes:

1. **Your mood.** What was your mood like before you became impatient? Were you struggling with something? Did you have a hectic morning? Are you worrying about things in your personal life? Your mindset going into difficult situations can exacerbate or eliminate the issue.
2. **Your moment.** What happened the moment before you felt impatient? If you were talking to someone, how was the conversation going? What specifically did you or the other person do or say to trigger you? If you were alone, what were you doing or thinking that caused your mood to change?
3. **Your material.** These are the material feelings, the physical reaction, to your feelings. What were they? And if you were talking with someone when you experienced impatience, what was your physical reaction? Did your heart start beating faster? Did you feel yourself getting hot? Did they look concerned or upset?

4. **Your meaning.** What story are you telling yourself about what just happened, and how is that story serving you?

REMEMBER

Patience, like empathy, is an internal practice with external results. It starts with identifying where you are right now — how you feel, what caused you to be impatient, how that impatience externalized itself in your body — and it begins to move externally with your opinion of the situation, because the opinion informs how you will operate next. The goal here is to identify exactly where you begin to derail so you can reign in your emotions before damage is done.

Let's look at this framework in action from my own personal life. Throughout the course of my career, I've worked in several different capacities. But the one constant has been what the crux of my work is: writing. No matter what role I was in, it somehow always ended up with me creating written content. And it's been this way for over two decades.

When you've been doing something for that long, you begin to notice patterns. And over time, I realized that I could write pretty much anywhere so long as I had quick access to a few things: a laptop, headphones, and a comfortable place to sit. I knew that I could listen to music, but it couldn't be anything I knew the words to or else I'd get caught up in those words making it harder to focus on my own. I also saw exactly what happened when I abandoned something I was writing. Let's break this down with the four M's:

1. **My mood.** Usually when I stopped writing something, I was feeling some sort of fatigue. There's of course the mental fatigue of nonstop creation for a specific period of time, but there was also the physical component. My head would start hurting and my eyes would strain a bit from staring at the glowing screen.
2. **My moment.** I could usually push through some of the fatigue if I was writing something that easily flowed out; but the exact moment I would stop writing is when I got to something that required me to switch up pace. Maybe I was having a difficult time putting into words what I was thinking. I might have had to stop writing to look something up to define or defend the words. Or something outside of writing, such as an email alert or a phone call, would switch my attention (even if only for a moment) and I'd lose my train of thought.
3. **My material.** No matter what happened in my moment, my material response would be the same: frustration that I lost my flow followed immediately by switching tabs or turning my attention away from my computer completely. I would immediately become thirsty or need to check on the laundry or even want to grab a quick bite.

4. **My meaning.** My meaning, the story I was telling myself every time I abandoned a piece of writing, was this: If it doesn't flow, it isn't worth finishing. I had attached my value as a writer to the ease of the process. When writing felt hard, I decided — without ever saying it out loud — that hard meant bad. That resistance meant failure. That the discomfort of being stuck was a signal to stop, not a signal to push through.

Working through the four M's established that I had a *meaning* problem. And meaning problems are sneaky because they don't announce themselves. They just quietly shape every decision you make. For me, the fix wasn't learning better writing techniques. It was learning to sit inside the discomfort of the hard part without immediately heading for the exit.

Leading and working with others means that you will have moments where impatience is inevitable. The purpose of this exercise isn't to bypass impatience entirely; it's to identify where in this process you are most susceptible to losing patience and abandoning ship. When you work through this exercise, your goal is to examine each of the four M's and pinpoint exactly what your internal trigger was that fanned the impatience flames. Once you know where you are most vulnerable to spiraling, you'll have a better grip on navigating that moment in the future.

Being Patient with Yourself First

Here's the thing nobody tells you about patience as a leadership skill: it starts with you.

As I began to unpack my relationship with my speech impediment, stuttering, something really surprising emerged. You see, I spent years viewing stuttering as hard; but I viewed it as hard in ways that weren't really that difficult. Yes, the physical act of stuttering is a challenge, as is the feeling of shame associated with being and sounding different. But the hardest thing was my own perception of it, and how impatient I was with myself as a result. So of course I was going to have a horrible relationship with my speech: I *hated* stuttering because I was so impatient with it!

Because I was so impatient with myself, I was also — without realizing it — impatient with everyone else. I felt deeply uncomfortable around other people with speech impediments or visible differences, so I was constantly running away from those situations. I couldn't give myself grace, and I most certainly wasn't handing it out free to others who struggled with something just like I did.

It wasn't until I learned to stay in the discomfort of stuttering — to resist the urge to escape it, to stop treating it as a problem to solve and start treating it as a part of my experience worth respecting — that I was able to genuinely practice patience with the people around me.

REMEMBER

Self-patience isn't self-pity. It's not making excuses for yourself or lowering your standards. It's extending the same quality of presence to your own process that you're asking yourself to extend to others. It's what allows you to say, sincerely and without performance, *I understand that this is hard. Take your time.* Because you've said it to yourself first — and you meant it.

TIP

Before you can transform patience from an idea to an action for anyone else, you have to practice it in your own life. Know what triggers your impatience with yourself. Know what stories you tell yourself when things feel hard. And learn to stay present inside your own discomfort long enough to get to the other side.

That is the work. And it is absolutely worth doing.

Everything starts with you: what you tell yourself, what you think you are capable of, and what steps you'll take to uncover difficult truths. Patience is no different.

Putting Patience into Action

Take a moment to think about a time when you knew you should have been patient. You could hear yourself scream in your own head to slow down. And yet, you did the opposite. You snapped, rushed, dismissed, or bulldozed your way through a situation that you know you should have handled differently. And the second it happened, you felt deeply disappointed in yourself.

We've all been there. We've all known what we should have done and yet we just couldn't make our way to the correct path. A gap exists that we are all constantly straddling: the space between *valuing* something and actually *living* it. You didn't lose your patience because you didn't value it; you lost it because valuing something and practicing something live in different parts of your brain.

Knowing you should be patient is not a skill. Reaching for patience in the moment you least want to; now that's a skill. You can absolutely think your way into patience in real time; all you need is a move. This section helps you to figure out what yours is.

Transforming patience from idea to action

When you are in the pursuit of patience, especially when you are starting from impatience, set yourself for success by attaching behaviors to your goals. Patience as a noun is an idea; but patience as a verb — an action — is a choice.

REMEMBER

Patience is a skill; you can start from where you are right now and improve that skill with targeted effort. In order to actively choose patience, you need to know what it looks like in real time:

- **Emotional regulation is physically calming yourself down.** Trying to avoid any emotional jumps isn't a solution. We are feeling beings, and trying to combat feelings by pretending they don't exist or without acknowledging them builds resentment. And resentment is horrible for your mental health. It can lead to anxiety, depression, chronic fatigue, and even higher blood pressure. When you aren't feeling your best, you are also quicker to shortness: you are more impatient and have a harder time getting back to being patient.

  Instead of running from your feelings — and attempting to fight your emotions into submission — learn to emotionally regulate yourself. How do you best calm down? It can be something as simple as counting to ten before you respond to something perceived as a threat. It can be deep breathing or even a half-smile to relax your facial muscles and promote a sense of calm. You can also walk away from the situation and vow to revisit it when you can think more clearly.

- **Mindfulness is self-awareness.** So many of us are mindful of what everyone else is doing, yet we have a much harder time being mindful — or self-aware — of our own behaviors. The reason why self-awareness is so critical to patience is because it forces you to know both what triggers you and what happens when you are triggered. Being *self-aware* means naming your emotions and identifying why you felt that emotion in the first place. It's accepting that you do indeed feel things and that it is absolutely okay to have those feelings.

  Identifying emotions isn't saying things like "I'm angry" or "I'm sad"; it's getting very specific about why you feel that way. Are you feeling ignored? Isolated? Blamed or judged? Do you think what just happened was unfair or that you couldn't speak up because you were being overlooked? Self-awareness is navigating your toughest moments with a mirror; you always know what you feel and why you feel it because you seek to see it clearly.

- **Cognitive reframing is rerouting toward productivity.** When you think of knee-jerk reactions, you often are referring to something loud like throwing your hands in the air from exasperation, rolling your eyes when someone annoys you, or raising your voice when you're angry. But most of your knee-jerk reactions are subtle, and it happens *somatically* (experiencing or processing something through a bodily sensation rather than through thought or intellect). Your body reacts to what's going on around you before your brain has a rational thought. So, when you find yourself in a situation that's making you uncomfortable, you physically react to it even if you think you're not. It's those small, unconscious reactions that trigger others, alerting them to your unease, disinterest, or impatience.

Your feelings drive your thoughts, and those thoughts turn into actions regardless of your intention. Rerouting those thoughts toward something positive and productive helps you cognitively reframe your situation by leveling up your mindset. Because you are already working on being both emotionally regulated and self-aware, cognitive reframing will look like changing those thoughts. You do that by checking the evidence — is what you are thinking and feeling true? Where's the proof? And if it's not true, why did you jump to the negative conclusion in the first place? Where did that come from, and why was that your first choice? (For more on cognitive reframing, check out the section "Exploring the Skills of Patience" earlier in this chapter.)

Creating an internal system to guide you toward patience

Once you've reached impatience, you need to get back on track. And, as easy as it is to blame the other person or the situation for your problems, this won't shift your mood and mindset to a productive place. The next time you find yourself in a moment where you feel the grip on your patience slipping away, ask yourself these four questions in this order:

1. **What was the trigger?** Identify exactly what happened. If you were talking to someone, identify what they said. If you were in a meeting, break down the series of events that lead to the discomfort. If you were alone, think about what specifically you were doing that caused you to feel impatient.
2. **Why did this trigger you?** This is where you go back to your meaning. Is there a wound underneath this trigger? Is there a pattern it's activating? For more information on the underlying causes of impatience, see the earlier section, "Uncovering the roots of losing your patience."
3. **How do you calm down?** Not eventually, but right now. Do you need thirty seconds? A glass of water? To write something down? Know your reset and have it ready at all times. This is your emotional regulation in real time.
4. **What do you want to get out of this interaction?** This is the question that really saves the conversation. Because when you remember what you actually want — for example, connection, clarity, resolution, or trust — it becomes a lot harder to justify blowing it up over the trigger that got you here.

Earlier in the chapter, I spoke about how impatient I was with myself as a result of my stuttering. And that self-impatience led me to be less patient with others. For me, going through this process helped me more accurately identify what my *actual* frustration was coming from. Here's how it looked:

1. **What was my trigger?** The moments I felt most impatient were when I wanted desperately to get my point across, and my stuttering just wouldn't allow me to do so in the way I wanted to do it. That interruption shifted my internal state from calm to anxiety to frustration.
2. **Why did this trigger me?** This goes to the underlying cause of my impatience with my speech: lack of control. It was the lack of control of how I sounded and also the lack of control of how I was coming across to others.
3. **How did I calm down?** In the moment, I usually pushed through and then stopped talking. I'd feel shame, and stew in embarrassment for a while. Eventually I would take a few deep breaths and jump back into the conversation. And then I would be hopeful that the next time, I'd be more fluent. Eventually, however, I had to learn that being patient meant addressing the underlying causes of my impatience: the frustration about my lack of control. I had to learn how to still have confidence in how I spoke, despite the fact that it wasn't like everyone else. Fascinatingly enough, I gradually learned that me being more patient with my insecurity led me to be more patient with everyone around me.
4. **What did I want to get out of this interaction?** I had to remind myself that I wasn't in a conversation to sound a certain way; I was there to contribute. Long term, however, I figured out that my worth wasn't tied to my fluency. People wanted to hear what I had to say, and they didn't care how I sounded. The only person making the whole thing weird was me.

Getting back to patience when you find yourself struggling to slow down means remembering the *why* of your interactions.

TROUBLESHOOTING WHEN IMPATIENCE CREEPS IN

Here are a few things you can do when you find your patience slipping away:

- **If you realized you rushed through a conversation:** Circle back, apologize, and have the conversation again. As an empathetic leader, one of your responsibilities is to assess the needs of your team in the moment. There are of course going to be conversations where someone will need a solution, but there will also be times when people just need your presence. As leaders, however, it's sometimes difficult to both decipher when that is needed and to take that extra few moments to give your direct report what they need. So, you rush through the interaction by solutioning instead of engaging. Sometimes, we don't even realize when we've let impatience creep in. To take that a step further, sometimes impatience feels like optimization. But at others, it looks and feels like dismissiveness. Fixing this misstep is a golden opportunity to build an even better relationship. Try this: "I've been thinking about our conversation, and I don't think I gave it the time it deserved. Can we revisit?" That simple sentence shows that you thought about that person. You came back. You are communicating that you value their time and respect their opinions. This kind of follow-through — when leaders misstep and own up to it — is what builds rabid support in teams.

- **If you've already interrupted someone:** Acknowledge what you've done and remind yourself that you can still recover. Interruptions, especially from those in positions of authority, can be interpreted as signals of dominance, disrespect, and disinterest regardless of the interrupter's intention. Interrupting essentially says that you were more interested in what you had to say rather than what they were saying. You fix this by owning up to it, apologizing, and letting them finish. A simple "I'm sorry — finish your thought," shows that you're paying attention not to just the conversation but to your behavior during it. We all mess up sometimes, and that's okay. It's how you recover that matters. In this instance, acknowledging what you've done isn't a weakness. It's self-aware. Yes, the interruption happened; but what you do next is what truly matters.
- **If you feel your body tensing up:** Your body is telling your brain that danger lays ahead. The body generates physical signals that precede conscious emotional awareness. Your jaw will tighten before you've consciously registered that you're frustrated. Your shoulders start creeping a bit further north before your brain has decided to be defensive. If you feel your body tensing up, use that an early warning system. Be aware of your physical sensations and how your emotional signals relate to them. When it does happen, pause and ask yourself where you are holding your tension right now: jaws, shoulders, chest, stomach, and so on. Before you respond, breathe and try to release that tension. Pausing for a few seconds to physically reset and emotionally regulate can save a conversation from turning south.
- **If you feel like patience is going to be all but impossible today:** Say so. Own it. This is an incredibly vulnerable thing to do, but telling the truth about your capacity is human. And leaders who consistently acknowledge their humanity — including their limitations and difficult days — are rated significantly higher in trustworthiness and relatability by their teams. Vulnerability doesn't erode authority; it builds it. It's okay to say when you're not okay. No one expects you to be perfectly *anything* — especially patient — all the time. People will understand if you're going through something outside of work that's causing you to be a bit snappier, or if you have a really bad morning and just can't get into the right groove. But in order for them to have that understanding, you need to be up front about how you're feeling. Patience begins with you; you create the environment for it to bloom or shrink.

IN THIS CHAPTER

» Recognizing perspective as a skill

» Digging deeper into understanding

» Exploring curiosity

» Putting your perspective into practice

Chapter 9
Pursuing Perspective

Everyone talks about empathy. Fewer people talk about what it actually takes to practice it: the specific, learnable, sometimes uncomfortable skills that turn a good intention into a leadership identity. This chapter is about one of those skills: Perspective. Not perspective as a vague concept or a motivational poster sentiment, but perspective as a discipline. The kind of discipline you pursue deliberately, practice consistently, and return to even — and especially — when it's hard.

This chapter defines what perspective-taking actually is and what it requires of you; it explores the two types of perspective and why you need both; it discusses the role of curiosity and how to pursue perspective. Chasing someone else's perspective is one of the most courageous things a leader can do. And by the end of this chapter, you'll be better equipped to do so.

Exploring Perspective-Taking

Perspective-taking is the deliberate act of stepping into another person's point of view. It's seeing the situation through their eyes, from their history, with their values and their concerns. Perspective-taking is not just recognizing that others have perspectives but actively inhabiting them.

You've been seeing the world through your own eyes your entire life, so perspective feels quite intuitive and even obvious. But the kind of perspective-taking that makes a genuinely empathetic leader is neither intuitive nor obvious. It is specific, practiced, and starts with understanding exactly what you're reaching for before you try to reach for it.

REMEMBER

Perspective, at its core, is the sum total of everything that shapes how a person experiences the world. Their history, their fears, their values, their wounds, their wins — all of it filters every interaction they have, every decision they make, and every feeling they carry into your one-on-ones, your team meetings, and your hallway conversations. No two people's filters are the same. And your job as an empathetic leader isn't to understand perspective in the abstract — it's to understand the very specific, very human perspective of the people right in front of you. That requires a particular set of skills:

- **Active listening.** We live in a world inundated with consumption. If you're anything like me, you are constantly checking *something* whether that be one of your several email accounts, text messages, any number of your social media feeds, current events . . . and this doesn't even include checking on other actual human beings such as your spouse, children, parents, and friends. It's an unforgiving, never-ending cycle that somehow always manages to make you feel bad for not checking enough but also checking too much!

  The world does everything it can to take your attention away from what is directly in front of you. It's for that reason you need to be all in on active listening. Give whoever is in front of you your undivided attention. Close your email. Put your phone on Do Not Disturb. Don't look away while someone is talking to you; maintain eye contact, nod, and summarize what they said to show that you heard them and are reflecting on what they've shared. For more on active listening, head to Chapter 10.

- **Awareness.** Chapter 8 discusses the importance of self-awareness when prioritizing patience: identifying what triggers you, knowing where that reaction comes from, and understanding how to cognitively reframe your behaviors toward something more productive. In perspective-taking, the awareness is now firmly on the other people involved.

  Awareness here means stepping completely out of your world and into someone else's. You do this by reminding yourself that your experience is not *their* experience; you may have gone through something similar as another person, but that doesn't mean you have full understanding of their experience.

  It is with that awareness that you are more equipped to really listen to another person's story. Practicing awareness in others looks like pausing and reflecting while you're in conversation with them. It's asking follow-up questions to clarify what was said and to touch on what was not. And it's doing a check-in every so often during the conversation to see where their energy is and if the conversation is still going in the intended direction.

» **Reading cues.** Author and University of California, Los Angeles psychologist Albert Mehrabian famously said that only 7 percent of our communication was verbal, with the other 93 percent split between tone of voice (38 percent) and body language (55 percent). This means that 93 percent of the time, words may not be spoken but communication is still happening. And you have an opportunity to learn more about whoever you are communicating with as a result.

People are constantly telling you who they are, what they're feeling, and how to talk to them; they just don't always use their words. So much of what you do is *somatic* (meaning related to the physical body as opposed to the mind). A small upturn of one side of your lip when you're feeling hopeful, lowering your head when you're feeling ashamed, or standing up a bit straighter when you feel threatened or on the defensive are very real movements that most of us have no idea are happening until someone else points it out.

Your job as a leader is to care. Your team needs to know that you care not only about their success, but also them as humans. And one of the hallmarks of caring is attempting to understand others; taking the time to get clarity, to learn more perspective, to see how someone thinks, and to check on how people feel creates a psychologically safe environment (which is important in creating high-performing teams).

TECHNICAL STUFF

Human beings are wired to connect, so it makes sense that one of the best feelings is when we know we are being understood by people who matter to us: our parents, our best friends, our partners, our bosses, and so on. Social neuroscience expert Matthew Lieberman takes this a step further. In his 2003 research described later in his book *Social: Why Our Brains Are Wired to Connect* (Oxford University Press, 2013), he found that social pain and social reward are processed in the same region of the brain as physical pain and pleasure. That means that being misunderstood has a similar mental impact on us as being physically harmed.

In order to properly pursue perspective-taking in your empathetic leadership practice, you need to understand the two types of perspective and how they work together to create the psychologically safe environment that all empathetic leaders crave: cognitive and emotional perspective.

REMEMBER

Both cognitive and emotional perspectives are required for true understanding to happen. Cognitive perspective gets you clarity; you know the facts and you understand the systems that back it up. It's following another's reasoning, seeing their perspective on the facts, and recognizing that what they believe is true to them. Emotional perspective encourages you to feel with others, acknowledging their feelings and making sure that they feel heard and safe.

Cognitive perspective

Cognitive perspective-taking is the "what" and the "why" of logic. Cognitive perspective-taking is all about the cognition: the mental processes of acquiring and understanding knowledge. It is practiced without emotional involvement; you understand someone's knowledge while remaining entirely detached from their feelings. In other words, you are actively and deliberately working to reconstruct someone else's reasoning. Cognitive perspective-taking:

- **Is the ability to step into another person's thoughts.** This is understanding how someone else reasons, what they believe, and how they arrived at their conclusions.
- **Focuses on intellectual content.** This is the pursuit of understanding someone's goals, assumptions, knowledge, and decision-making logic.
- **Draws on information.** One of the most important factors in perspective-taking is clarity. Did you hear what was actually said or did you hear what you wanted to hear? Did you retain the speaker's message or just your opinion on what they said? Drawing on information means you are focused on both context and observation to build an accurate mental model of another person's perspective.
- **Is associated with accuracy.** The goal in cognitive perspective-taking is to correctly map how someone else sees a situation.

Emotional perspective

Emotional perspective is "all the feels!" It's understanding what someone else feels, and why it makes sense that they feel it. You're not just reconstructing their logic, you are dissecting, examining, and exploring their inner experience: the weight, the texture, and the emotional impact. Beyond just understanding what another person's position is, emotional perspective attempts to understand what it is like to be them at this very moment. Emotional perspective:

- **Is the ability to step into another person's feelings.** Beyond just sensing what another person is experiencing emotionally, emotional perspective-taking is pursuing the *why* of those emotions as well.
- **Focuses on the affective content.** Also known as someone's emotional needs, emotional perspective-taking centers someone's fears, frustrations, joys, grief, and any other emotional needs they are expressing.
- **Draws on attunement.** Attunement is one of the dark horse skills of excellent leaders; all of them have it but most of them rarely discuss it. Being *attuned* with others means you are connecting on a deeper level because you

validate their emotions, mirror their expressions, and respond to their needs beyond just their words.

- **Is associated with connection.** The goal here is making the other person feel genuinely seen and less alone.

GROUPING VULNERABILITY WITH PERSPECTIVE

The act of vulnerability is always impressive. You see someone doing something that you deem as scary, intimidating, or even impossible and you immediately want to lean in. It elicits that sort of response because it humanizes people, and we all desperately need to be reminded that we are not the only person in the world who struggles with fear or insecurity.

When I first got started speaking at events, I felt deeply insecure about stuttering. I was worried that people would judge me or think I wasn't smart; and I was really concerned that people wouldn't think my message was worth listening to. I had it in my mind that others viewed people who stuttered as less intelligent. Think of the way stutterers are portrayed on television: usually bumbling idiots and the butt of a joke. I was deeply concerned that I would be received like that.

Save for a few moments, that's not at all what happened. I quickly learned that people are always willing to listen and to learn so long as you are willing to share. But an even more valuable lesson was one of reciprocity. I had to be comfortable with being openly vulnerable, but I also had to be comfortable engaging with the vulnerability of others. Because vulnerability, as it turns out, is mutual.

When you think of pursuing perspective, you're mostly referring to pursuing the perspective of those you align with in the most important ways. You agree on some core beliefs, such as religion or politics, and you enjoy some of the same hobbies. You give your family the benefit of the doubt because of your shared history and unconditional love. And you seek out partnership with people who share a similar vision of your future together. Being vulnerable with people like these is easy; there's a steadiness in the relationship, a foundation so strong and resilient that vulnerability feels like a deep comfort.

Real perspective-taking, however, comes from a reciprocal experience of vulnerability. And you being vulnerable is only half of the equation; allowing another person, whose perspective is so different that it could make you uncomfortable or even angry, to be vulnerable with you is equally as impactful. Getting the perspective from a person you disagree with is an act of vulnerability on both parts: you as the listener and them as the speaker.

Deconstructing Understanding

Empathy may be the star of the show — and rightfully so — but empathy doesn't exist by itself. It's built, brick by brick, with understanding. Before you can feel with someone, you have to get them. And before you can lead with empathy, you have to know what understanding looks like in practice — because it's not a single lightbulb moment, a nod across a conference table, or a well-timed "I hear you." It's layered. It's progressive. And sometimes it's genuinely difficult work. Like any skill worth having, it helps to first take it apart before you put it to use. Understanding isn't just the soft part of empathetic leadership. It's an integral part of its DNA. This section explores the skill of understanding.

Figuring out why understanding is so hard

Learning something new is an act of vulnerability that requires cognitive effort, focus, and resilience. It also requires understanding; you can't "learn" if you don't "get." But, just like learning new things, understanding new concepts, experiences, and — especially — people can be painful.

TIP

It's helpful to know why exactly something is hard so you can seamlessly circumvent those challenges. Here are a few reasons to keep in mind when understanding seems so difficult to do:

- **Confirmation and cognitive biases.** You have a lifetime of experiences that shape your beliefs. You believe your view is the correct one because your existence is the proof. But two things can be true at once: that your experience is valid and someone else's completely opposite experience is too. Your confirmation and cognitive biases make it difficult to fully accept or even consider alternate viewpoints.
- **Emotional filters.** Emotional regulation is such an underrated skill yet feels almost impossibly challenging to achieve. This is not your fault; big emotions can trigger a fight-or-flight response, and that basically makes the rational part of the brain shut off. It's even more difficult to regulate when you are tired, hungry, or experiencing sensory overload. Add in any level of stress or burnout, and you're fighting a losing battle.
- **Lack of accurate information.** This can be as simple as not having a singular piece of small information or as big as not having any context about a person's mental or emotional state. Beyond that, not knowing that you do not have all of the correct information adds frustration to the mix, making understanding even more elusive.

» **Power dynamics.** Just because you have experienced something in the past, it doesn't mean that you completely understand what that current experience is like for another person. Think about when you first entered the workforce; so much of the world was likely very different than it is now. Advancements in technology continue to shift what work looks like for everyone, and societal pressures continue to evolve as time marches on. As you climb up the ladder, you forget what it's like at the previous rung and you most likely do not realize this is happening. This is especially important to remember as you are developing your empathetic leadership practice. Consistently remind yourself that you don't know what it's like to be in a role you previously held at this current moment, and that the gap between what you experienced then versus what another person is experiencing now makes understanding much harder for you.

Understanding yourself first

When Ethan was first promoted to being a people manager, he was thrilled. I met him in one of my in-house empathetic communication workshops, and it was clear he was a high-performing young leader. Promoted when he was barely out of his mid-twenties, he'd spent his early career being constantly commended for his many successes. Ethan had always loved his experiences with mentors earlier in his career, and he knew he wanted to create a similar experience for those who came after him. He led his team of 15 full-time employees and 25 contractors with what he thought was excitement, full visibility, and very specific processes. So, when it came time for his first 360-degree review, he went into it feeling confident. He'd never mis-stepped before, and he felt that this moment would be no different.

He was very wrong.

Like most first-time managers, Ethan's 360-degree was a list of grievances. He was a severe micromanager, watching every detail and requiring approval for even the most menial of tasks. He rarely showed gratitude, preferring instead to focus on what needed to be improved instead of pointing out what went well. And he hoarded information, which came across as ineffective communication.

The lesson of Ethan's experience? Before you can understand others — their experiences, their behaviors, and their preferences — you first need to understand yourself.

TIP

Knowing how you react to things, what your approach is to discomfort, and when exactly things take a turn gives you a path to follow when doing the same for others. Understanding is more than a single "I get it" moment; it's a progressive and layered experience. Let's break down exactly what that step-by-step experience looks like, and how this played out for Ethan:

1. **Informational.** The first step in understanding is just knowing the straight facts. You can comprehend, analyze, and synthesize the raw data. And the information is 100 percent correct. For Ethan, the informational understanding was simple: His behavior was controlling and his team was not happy about it.
2. **Contextual.** Next you need to contextually understand the situation; you can interpret information, language, or behaviors as they relate to their environment. To fully grasp the context of his behavior, Ethan had to ask himself why he was doing this. As it turned out, one of his managers earlier in his career was blamed for their team's failure. Ethan was deeply fearful that the same fate would befall him if he didn't do well in his role.
3. **Emotional.** Recognizing the felt experience, or knowing how it feels to be in a certain situation, is where empathy begins to peek through. Though you may not have lived the exact same experience, you understand the emotions that can be tied up into it. In Ethan's case, he felt chronic anxiety about being blindsided, and that realization helped him better understand where those behaviors were rooted.
4. **Meaningful.** Meaningful understanding is when you appreciate that the situation will be experienced with a different gravity for everyone. While one person views sending one-too-many emails as a minor inconvenience, another may view it as acutely unprofessional. Ethan kept digging for the meaning behind his performance, and he finally got it; he felt like trusting his team was a risk he couldn't afford, so he micromanaged.

This process of understanding yourself is more than getting the full picture; it is the beginning of self-empathy. Practicing being kind to yourself, understanding the why behind your actions, and doing so in a non-judgmental way helps you do the same for others. You understand what it takes and how it feels, so you can then walk those same steps in your pursuit of perspective. As for Ethan, his first 360-review was a painful yet powerful exercise. It helped him figure out how to be a better manager to his team, but — maybe more importantly — he walked away a better person because he confidently knew how to understand people.

REMEMBER

Understanding is a four-step knowing process. You begin with knowing the facts; you can accurately state what happened. You then know the context surrounding the circumstance; you grasp the situation around those facts. Next, you know the felt experience; you address the shame, fear, stress, or any other feelings associated with being (and feeling) in that situation. Finally, you know the meaning for the person experiencing it; you appreciate what is at stake for that specific individual even though it is different for everyone.

THE COMPOUNDING EFFECT OF UNDERSTANDING

The year after I got married was gearing up to be the busiest, most lucrative year of my career. I gave keynotes at several household name companies. I'd traveled to Nigeria and Kenya to speak at conferences with some of the brightest minds in the tech space. And I was fielding inquiries and sincere interest from some of the most respected organizations on the globe. My calendar was filling up and I was excited to spread the empathy message to more companies and conferences around the world.

And then, right before our first wedding anniversary, the world shut down. That's right: 2020 was supposed to be *my* year. But one by one, that packed calendar started to clear up. Gigs were postponed. Then cancelled. And I was devastated. I remember watching the news and feeling a sense of relief that I wasn't the only person on the brink of losing everything I'd worked so hard for. Then I immediately felt a massive sense of guilt for being upset about my career when other people were literally losing their loved ones.

But as the year rolled on, something started to shift. I have a LinkedIn Learning course called "Communicating with Empathy" that had been doing marginally well since it's 2017 release. During the global COVID-19 pandemic, however, it absolutely exploded. People were yearning for a sense of connection, of normalcy in the chaos. And improving communication gave people calm. We as a society had to learn better communication skills just so we could support and be supported by others in the most effective way possible since everything was virtual.

Those enhanced skills were pivotal in managing the psychological distress so many of us felt; it was crucial to calming our anxieties, fears, and quelling the social isolation. As the virtual events picked up, I started having conversations with people about how the pandemic better helped them understand the struggle of others. It changed how we listened to people because we could better understand their feelings on a contextual and emotional level. We experienced unprecedented levels of trust because we were all going through something really miserable, and we were doing it together. Even how we spoke shifted, with many of us leading more with honesty and openness and a willingness to learn about what others were going through.

It's one thing to be heard, but being understood? That feels real and sincere to people. It's something that people can take with them, spreading that understanding to others on the team or in the world at large. Every layer of understanding you develop about a person generates more understanding, more trust, and more capacity for connection. Understanding is not a moment. It's a practice that pays dividends.

Questioning Your Way to Deeper Perspective

Humans are consumers by nature. We spend countless hours a day discovering new information via social media, books, or television shows. We're constantly buying things, eating, reproducing — all of which are necessary for our basic survival. Yet, somehow, we've managed to give consumption a bit of a bad rap. But consider this: What if consumption is just an act of curiosity?

TECHNICAL STUFF

Interestingly enough, curiosity isn't something that is heavily studied. Researchers agree that being curious is an incredible motivation for learning, influential in decision making, and one of the healthiest things you can do for personal and professional development. However, it is difficult to define, measure, or manipulate in standardized laboratory settings.

Psychologists do, though, have a few things they agree on when it comes to being curious. Put simply, curiosity is the strong desire to know or learn something new. Curiosity looks like:

- Initiation of humor and playfulness.
- Non-defensive attitude.
- Positive emotional expressiveness.
- Tolerance of uncertainty.
- Unconventional thinking.

Do you notice a trend? These all require a relaxed sense of self. Every single one of those traits is only possible when a person isn't busy protecting themselves. Let's look at these again with a bit more development:

- In order to have humor and playfulness, you can't be guarded. These two traits require a levity and openness.
- For a non-defensive attitude, you must have a strong sense of identity and not feel threatened easily.
- Positive emotional expressiveness requires feeling safe enough with yourself to show what's happening inside your head.
- With a high tolerance for uncertainty, you don't need to be right to feel okay. In fact, you love not knowing the answer because it's an opportunity to discover.

» A penchant for unconventional thinking means you're comfortable with coloring outside of the lines because you don't fear judgment.

WARNING

But the deepest thread is this: Curiosity is essentially egoless. It can't coexist with the need to look good, be right, stay safe, or maintain control. The moment self-protection enters the room, curiosity leaves. If your sense of safety is tied to being right — to your way of seeing things being the correct way — then stepping into someone else's perspective feels like a threat, not an exercise.

Let's go back to those traits one more time and look at them through lens of pursuing perspective-through curiosity:

» Rigid people make rigid perspective-takers. You can't fully engage in the humor and playfulness curiosity requires if you refuse try on another person's costume, or if you do it as if it's a joke. Perspective-taking is using your imagination — your creative side — to see a bigger world.

» Someone else's perspective is going to challenge your own; that's the whole point. If that perspective makes yours incomplete or wrong, a defensive person rejects the new perspective to protect the old one. A person with a non-defensive attitude celebrates both by holding both simultaneously.

» Pursuing perspective is an emotional act, not just an intellectual one. If you dismiss positive emotional expressiveness, you can still reconstruct someone's situation, but you'll miss their feelings entirely. Curiosity means being emotional.

» The rush for closure and certainty is where curiosity goes to die. Someone else's perspective may not be finished; it can be contradictory, unresolved, and uncomfortable. Having a tolerance of uncertainty means that need for a perfect resolution is traded for a dalliance with chaos. Being curious when pursuing perspective means sitting inside the mess, not trying to fix it.

» Every other person's perspective is, to some degree, unconventional thinking to you. It follows rules you didn't write, values you didn't choose, and experiences you didn't have. Stepping into it requires you temporarily suspending your own framework, which is one of the most unconventional (and not to mention curious) things a person can do.

REMEMBER

Perspective-taking is often thought of as a technique. You are encouraged to walk in someone else's shoes, ask more questions, and listen more. But to really pursue perspective — to seek genuine understanding — requires curiosity. And without a relaxed sense of self, you'll perform it rather than practice it. That's the big difference between leaders who center empathy and those who do not. Leaders who merely perform the act of pursuing perspective will just take the parts of what others share with them to confirm what they already believed. To truly pursue perspective — and, as a result, to lead with empathy — you need to be curious.

Practicing Understanding

Now's the time to put your empathetic leadership — specifically when it comes to your pursuit of perspective and understanding — into practice! Pursuing perspective as a leader can be broken down into three key behaviors: identifying, seeking, and following up and following through. This section digs into these behaviors.

Identifying biases, assumptions, and judgments

We are all biased. And being biased doesn't make us bad people; it just makes us human. How? Because your biases are developed over a lifetime of being uniquely you: your education, race, ethnicity, gender, sexuality, socioeconomic status, religion, and a host of other things. The problem is never about we as humans being biased; the problem is how we as humans use our biases as weapons against communities we view as being misaligned. We take those biases — those literal opinions — and discriminate, isolate, judge, and harm others.

TIP

In order to really pursue perspective, you first need to know what your biases are, where they originate, and how they could impact your ability to be both impartial and invested. This requires self-awareness, honesty, and patience. This is the identification phase of perspective-taking. Here's what this looks like in real time:

- **Audit your thoughts.** What are you thinking and why are you thinking it? You approach the world from a biased place. Instead of being ashamed of those biases — judging yourself harshly and trying to convince yourself that you shouldn't be biased — examine them. Where do they come from and what is their origin story? Was this opinion ever different from what it is now? If so, how did it shift? If not, do you have any evidence that this opinion is indeed true? And have you seen anything in the world that challenges that belief? How did that change what you think now?

  Auditing your thoughts means viewing them from a place of curiosity, not scrutiny. This is your opportunity to dissect your beliefs, poring over them like you're an archeologist; each and every stroke of that brush could uncover a great discovery that changes everything. That is the excitement and the precision you need when auditing your thoughts.

- **Analyze your circle.** Humans gravitate toward others who we see at least a little bit of ourselves in whether it be similar hobbies, backgrounds, professional aspirations, or attitudes about the world. We don't want to be alone, so we seek out the camaraderie of those who reflect at least a part of ourselves back to us; that makes us feel seen, heard, valued, and that our opinion is truly valid.

  The problem here is that you can end up in an echo chamber. It's not only really difficult to get a genuinely diverse perspective but also to find the strength and resolve to even hear another perspective. Analyzing your circle means scrutinizing what you are constantly consuming and evaluating its effect on your ability be curious when it counts. Chapter 11 considers the impact of empathy on groups, but for now recognize that you are deeply impacted by the thoughts, opinions, and perspectives of those people you are with most frequently. Is that to your benefit or to your detriment?

- **Identify your triggers.** Can you pinpoint the exact moment in a conversation when you go from confident to uncomfortable? And can you identify what exactly about that moment caused the shift? How about your reaction to that discomfort: where does your mind go, how does your body feel, and what exactly do you want to say in response to that feeling? The biggest reason perspective-taking is so challenging is because it forces you to not only be uncomfortable but also sit in that feeling with the person who is at the same time causing it.

  Identifying your triggers means being aware of the situations and conversations that frequently cause you discomfort and make it difficult for you to really engage in other perspectives as a result. Remember that pursuing perspective means knowing both what triggers you and what you do to avoid discomfort, because in that avoidance you are less likely to get the perspective that you seek. To find out more about triggers, head to Chapter 8.

- **Slow down decisions.** When you don't check your biases, they turn into assumptions. Then all of a sudden, you've judged someone — developed an entire opinion and reached a full conclusion about them — based on some thing that is probably somewhat inaccurate. That's unfair to them, and it's also unfair to you; hearing about others' experiences is a really beautiful way to learn, grow, and build community. Immediately judging and making assumptions about them destroys that possibility. No one wins.

  Despite seeming nearly impossible much of the time, you need to slow down. Everything discussed in this section requires intention. When you rush, you lose the ability to make sound decisions. Slowing down your decision means slowing down your thoughts; when you know what you're thinking — and why you are thinking it — it's easier to correct your course.

REMEMBER

Not wanting to engage in someone else's opinion about a subject you feel passionate about does not make you a bad person; it makes you a completely normal human operating exactly how you are supposed to. That's why pursing perspective is challenging, because your default is to be egocentric; your view is *the* view. The pursuit of perspective means being self-aware, honest, and willing to question your reactions.

Seeking context, conversations, and conclusions

When you're seeking answers, what are you really after: the truth or what you want to hear? It's okay to be honest; we're all friends here!

WARNING

As discussed earlier in this chapter, being biased is a completely normal part of being human. It's proven by science. Humans suffer from cognitive biases. You are deeply influenced by confirmation bias and that distorts your reality; it prevents you from seeing situations objectively and truly understanding another person's view. Instead of hearing what another person says to you, you hear *your opinion* of what they said. To add to that, you don't know what you think you know about other people. You are operating with an information deficit because you do not know what is going on in another person's life. Imagine how many arguments have happened because people have jumped to conclusions based on flawed information!

TIP

Pursuing perspective is just that; you are in constant pursuit — always seeking — that missing information. Being an empathetic leader means accepting that your knowledge is limited. Your job is to seek context through conversations before coming to any conclusions. Here's what that looks like in real time:

- **Pause your narrative.** You've already addressed your biases by examining them and determining if they have merit (see earlier in this chapter). You're self-aware enough to know that those biases may be clouding your judgment and forming a narrative that will harm your ability to really hear what another person is saying. Seeking context means first hitting pause on that narrative. Remember that your brain isn't defaulting to hear what people say, it puts their words and feelings through your own filter. Turn that filter off and really listen.
- **Ask questions.** You can't discover something new if your information is flawed. Clarity is just as important as context. Asking questions is critical to perspective-taking because they help reframe the narrative you've been holding on to. Your questions help further reduce your assumptions, and they allow the speaker to reveal more of themselves. This fosters deeper exploration and better relationships.

» **Listen to the answers.** I know this seems obvious and a bit insulting. Of course, you have to listen to what people say to hear them; you began learning that the moment you were born! But sometimes it is genuinely difficult to really listen. You might be uncomfortable with the conversation, so you get defensive. You might disagree with them, so you don't want to hear what they have to say. Or maybe you're listening with your filter on, so you may have heard someone discuss their personal experience but it was with your narrative as the foundation. Listening isn't always comfortable, but it is invaluable and it's the only way you'll get the perspective you pursue.

TIP

Listen to learn. Listen to respond. Listen to build community. Do not listen to judge.

Following up and following through

REMEMBER

Identifying your biases and seeking context through honest conversation are both tremendous acts of empathetic leadership. But perspective-taking doesn't end when the conversation does. Your follow-up or follow-through is where your commitment to understanding becomes visible and where trust is either quietly built or loudly broken.

Following up means circling back. It's checking in after a hard conversation to see how someone is doing. It's referencing something they shared with you weeks later, because you actually retained it. It's letting people know that what they told you mattered enough to stay with you. These are small acts that carry enormous weight because they signal something most people rarely feel from their leaders: *I wasn't just listening in that moment, I was actually paying attention to you.*

Following through means doing what you said you would do with what you discovered. If someone shared a struggle and you committed to addressing it, address it. If you promised to advocate, advocate. Nothing unravels trust faster than a leader who listens beautifully and intently and then doesn't take any action to show that they actually care. The follow-through is the proof of the perspective.

Together, following up and following through closes the loop on perspective-taking, transforming it from a one-time exchange into an ongoing practice that compounds over time.

3 Leading Others with Empathy

IN THIS PART . . .

Discover how to communicate with empathy.

Unpack the minefield that is empathy in groups, and find out how to lead groups from an unbiased place.

Lead with empathy while also having authority and influence.

Plan how to act when you have empathy failures.

IN THIS CHAPTER

» Understanding empathetic communication

» Discovering how to speak and listen with empathy

» Hurdling the difficult barriers to empathetic communication

Chapter 10

Forming Real Connections with Others

As a keynote speaker, I spend a lot of time talking to people. They always want to approach me after my talks or workshops and tell me a part of their story, and I always love to hear them. I've truly heard it all; from the woman who struggled work while dealing with bipolar, to the first-time manager trying to figure out how to run a meeting properly, to the many people who learned that they are not the only ones being deeply impacted by their insecurities in the world.

But the most repeated sentence I hear is: "I suck at communication." This is such a fascinating sentiment because we are always communicating. And, whether we like it or not, people are always receiving our message. This chapter discusses how to confidently form that message in every aspect of your communication through the lens of empathy.

Defining Empathetic Communication

REMEMBER

People are constantly telling you how to communicate to them, and most of the time they don't even realize they are doing it. But the information relayed in their tone of voice, body language, eye contact, what they don't say, and their silences speak volumes. Yours do as well. You enter a room, and you are communicating with others just by standing there. What do you want to relay when you're speaking? How do you want people to feel when they're with you? What do you want them to feel when they walk away? And most importantly, what do you want to discover about them from this interaction? And what do you want to discover about yourself?

Those questions are woven into the real definition of empathetic communication. It's truly a two-directional act — it's not just what you transmit, but also what you receive. Let's get further into this.

Empathetic speaking: What you transmit

When you see the word *communication*, most likely the first thing that comes to mind is what you say. That makes sense; we prioritize speaking because it is the fastest and most instinctual tool for interaction. It's how we convey emotion, intention, and information. And it's the most impactful way to show others what you are capable of intellectually.

TIP

To dissect the purpose of empathetic communication, it's easiest to start with what immediately springs to mind: speaking. Use these five cues when approaching a conversation:

- **What is the context?** Is this a casual catch-up or a serious dialogue? Are you speaking to one person or several? Is this a meeting or a water-cooler chat? The context is the surrounding circumstances of the situation you are walking into.
- **What is the goal?** What is the overarching message you want to get across? And what do you want the result of sharing this knowledge to be? Your goal is your guiding light; it's the thing that keeps you on track when things get a bit off, and it's what to remind yourself of when you run into difficulties.
- **Who is your listener?** What do they need from you right now? What information will propel them forward? What is their mood and mindset? Are they in the best headspace to hear what you have to say? How does that impact what you'll say? How do they need to receive that information in order to really embrace and understand it? Your listener is operating at their own pace, speed, and bandwidth. When you are considering your listener, remember that just because you know what something means does not mean that they will also. Choose your words and tone according to how it will impact them.
- **What is your plan?** What words will you use to get your point across? How will your tone and body language align with it? Your plan changes according to who your listener is and what they need from you in that moment. Generally,

when you are approaching conversations, you have a good idea of what you want to say. Remember, though, to plan for a pivot if necessary. Not all conversations transpire as they are mapped out in our heads; always be prepared for a curve ball.

- **What are your next steps?** How do you want the person you are speaking with to feel immediately after they leave? What do you want them to think about you and the interaction? And, of course, what do you want them to do as a result of this conversation? Empathetic speaking as a leader is always action-oriented, and not just because it involves a task. You want to speak as if this interaction could change the course of someone's day.

Empathetic listening: What you receive

We spend so much time thinking about what to say that we rarely stop to examine how we receive what others say to us. But empathetic listening is an active, intentional practice — and like any practice, it has a framework.

I break empathetic listening down into a simple ABC mnemonic. These ABCs aren't about being passive or simply staying quiet while you wait for your turn to speak. They're about showing up to a conversation as a genuine receiver: open, aware, and committed to understand over responding. Because what you receive in a conversation is just as important as what you give.

TIP

My ABCs of empathetic listening are:

- **Accept, don't advise.** A part of the reason I think listening is so challenging is because you desperately want there to be movement. We all do, and we all view that movement as speaking. Because when you speak, you feel as if you are moving the conversation forward. But movement isn't always vocal. Sometimes movement is sitting in silence, because that silence is what stirs movement in the other person.

  Another part of the reason listening is so difficult is because it's hard to just accept another person's words. Listening without then immediately jumping in to speak can feel like you aren't doing enough in the moment to be supportive of the speaker. The stillness is disturbing and feels devoid of action, so you rush to speak to inject life into the interaction.

  But accepting what a person says without advising them means you are in the conversation to actually listen. You're not there to judge, suggest, or create unnecessary movement. You want to just hear them and allow them to feel the benefits of being heard.

The whole point of empathetic listening is to do just that: listen. Next time you are in a situation where someone just needs to vent, adjust your mindset so you don't immediately want to speak. Approach the conversation from the point of a listener, not an advisor.

» **Beware of your bias (and your body language).** I truly cannot stress this enough: We are all deeply biased. That's a part of our humanity and there is absolutely nothing wrong with it. The issues arise when you use your biases to diminish the value of other people. In doing so, you eliminate your ability to view their experiences as worthy.

  Your biases get in the way of listening because they take away your ability to hear correctly. This is the result of expectation bias. *Expectation bias* is where individuals perceive, interpret, or act on information based on what they expect to happen, rather than the reality of the situation. This is rooted by the work of psychologist Robert Rosenthal whose 1960s research found that expectations can influence experimental subjects.

  You unconsciously filter out information that does not match with your own opinions. As an empathetic listener, you know where you are capable of being biased so you keep those potential biases in mind when you are listening to others.

  Be aware of your body language cues as well. Your body is constantly communicating your feelings — both good and bad. An *open stance* — with a relaxed face and unguarded posture — shows comfort and receptiveness, while a *closed stance* — with crossed arms or a clenched jaw — indicates anxiety or defensiveness. Your body language can also emit engagement or boredom, honesty or deception, and emotional intensity.

» **Chase clarity to avoid confusion.** Confusion is a mental obstacle; when our brains can't comprehend a situation, this quickly shifts toward anger. That anger results in combativeness, frustration, and cognitive dissonance. To avoid confusion, you must pursue clarity.

  Always take a moment before you respond to take a breath or two; I know the quiet feels uncomfortable but it's necessary. It's in that quiet before you respond that you can process what was said, because you can't process what you heard *and* speak at the same time. Take those few moments to accept what was said to you and to remember your biases.

  When you begin to speak again, remember that listening doesn't end when the speaker stops talking. Listening continues to happen when paraphrasing and asking follow-up questions about what was just spoken.

Listening is an exercise in clarity. Getting clear on what was said to you — not what you think you heard and not your opinion of what was said — is a core part of empathetic listening.

TIP

Practice your ABCs in low-stakes conversations first — a casual chat with a teammate or a check-in with a friend. Empathetic listening is like a muscle, and just like any muscle it needs reps before it's ready for the heavy lift.

Communicating with Empathy

Every relationship in your life — personal or professional — lives and dies by how well you communicate. And communication is so much more than the words you say. It's what you do when you're not speaking (see the preceding section). It's the stories you tell yourself before you walk into a hard conversation. It's whether the person across from you feels seen when they leave the room. Communicating with empathy means paying attention to all of it — and this section shows you how to do so.

Empathy is a collaborative endeavor; it's driven by perspective-taking, curiosity, and open as well as closed questions. For more information, check out the nearby sidebar "Open and Closed Questions."

OPEN AND CLOSED QUESTIONS

Real empathy starts with the questions you ask. You of course want clarity on the information presented to you, but you also need to understand the meaning behind what was said: why a person feels the way they do, what inspired their opinion, and how their experience shaped their passion. For this reason, it's important to know the two types of questions you ask and how they impact your listener. *Closed questions* — ones that invite short, specific answers such as yes/no or a single fact — are for clarity. *Open questions* — ones that invite explanation and can't be answered in a single word — usually start with words such as *what, how,* or *tell me about.*

When it comes to empathetic leadership, open questions tend to build trust and understanding because they signal genuine curiosity rather than just gathering information. Closed questions are useful for quick confirmation. Something to keep in mind when it comes closed questions is that they can very quickly shut down a conversation if overused. To be empathetic, use closed questions for clarity (to get the facts) and open questions for curiosity (to learn *why*).

Realizing that conversations are two-way streets

A conversation is not a monologue with a pause in the middle. But if you're truly honest with yourself, that's probably closer to how most of your conversations actually go — you speak, they speak, you wait, you speak again. The listening part is treated like a rest stop between your real destinations. Empathetic communication blows that model up entirely. In a true two-way conversation, listening isn't the break. It's half the work.

Listening is just as active as speaking

Most of us approach conversations in a similar way. You know what you want to say, and you develop the words and phrasing in your head. You know the message you want to get across, the feeling you want to emit and exactly how the other person should embrace what you say and run with it. Then, you say your piece. You speak with passion, excitement, and confidence. When you're finished, you revel in your feat. Then, you wait. What are you waiting for? Your turn to speak again.

This is all sounds fine, but something's missing. Listening.

WARNING

Most of us focus on *our* side of conversations. The most we think about our listener is if they heard us and if they accept what we have to say as truth. This is especially egregious during difficult conversations. Anger triggers a fight-or-flight response, and that prioritizes survival over rational thought.

TIP

To make sure you are an actively engaged listener, remember these three things:

- **Be present.** The world makes it really difficult to focus on what's directly in front of us. We're constantly getting alerts from emails, text messages, social media, the news, and the list goes on. The system we live in is begging for our attention constantly, so being present in the exact moment that you're in is nearly impossible. But being present — fully engaging in the moment — improves your mental and physical health by lowering your cortisol levels, decreasing nervous system activation, and breaking the cycle of worry. And? You give the person speaking the gift of your attention, your interest, and your investment.
- **Mirror the speaker.** I realize that many people view this as a manipulation tactic. But this isn't why you are doing this. For you, matching the speaker's energy is an exercise in attention. In order to be successful at mirroring them, you have to invest most of your energy into examining them. A natural

extension of the ABCs of empathetic listening (discussed earlier in this chapter), matching their energy forces you to be deeply interested and curious in what they're both thinking and feeling.

» **Use non verbal cues.** Non verbal communication is a huge part of how we emit messages to others. This happens when we're speaking, yes, but it's especially important when we're listening. Because when we're not talking, we are communicating just as loudly as when we speak. Be sure to nod, maintain eye contact, and adopt an open posture. Give your speaker the non verbal cues that you are invested in the conversation.

REMEMBER

Many people view listening as a break. It's their opportunity to regroup, think about what they just said, and plot what they want to say next. You, as an empathetic communicator, know better than this! You know that listening is not passive; it is an active part of every conversation.

Listening to learn and speaking to share

Listening to learn is a deeply layered experience. You're of course learning the content of what someone is saying. Beneath that, you're learning how they feel about it. Another layer deeper, you're learning what they need. And even further — if you're paying close enough attention — you're learning something about yourself and how you're showing up as a leader.

Each of those layers requires a different kind of attention. Because so much of what's communicated isn't said. Some of the data you're receiving in the conversation is in the hesitations, deflections, changes in tone, and what people skip over. Listening to learn means tuning into the subtext of a conversation, not just the actual text.

This then changes the meaning of speaking, because you're not just delivering your message. You're sharing what you've learned from them as well as how that information has shifted your own thinking. Sharing — and I mean really sharing, not just reporting — requires a degree of vulnerability that many leaders are uncomfortable with. That vulnerability, modeled by the leader, creates the conditions for the whole team to communicate more openly.

REMEMBER

As you move more toward this empathetic model of communication, you'll notice that others will start to do the same. Empathetic communication is contagious. How you as the leader shows up in a conversation sets the tone and gives the other person permission to match your energy. As the leader, you almost always set the register of the room.

TIP

Your speaking habits reveal a lot about your listening habits. How much you talk in a conversation is often a direct reflection of how much you're listening. Leaders who dominate conversations aren't bad people — they're just deeply conditioned to perform competence through speech. The next time you're in a meeting or a one-on-one, audit your talk-to-listen ratio. If you find yourself doing more than 50 percent of the talking, ask yourself: "How much am I learning?"

Debugging your head: Your empathetic communication mindset

One of my favorite hobbies is fitness. It's been a constant in my life for two decades, and I feel my best when I'm consistent with my workouts. It's obviously a good thing for my physical health, but mentally it helps me be stronger. I'm able to concentrate and focus more on my daily work tasks; have a larger emotional capacity for my family; and I can better engage with friends and associates. My mindset in the gym greatly mirrors my mindset in my life as a whole.

Controlling your mind — and your mindset — is an incredibly powerful activity. As American industrialist and business magnate Henry Ford so correctly pointed out, "Whether you think you can or you can't — you're right." This is also true for your communication; if you think you're bad at it, you won't try as hard to improve it. You've resigned yourself to believing your current mindset as a fact.

To be an empathetic communicator, you need to get into the correct mindset. Just as we are constantly communicating with others, we are also constantly telling ourselves stories. And these are stories about who we are, what we're capable of, and who we want to be. These stories form your mindset; they are the baseline of who we present to the world (even if we don't realize it).

Who you are now is a great starting point for who you want to be, but first you need to figure out where your mindset is currently and where it needs to be in the future. Think about your answers to these questions (maybe even write them down):

» **What do you tell yourself about yourself now?** What is your self-talk (*self-talk* is your internal monologue)? Who do you tell yourself you are? What are the actual words you use when you are talking to yourself in your head? I know this sounds silly, but what you say to yourself really does jolt (or crash) your abilities. A 2021 study published in the science and technology journal *Nature* (`nature.com`) found that positive and negative self-talk directly modulate brain states to improve (or hinder) cognitive performance, emotional regulation, and behavior control.

» **What do you want yourself to look like in the future?** What kind of communicator do you want to be? How do you want people to feel? What do you have to say to yourself — your self-talk — to get you in the correct mindset to create an empathetic environment for you team?

Once you've answered those questions, it's time for the transformation.

TECHNICAL STUFF

To make that mindset shift, you need to go from transactional to relational communication. Here's a quick primer on these two types of communication:

» **Transactional communication.** This form of communication is task-oriented; the goal is to be concise and to get things done. The characteristics are short-term, self-serving, and often impersonal. Think of these as quick email exchanges, text messages, or conversations where you're doing something transactional such as scheduling a meeting or ordering lunch.

» **Relational communication.** This is where you begin to build rapport, trust, and a mutual understanding. This type of communication is characterized by empathy, has a focus on the long-term relationship, and emotional investment. An example of this is when you begin a team meeting with personal check-ins before discussing business.

Most leaders communicate transactionally, and that makes perfect sense. Their goal is to complete tasks and to make sure your team does the same. Information goes in, information comes out, and problems get solved. To communicate with empathy, concentrate on communicating relationally. Every conversation is a relationship moment first and a business relationship second. Debugging your head starts with recognizing which mode you default to and why.

Formulating your communication phrases

Our lives are made up of habits and patterns. Most of us wear the same few items of clothing, drive the same way to work, order the same coffee, and eat the same few meals every week. It may get boring, but it's effective in getting us through our busy and highly scheduled days.

CHOOSING THE RIGHT SELF-TALK WORDS

To be a more empathetic communicator, focus on words that encourage empathy: listening, perspective, appreciate, understand, together, and validate.

Write these words down and put them into your self-talk rotation.

It's smart to take a similar approach to the way you communicate with empathy. It's easier to stick to something when you have some foundational elements right there to lean into when things get sticky. Communication is no different. If you know what to say, what to avoid, and what to look out for, you have a much better chance of success.

Phrases to avoid

Let's get this out of the way first: You've probably used one or more these phrases before. Don't beat yourself up too much! Every leader has done the same thing. These words and expressions usually slip out of our mouths when we don't know what else to say or when we're uncomfortable with someone else sharing their emotions.

WARNING

The problem is that every single one of them communicates the opposite of empathy and the people receiving it never forget this. Though they aren't being said with malice — they're mostly used on autopilot — they still have a huge impact. Here are a few of those phrases:

- **"Why did you do that?"** This is not a question; this is an accusation. And people immediately go on the defensive when you pose it. Remember that empathy is driven by curiosity. Saying this takes the conversation from an opportunity to learn to a debate. And when is the last time you entered a debate with any other goal than winning?
- **"At least. . ."** You're probably saying this with good intentions, but it is an empathy killer. What it communicates is "Your pain is inconvenient and I need you to shrink." This phrase minimizes what a person is going through by comparing it to something that you deem worse.
- **"I know how you feel."** No two people have the same experience. And even if two people encounter the same situation at the same time, it won't translate in the same way. So no, you do not know how they feel. You do not move through the world the same way they do. You don't have the same life experiences; the same ideology or culture; and you don't process information the exact same way. Saying you know how someone feels doesn't center the speaker; it centers *you* and your opinion of their experience.
- **"You shouldn't feel that way."** Phrases like this are particularly damaging because they don't just dismiss the emotion — they make the person feel wrong for having it in the first place.

Phrases to use

When considering the phrases to say when trying to be empathetic, you have one of three goals: create space, reflect reality, or transfer power. Creating space is an invitation for vulnerability and/or collaboration. Reflecting reality is a deeper dive into what is actually being said and felt. Transferring power enables the other person to speak autonomously.

TIP

Here are a few great phrases to keep in your back pocket:

- **"I'm listening."** This signals a shift from the passivity of merely not speaking to actively engaging. You are giving this person your full presence and attention. In a world full of constant distractions, you saying *I'm listening*. This shows you are unwilling to be interrupted by any outside factor.
- **"Take your time."** As a person who stutters, I have a deep fear of taking too much time when I speak. I know that people don't always have the patience to listen, especially when they have to listen harder and longer to hear what I have to say. And I've always felt particularly self-conscious about how long it takes me to say things. The most comfortable I've felt when speaking to others — especially when I'm feeling nervous or insecure — is when they say to me "Take your time." I know I'm safe to speak freely, and I just feel a bit more confident. This is patience made verbal.
- **"Can I clarify?"** Repeating what someone says back to them — doing so in a calm, curious way — tells them that you not only heard them but also want to make sure you heard them correctly.
- **"Help me understand."** You can very quickly foster connection by simply asking to better understand because it transfers the power to the other person. You as a leader are generally going into conversations with a power imbalance that favors you. Because of that, it's your responsibility to step out of the "expert" role and invite the other person to lead.
- **"Your experience matters to me."** You don't realize it, but many times in conversation you aren't speaking to or about the person; you're speaking to and about their experience. When you as a leader say "That sounds really hard" or "I understand this has been difficult," you center the circumstance. When you say "Your experience matters," you are centering the person. This phrase shifts the conversation from what happened to who it happened to.

Phrases to use with care

WARNING

Some phrases mean well but don't land how they are intended to. Empathetic phrases without empathetic presence are just vocabulary; and often those phrases do more harm than good. Here are two to be particularly careful of in conversation:

- **"I hear you."** In the right hands, this statement can be incredibly validating. It can confirm to the speaker that they are being listened to, acknowledged, and understood without judgment. But there is nuance here, because hearing someone is a stone's throw away from being the least you could do. True empathetic communication doesn't just receive; it reflects. It shows the other person that you both hear their words and understand the weight behind them.

  I hear you has become a placeholder for people to use when they're trying to signal empathy without actually demonstrating it. When you use *I hear you* in this way, it doesn't feel like validation. It feels like a pivot, a way to shut someone up so you can jump right in and take over.

  Here's how you make this phrase work: have some proof. Show the listener that you heard their feelings, not just the facts (for example: "I hear you — this has been going on for a long time and you're exhausted by it."). Show them you've heard enough to know you need more detail (for example: "I hear you — and I want to make sure I'm understanding this correctly.").

- **"You should. . ."** Accepting what people say without advising them on what to do is discussed earlier in this chapter (see the section, "Listening to learn and speaking to share"). Any sentence that starts with *You should* is an advisory statement masked as comfort and support. Instead of listening to learn and experience the speaker's feelings, you listened to diagnose and fix. I've rarely heard a *You should* statement that's not coming from a good place; the issue is what it implies. And what the speaker hears is that you think they are handling their situation in the wrong way.

  When people are sharing something difficult with you, they might not be coming to you for a solution. They might just want to be heard. When you start *should-ing* all over the conversation, it skips the human part of it: the connection. That can signal your discomfort with sitting with that person in their problem; you as leader need to discover how to navigate these moments with calm and patience.

Overcoming the Barriers of Communicating with Empathy

Here's the thing: Most leaders actually want to communicate with empathy. The intention is there. What gets in the way is everything else — the packed calendar, the power dynamic, the ego that no one wants to admit to, the cultural assumptions baked so deep you don't even realize they're there. Empathy doesn't fail because leaders stop caring. It fails because something is quietly blocking it, and most people never stop long enough to figure out what that block is.

That's what this section is for. It identifies the barriers — the real ones, not the polished version — because you can't work around what you haven't looked at directly. Some of these will feel obvious. Some will feel a little uncomfortable. Either way, pay attention to your reaction. That's usually where the real work is.

WARNING

These are the barriers to watch out for:

- **Cognitive overload.** You are stressed, overstimulated, decision-fatigued — and it's a lot. And when your brain is full, empathy is one of the first things to go. It's neurologically expensive to hold space for another person's emotional experience while managing your own. Leaders who are chronically overwhelmed will default to transactional communication simply because it requires less of them mentally and emotionally.
- **Cultural and generational differences.** At any given time, there are up to five generations actively in the workforce. What feels empathetic in one culture or generational context can feel intrusive, patronizing, or inappropriate in another. You as a leader can't apply a single empathy template across your entire team; that just plain won't work because not every will receive it the same. You have to have cultural and generational humility so you can recognize your default is not universal.
- **Ego.** This is probably the most pervasive barrier because it's the least acknowledged. Ego makes you show up needing to be right, needing to be the smartest person in the room, and needing the conversation to validate your existing perspective. Ego makes listening feel like losing. And you cannot communicate with empathy when you're more invested in winning than understanding.

  So how do you combat this? Watch how you respond when you're wrong. Because being wrong is the ultimate ego test. Some leaders double down; some deflect blame; some minimize the error; and some own it cleanly.

The ones that own their mistakes are the ones worth following, and that type of leader is who you should strive to be. How you handle being wrong teaches your team if it's safe to be honest with you. A leader who can say "I was wrong about that and here's what I'm going to do differently," is a leader people trust with their truth.

- **Power imbalance.** Leadership comes with authority, and authority — even when done kindly — creates distance. People edit themselves around power. They soften their feedback, omit their real feelings, and tell you what they think you want to hear. That editing makes genuine empathetic communication nearly impossible unless the leader actively works to flatten the dynamic and create psychological safety.

  To combat the power imbalance, make it safe to disagree with you. If your team never pushes back, never challenges your ideas, and always seems to agree with your decision, this is not harmony. Another tip? Watch how you enter a room. Power communicates before you speak a single word. How you physically enter a space, where you sit, whether you initiate warmth or wait for others to approach you — all of these send signals about accessibility.

- **Urgency.** There are always going to be a million things to do. Your calendar is back-to-back and your inbox never empties. You have two meetings to prep for, your kid's doctor's appointment to reschedule, and . . . wait, what are you cooking for dinner again? And who is picking up the dog from the groomer? Urgency communicates — loudly, I might add — that the task matters more than the person, and people feel that. And busyness? It is one of the most socially acceptable barriers to empathy because it's so easy to justify.

  To combat this, reframe what "productive" means. The biggest mindset shift is recognizing that a conversation where someone felt truly heard is not time wasted — it is leadership work. If leaders measure productivity purely by tasks completed, human connection will always feel like a detour. Redefining productivity to include relational communication changes how you allocate your time and attention.

REMEMBER

The barrier is never the problem itself — it's your willingness to look at it. Every leader has a reason their empathy breaks down. The ones worth following are the ones who stopped using that reason as an excuse. You don't have to be perfect at this. You just have to be honest about where you get stuck. Awareness is not weakness — it's the starting point for every leader who actually gets better.

IN THIS CHAPTER

» Differentiating empathy and conformity

» Understanding the role of science

» Exploring empathy in a group setting

» Basing your decisions on human data

» Building processes that encourage group empathy

Chapter 11
Leading Groups with Empathy

You are a part of quite a few groups. Some of them you actively choose — such as your friend circle and the organizations you join because they reflect your values. Some you find yourself in unexpectedly — a task force, a cross-functional project, or a community shaped by circumstance. And some you are just born into — your family, your culture, and your nationality.

What all of these groups have in common is that they require something from you empathetically that one-on-one relationships don't. The dynamics are more complex, the competing needs are louder, and the opportunities for misunderstanding multiply with every person added to the group. Leading with empathy in a group setting isn't just harder than leading one person; it's a fundamentally different skill. And most leaders have never been taught how to do it. This chapter helps you find your path.

Dissecting Conformity

In 2004, empathy had a bit of a moment even though no one realized it at the time. The first thing that happened was the launch of Facebook and, as a result, mass-adopted social media. Social media in general makes it difficult to form deep, local bonds despite expanding the capacity for global awareness and rallying, but it also frequently reduces empathy to superficial reactions.

And then? There was *Mean Girls*. Stick with me on this one.

For those unfamiliar, this 2004 movie followed the story of a homeschool teenager as she transferred to a suburban high school and plotted to dethrone the school's reigning "Queen Bee." It's a fascinating look into social hierarchies, group dynamics, and why empathy is so hard to have for people you don't view as "one of us." The main character, Cady Heron, learns very quickly that the way to not eat lunch alone in a bathroom stall isn't to just be nice and accept everyone as they are; it's to show people what they want to see. And it works — she climbs the ranks and becomes the most popular girl in school. But her downfall? It's the exact same thing that sparked her meteoric rise in not just her social group but also her school at large in the first place: conformity.

REMEMBER

Here's the tension at the center of group empathy that people talk about enough: Groups don't naturally produce empathy. They produce conformity. The social pressure to align, agree, and belong is one of the most powerful forces in human psychology. And it works directly against the kind of genuine curiosity and perspective-taking that empathy requires (for more on perspective-taking, see Chapter 9).

So, what is conformity, and how is different to empathy? And how does conformity impact empathy? *Conformity* is defined as the act of aligning your attitudes, beliefs, or behaviors with social norms, group expectations, or established standards. Most of the time, it stems from a desire or need to fit in, gain acceptance, or adapt to perceived pressure from others.

Think about the last time you were in a group setting where someone expressed a view that went against the grain. What happened to that person? And more importantly, what happened inside you? Did you feel the pull to distance yourself from them, even slightly? That pull is conformity at work. And it is always in tension with empathy.

Psychologists and sociologists agree that conformity is generally broken down into four distinct categories based on your internal motivations:

- **Compliance.** *Compliance* is public conformity without private agreement. You go along with the group — you say the right things, nod your head when you're supposed to, and exhibit the expected behaviors — while internally holding a completely different view. Unlike normative influence that is driven by the desire to belong, and informational influence that produces genuine belief change, compliance is purely performative.

  WARNING

  As a leader, be vigilant about compliance. In environments where empathy is low — where disagreement is risky, where emotional expression is coded as weakness, where the leader's reading of the room is understood to be the correct one — compliance becomes the dominant adaptive strategy. It's what psychologically healthy people do when the environment isn't safe enough for authenticity, but they still need to function.

  REMEMBER

  Compliance kills empathy in two distinct ways. First, it prevents you — the leader — from being able to practice empathy accurately. You don't have the correct information because people aren't giving it, so the signals and emotional data you rely on to properly engage with your team just isn't available. And second, compliance prevents your team members from practicing empathy. When everyone is performing a version of themselves rather than being themselves, genuine human contact becomes difficult. People don't know each other well enough to empathize accurately because they've only ever seen the performed version. The interpersonal distance that compliance creates isn't just about the leader–team relationship. It runs through every relationship in the group.

- **Informational influence.** *Informational influence* is when you conform because you believe the group has accurate information or a better understanding of a situation. Informational influence is conformity driven by a genuine belief that others know better than you do; you go along because you've concluded that the group's reading of the situation is more accurate than your own.

  This is different from normative influence in a critical way: Informational influence produces actual private belief change, not just public compliance. You aren't secretly disagreeing and going along anyway. You have genuinely updated your view, and that makes it both more powerful and more difficult to correct.

  WARNING

  On the surface, informational influence seems thoughtful and a bit more measured than its normative counterpart. But it is actually one of the primary drivers of *groupthink*. When a group has strong shared identity and a dominant interpretation, dissenting information gets filtered out not through suppression but through genuine disbelief. People don't ignore contradictory evidence because they're afraid; they ignore it because the group's shared frame has become their own frame, and evidence that doesn't fit the frame simply doesn't register as credible.

So, the loyal and well-meaning team that unanimously agrees with a bad decision isn't necessarily full of people who were too afraid to speak up. Some of them simply stopped being able to see the alternative. And that's how it suppresses empathy: by stopping people from feeling it in the first place.

» **Internalization.** The deepest form of social influence, *internalization* is what happens when values, beliefs, or behaviors become genuinely your own. Not because you're afraid of social consequences or have deferred to someone's expertise, but because you've absorbed it into your identify and value system. The defining characteristic is that internalized beliefs and behaviors persist in the absence of any external pressure. No one is watching. No reward is attached. The surveillance is gone. And the person still behaves consistently with the value because it's now theirs.

REMEMBER

Internalization is the endgame for empathetic leadership. Every other form of influence produces empathetic behavior conditionally. Normative influence produces it when the social environment rewards it. Informational influence produces it when the shared framework supports it. Compliance produces it when the incentive structure requires it. But internalization produces it always, because the person has genuinely come to believe that understanding and caring about other people's experience is right, important, and part of who they are.

How, then, does internalization actually happen? Well, here's how it doesn't: through instruction. You cannot tell someone to just value empathy, and then they go off and do it. It happens through repeated experiences that demonstrate that empathy produces something real and meaningful. It happens when someone practices genuine perspective-taking and it visibly changes an outcome. When a leader extends real understanding to a team member in a hard moment and the relationship deepens in a way that produces better work. When a group moves through conflict with honesty and care and comes out more cohesive than before. These experiences don't just teach empathy as a skill. They demonstrate empathy as a value — as something that matters, that works, that produces a kind of human connection and organizational effectiveness that other approaches can't replicate.

» **Normative influence.** Arguably the most common kind of conformity, *normative influence* is conforming to be accepted and liked by the group or to avoid rejection. This usually involves quite a bit of outside pressure and influence to fall in line, and often times we do.

TECHNICAL STUFF

Social psychology pioneer Solomon Asch conducted what became to be known as the Asch conformity experiments in 1951 that proved that people will knowingly give incorrect answers to match a unanimous group's obviously false judgments. I know what you're thinking: how obvious could it have been if people gave wrong answers? The participants were asked to match line lengths — an objectively simple task with an obvious correct answer. When asked privately why they gave the incorrect answer, they all said that the social pressure to align overrode what they could see with their own eyes.

If people will deny an obvious visual reality to avoid social friction, imagine what they'll do with something as ambiguous and uncomfortable as emotional truth. Normative influence is why people say "I'm fine" in team meetings when they're not. It's why no one names the difficult thing in the room. The social cost of being the one who breaks the consensus is real, and people feel it viscerally.

REMEMBER

Normative influence is what makes group empathy incredibly difficult. It is also, however, the mechanism that makes group empathy scalable. If you change the norm in the group to be that of pursing empathy, you will be able to change what people feel pressured to do.

REMEMBER

The reason this matters for leaders is that you set the norm. If your group culture rewards agreement and punishes deviation, you have built a conformity machine, and most forms of conformity are the enemy of the honest, varied, sometimes uncomfortable input that good decisions require. Empathetic leadership in groups means actively resisting that pull. It means creating enough safety for people to disagree, enough curiosity to actually want to hear why, and enough self-awareness to notice when you are enforcing conformity without meaning to.

The work of empathetic leadership, at its deepest level, is the work of creating the conditions under which people move from the first three forms — normative, informational, and compliance — toward internalization. It's slow. It requires sustained modeling, real experience, honest narrative, and genuine autonomy. But when a group has genuinely internalized empathy as a shared value, you have something that doesn't need to be monitored, mandated, or maintained. It maintains itself. And that is the only kind of group culture that actually lasts.

Unpicking the Science of Empathy in Groups

"On Wednesdays, we wear pink." One of the most iconic lines in *Mean Girls* belies a core truth: We all want to belong. To a mission, to a person, or to a group. When Karen, one of the popular "Plastics" group, invited Cady to sit with them that next day — a Wednesday — Karen was letting her in on their social code: to belong in this group, you have to dress a certain way. Behave a certain way. Be a certain way. And then? You're one of us.

TECHNICAL STUFF

The reason why we strive so hard to belong somewhere is evolutionary. We are highly social beings and, throughout human history, relying on a group meant a higher chance of survival. While modern life has changed significantly, our primal instinct for socializing remains. We feel much more secure when we're surrounded by our peers. And then there's our identity and our self-esteem; namely, *social identity theory*. Formulated by social psychologists Henri Tajfel and John Turner in the 1970s and 1980s, social identity theory explains that our sense of self is deeply tied to the groups we belong to; we categorize people, identify with groups, and compare ourselves to others to boost our self-esteem, which often leads to in-group favoritism and out-group bias (in-groups and out-groups are discussed in the later sections, "Intragroup empathy" and "Intergroup empathy" respectively).

It's for that reason that if you agree with someone, empathy comes more easily. Because we adopt the identity of the groups we belong to and internalize their values, we end up aligning our behaviors with group norms and — like Cady — we wear pink on Wednesdays, because that's what we do.

Simple, right? Well, not exactly. Research shows that both in-group and out-group empathy is quite challenging. Most people find genuine empathy in group settings difficult and uncomfortable even with people they like, even in groups they chose, and even when everyone is nominally on the same side.

TECHNICAL STUFF

Why? Because groups activate a completely different set of psychological mechanisms than one-on-one relationships do. The brain processes group membership through the same neural pathways it uses to assess threat and safety. In-group members feel familiar, safe, and deserving of empathy. Out-group members feel different, uncertain, and — at the neurological level — slightly less human. This isn't a character flaw; it's biology. But biology isn't destiny, and understanding the mechanism is the first step to overriding it.

Research on this is consistent and may make you a little uncomfortable. Studies on *mirror neuron activity* (which fire both when you act and when you watch someone else do the same action) show that we physically resonate less with people we perceive as different from us. Research on perspective-taking shows that we are significantly worse at accurately modeling the inner experience of out-group members than in-group members even when we think we're being fair.

Empathy researcher and social psychology professor Daryl Cameron's work on empathy in groups found that people often engage in what he calls *motivated empathy regulation;* they unconsciously choose not to empathize with certain people because the emotional cost feels too high. This means that leading with empathy in a group setting requires something more deliberate than just caring about people. It requires structure, practice, and a willingness to override instincts that feel natural but aren't serving anyone.

That's why the following sections focus on understanding the benefits and challenges of both intragroup (within your current group) and intergroup (outside of your current group) empathy.

Intragroup empathy

As Cady Heron quickly found out in *Mean Girls*, groups are incredibly difficult to navigate; especially if you're not fully versed on the status quo. She changed herself to fit in with The Plastics — shifting the language she used and wearing clothes that weren't her style — so everyone could see that she belonged, especially those three members already on the inside. But, as time went on, she began to actually become one of them.

The empathy she sought through "playing the part" turned into who she actually was. And that clouded her true vision of herself more than anything else. It's that trap that all of us must do our best to avoid when it comes to intragroup empathy.

REMEMBER

Intragroup (in-group) refers to group dynamics within the confines of a specific group. These dynamics are where most leaders spend the majority of their attention. And that is for good reason. The health of your immediate team, department, or community is the most direct expression of your leadership. But intragroup empathy is trickier than it looks, because being in the same group doesn't automatically produce understanding; it only produces proximity. That trickiness shows up in a few key ways that leaders need to watch out for:

- **Leadership lookouts.** The biggest trap you need to be aware of is *selective empathy*; you connect more deeply with certain team members without even realizing it. We all have natural affinities for certain people, but the problem arises when those preferences turn into favoritism. You begin to filter opportunities, support, and recognition, and your team notices these tendencies long before you as the leader realize you're displaying it.

  As the leader, you are always a character in the group's story whether you intend to be or not. Your moods are contagious. Your attention is currency. The people you engage with most become implicitly more valued, and the people you overlook feel it even if you never said a word. Intragroup empathy in leadership means being conscious of the signals you're sending at the group level. This means not just in your one-on-one relationships, but in every room you share with your team collectively.

» **Psychological impact.** Empathy should be reframed from a soft skill to a non-technical one. Soft skills often get dismissed as fluffy, innate and secondary; they are anything but. According to the Association for Talent Development (ATD), culture lacking empathy and compassion results in 30 percent less creativity and 38 percent of employees in such cultures intentionally reduce their work effort. That's not a soft finding; that's a direct productivity hit. On the flip side, research also shows that empathy fosters psychological safety, encourages an open exchange of ideas, and enhances both individual and team creativity.

Within any group, individuals are navigating their own psychological needs simultaneously: the need to belong, to be seen, to have status, and to feel competent. When these needs aren't met, they don't disappear; they show up in other ways. Such as passive resistance, conflict that looks like it's about the work but is actually about feeling invisible, or the person who goes quiet in meetings. And nobody thinks to ask why. Intragroup empathy means staying curious about what's happening beneath the surface for each individual even when the group looks to be functioning fine.

» **Social dynamics.** Google's Project Aristotle (`https://rework.withgoogle.com/intl/en/guides/understand-team-effectiveness`), the renowned research initiative to discover what makes team highly effective, found that psychological safety was the single factor differentiating high-performing teams from their counterparts. When people feel safe, they are more willing to share ideas, admit mistakes, and take the interpersonal risks that drive innovation.

Empathy is what creates that safety. Research by ATD comparing companies in the highest versus lowest quartile on organizational trust and leadership empathy found that employees at high-empathy organizations reported 75 percent higher engagement, 50 percent better retention, and 40 percent less burnout.

Groups develop their own social norms faster than most leaders realize. And those norms determine what emotions are safe to express, whose voice carries weight, and what kind of experiences get acknowledged versus minimized. In a low-empathy intragroup environment, the social norm becomes performance: Everyone presents their best, most capable, least complicated self. Which means you as the leader are always working with incomplete information, and the team is always spending energy they should be giving to the work on managing their image instead.

REMEMBER

The relationships within your group are not your relationships to manage, but they are yours to protect. When conflict exists between team members, when someone is being subtly excluded, when the quiet person in the corner has stopped engaging, these are empathy failures at the relationship level that compound into culture failures over time. An empathetic leader notices and responds, not by playing therapist, but by creating conditions where people feel safe enough to work through what's hard rather than around it.

Intergroup empathy

"Where you sit in the cafeteria is crucial." When Cady first met what ended up being her true friends Janis and Damian, they knew she was a floppy fawn. Cady had no idea that what she was stepping into in the terrifyingly intimidating dynamics of the social hierarchy that is high school. So, during their first lunch period together, they gave her a guided tour of the cafeteria and the cliques within the school. The broader concept this demonstrates is that you feel a deep connection to and identity with who you spend the most time around. And we gravitate toward those people every chance we get — even at work (explore connecting with others more in Chapter 10). Because we feel such a strong attachment to our groups, we are naturally inclined to be wary and judgmental of those on the outside. That makes intergroup empathy difficult.

REMEMBER

Intergroup refers to the interactions or conflicts between two or more different groups. If intragroup empathy is hard (see the previous section), intergroup empathy — what happens between separate groups — is where things get genuinely complicated. And it's where most organizations have their biggest unresolved problems.

WARNING

It is natural for people from different departments, different functions, different nationalities, and different cultures to be in chronic low-grade conflict with each other. And in almost every case, at the root of that conflict is a failure of intergroup empathy — an inability or unwillingness to genuinely understand the experience, pressures, and perspective of a group that isn't your own.

That failure shows up in a few key ways leaders need to watch for:

» **Leadership lookouts.** As a leader operating at the intersection of groups — whether you're managing a cross-functional team, leading a diverse organization, or navigating a merger — your job is to be a bridge, not a wall. That requires something genuinely difficult: holding multiple group realities simultaneously and treating each one as legitimate, even when they're in direct tension with each other.

Don't be the leader who takes sides; that makes the intergroup empathy problem worse. The leader who can genuinely say "I understand why both groups feel what they feel, and here's how we move forward together" is extraordinarily rare and extraordinarily effective.

- **Psychological impact.** It is difficult to relate to those outside of our own group and the resulting conflicts and tensions that causes. But what happens if we actually succeed at intergroup empathy? Research on intergroup contact theory found that meaningful contact between groups reduces prejudice and increases empathy, but only under specific conditions: equal status, common goals, cooperation, and institutional support. When those conditions aren't present, contact can deepen division rather than reduce it.

  This has profound implications for how you structure cross-functional work, how you run all-hands meetings, and how you handle conflict between groups. Throwing people in a room together and hoping empathy emerges is a wish not a strategy.

- **Social dynamics.** My deep and personal affinity for *Mean Girls* aside, it is an excellent breakdown of how we as humans approach intergroup social dynamics. People naturally categorize themselves and others, and this categorization often leads to unmerited favoritism toward one's own group ("us") and prejudice or suspicion toward those outside of it ("them"). It's tribal by design because humans evolved to feel stronger loyalty to their immediate group than to outsiders — a survival mechanism.

  In modern organizations, this shows up as the marketing team that doesn't understand why engineering moves so slowly, the field team that feels invisible to headquarters, or the new hires who can't crack the culture that the tenured employees built and protect without realizing it. Every one of these is a social empathy gap between groups. And left unaddressed, they calcify into us-versus-them dynamics that no amount of team-building exercises will fix.

WARNING

Intergroup relationships are built one interaction at a time, and they're destroyed the same way. A single moment where someone from one group feels dismissed, stereotyped, or unseen by someone from another can set back months of progress. This is why empathetic leaders are deliberate about cross-group interaction — they create the conditions for real contact, they model genuine curiosity about other groups' experiences, and they treat intergroup tension not as a people problem but as a leadership opportunity.

Rewiring Your Brain to Have Empathy in a Group Setting

One of the narrative framing devices used in *Mean Girls* was Cady comparing her experiences in a traditional high school setting to her experiences around the animals her parents — both zoologists — researched in Africa. The first time she felt jealousy and anger toward the "Queen Bee"— Regina George — the actors transform into primal beasts, attacking each other as if they were animals in the wild. Because that's how it would have been settled in the animal world. This allegorical choice shows how our basal instincts as humans aren't that far off from animals. But what separates us from our primal origins is choice. Our *cerebral cortexes* (the outmost, wrinkly layer of the brain) are massively enlarged, giving us much more ability to process abstract thought and develop language. Our brains are also highly specialized for complex social cooperation and abstract problem-solving.

Our brains are also malleable. The default toward in-group favoritism and out-group distance is real (just like in the movie), but it is not fixed. Research consistently shows that deliberate perspective-taking practice, meaningful cross-group contact, and conscious interruption of automatic categorization all produce measurable changes in empathic response over time.

TIP

What does this look like practically? It means noticing the moment your brain categorizes someone — that quick, automatic read of who they are and whether they're like you — and pausing before you act on it. It means deliberately seeking out the perspective of the person in the room whose experience is most different from yours, not as a political gesture but as a genuine act of curiosity. It means building the habit of asking, before any group interaction, whose voice you haven't heard yet and why. Here's how you do that:

- **Be curious, not judgmental.** There will be times when one of your team members expresses a controversial or frustrating opinion. It will be very easy to judge them, but reject that urge with everything you have. Instead, replace that judgment with curiosity.

  Curiosity creates a pause between stimulus and reaction and, in that pause, your brain starts to build new neural pathways. Over time, this practice rewires your default response from defensiveness to openness. A simple reframe helps. Instead of thinking "I can't believe they said that" try thinking "I wonder what's behind that." You don't have to agree with someone to be genuinely interested in them. And more often than not, that interest is what makes them feel seen — and that is the whole foundation of group trust.

- **Engage in perspective-taking.** The true cornerstone of empathy, *engaging in perspective-taking* means consciously imagining yourself in another person's position. You do this by actively setting aside personal biases so you can better understand the thoughts, emotions, and motivations of others.
  To do this in a group setting, you as the leader have to actively invite diverse viewpoints. To learn how to do this, head over to Chapter 9 where we discuss pursuing perspective.

It's incredibly challenging to go against the grain; the fear of dismissal, the threat of reprimand, and the possibility of being viewed as incompetent is very real. Your job as a leader is to encourage your team members to speak their unique perspectives, especially if they might disagree.

Something that I drive home in my talks is that you, as the leader, need to tailor your communication for every interaction. And that's exceptionally important when you're dealing with a group. The point of speaking to anyone is to get your point across; why would you speak in a way that fails at that mission? It's important to express your ideas in a way that all of your recipients can connect with; this means being intentional and measured in how you speak to your team. Finally, it's important to be humble. It's important to remind yourself that when you're pursuing perspective-taking, especially in groups, that you don't have the full picture. Humility quiets your ego, allowing you to prioritize understanding over being right. This fosters a collaborative environment where all members feel safe sharing ideas, leading to better collective problem-solving and stronger team cohesion.

- **Participate in shared goals**. Working collaboratively on a common task naturally aligns brain activity and builds camaraderie. The brain finds it much easier to feel empathy for people it perceives as being on the same "team."

  One of the most reliable ways to build that perception — especially with colleagues you find difficult — is to build something together. When your group works toward a shared goal, you experience small moments of mutual struggle, mutual investment, and mutual reward. Those moments stack up neurologically. They move a person in your mind from "other" to "ally." This is why team-based challenges, co-created projects, or even just collaborative problem-solving meetings can do more for group empathy than any workshop or conversation about feelings. You're not just building camaraderie, you're giving your brain evidence that these people matter to your success, and that changes how you see them.

- **Practice active listening.** *Active listening* — the practice of being fully present in a conversation — is crucial for empathy to have a chance of succeeding. You have to remove distractions, pay attention to nonverbal cues, and paraphrase and reflect on what you just heard before you respond. And this isn't just in one-on-one situations, but also complicated dynamics of a group.

  So how do you practice active listening in groups? First, shut off your inner rebuttal. This is that thing you do when you're supposed to be listening to what a person is saying but you're actually mentally preparing your counterargument. It's okay; we all do this at one point or another. The trick is to catch yourself in the act and correct your course. Instead, focus entirely on what the person is saying to you rather than planning your attack. Also, avoid side conversations. This includes the conversations you have with whoever is standing next to you as well as the ones happening via technology. That's right, scanning your device is akin to verbally interrupting someone. When you look at any of your devices, you're breaking focus. You likely think you're multitasking, but true multitasking is an overwhelming myth; research argues that only two percent of the population is naturally equipped to multitask effectively and, put plainly, people who claim to be great at it are often the worst. Start paraphrasing and summarizing what someone says to you before you introduce your own ideas to the conversation. Often times in conversation, we don't hear what people say. We hear our opinion of what people say. Summarizing what people said to you provides clarity and helps you stop whatever bias you are holding before it goes any further.

The rewiring isn't comfortable. Growth rarely is. But the leaders who do this work — who actively practice empathy across difference rather than just within their comfort zone — develop a range and a depth of human understanding that makes them more effective in virtually every leadership situation they encounter.

Making Decisions Based on Human Data (Not Just Feelings)

An incredibly intimidating thing for me — a naturally shy and introverted person — is the concept of *working a room* (connecting with people, reading the energy, and making genuine connection rather than just being present in a group). This may sound unbelievable coming from a professional keynote speaker, but groups of people intimidate me. I never know who to talk to or what to say. Can I just walk up to them? Am I interrupting their conversation? Do they even want to talk to me?

And then, of course, there's the anxiety of my stuttering — specifically, I have some insecurities about sounding a certain way. When I'm speaking to a new person, I don't want to sound different or abnormal which makes them uncomfortable; and because I feel insecure, it makes them even more uncomfortable and less likely to actually want to talk to me.

That's a part of the reason why public speaking actually made these group situations easier for me; anyone I speak to after a talk knows I stutter, they know what I do for a living, and they already have a topic they want to discuss. In the beginning, pursuing public speaking was about growing my confidence, expanding my network and building my career. Over time, though, it really did stop being about me. It started being about the message people received and the community the audiences were able to cultivate as a result of it.

My stutter was the data that changed everything, but only when I finally shared it. Imagine giving every person in your organization that same gift: allowing them to be known before they have to prove themselves. That's what human data does.

REMEMBER

Human data means the information you gather about a person — their motivations, fears, and needs — by listening and observing closely, rather than assuming. Being in a group makes rational, unbiased empathy incredibly difficult. The social pressures, the conformity pulls, the in-group biases; all of these distort your perception in ways that feel like clarity but aren't. This is why empathetic group leadership can't rely on feeling alone. It has to be paired with deliberate data collection about the human experience of the group.

What does that mean practically? It means:

- **Creating anonymous channels for feedback.** So that the people least likely to speak up in a group setting have a way to be heard.
- **Paying attention to who is absent from the conversation.** I mean this both literally and figuratively; be sure to treat that absence as information rather than coincidence.
- **Running pulse checks.** Not just on performance metrics but on how people are actually experiencing the work and each other.

Human data through engagement surveys, stay interviews, listening sessions, demographic breakdowns of who is speaking up and who isn't, is how leaders get the fuller picture. This doesn't replace empathy; it makes empathy accurate.

My post-keynote dynamics made me more comfortable, but they were also bidirectional. Because of the nature of my talks — the vulnerability, the rawness, the discomfort — people felt known and seen, and that resulted in them showing up more honestly and openly. Collecting human data isn't just about you as the leader getting smarter. It changes the group dynamic itself. It signals to your team that their experience matters, and you're actually trying to understand it.

TIP

The leaders who do this well aren't the most emotionally expressive ones in the room. They're the most observant. They're tracking patterns and they notice when someone who used to contribute has gone quiet, when a group that used to collaborate has started to fragment, when the energy in the room before a meeting and after it tells two very different stories. That is human data. And it is some of the most important data a leader can have.

WARNING

As a leader, keep the following thoughts in mind when you're attempting to encourage empathy on your team:

- **Conformity pressure distorts gut feelings.** Social conformity, discussed earlier in this chapter, impacts decision-making. When you rely on how the room felt, you're often reading conformity and not consensus. Human data gives you an actual read on sentiment before social dynamics kick in.
- **Empathy gaps can exist in decision-making.** Research shows that empathy narrows as group sizes increase. Humans are wired to feel more for individuals than for groups, so without *intentional systems* (the deliberate processes and structures a leader builds that make empathy a consistent practice rather than something dependent on mood or memory), group decisions get made on instinct rather than on what the data actually shows about *collective impact* (the combined results of a group's individual actions and attitudes).
- **Whose voice gets counted and whose doesn't.** Groups tend to platform the loudest or most central voices, and those voices become representatives of the whole. Be sure to use data tools such as surveys, pulse checks, and anonymous feedback to reveal the gap between who speaks and who's actually present. This is an empathy failure with a data solution.

Encouraging Group Empathy

Individual empathy is a virtue. Structural empathy is a strategy. And in group settings, the virtue has a real impact only if the correct structure is in place. You cannot rely on everyone in a group to naturally extend empathy in the directions it's most needed. You have to build it in.

TIP

In my work, building that empathy looks like leaning into the vulnerability. I found that there is value in transparency, in taking enough of an emotional risk to possibly form a deeper connection. Because I teach audiences and teams empathy skills, I focus on building processes that can make people feel comfortable and confident enough to take those kinds of risks. I tell stories about my struggles as a stutterer, my failures because of stuttering, and what I did personally to try to right my own ship and change my life. It's in those moments that people begin to not only forgive themselves for falling prey to their insecurities but also begin to extend their teammates and colleagues grace. What could this look like for you and your team? Maybe it's actively creating space for minority viewpoints rather than defaulting to the loudest voices. It could look like decision-making processes that require perspective-taking as a step; you can explicitly ask, before a decision is finalized, whose experience hasn't been considered and what they would say. It might look like onboarding and team rituals that highlight the person behind the role, creating the kind of familiarity that makes empathy easier to extend.

Whatever you choose to focus on, make sure one thing is crystal clear: accountability. Groups need to know that dismissing someone's experience, talking over a quieter voice, or defaulting to in-group favoritism has a consequence — not a punitive one, but a corrective one. An empathetic leader names bad behavior when it happens, models the alternative, and returns to empathy and accountability consistently enough that the group internalizes both as a norm rather than an exception.

The goal isn't a group where everyone agrees, or where everyone feels comfortable all the time. That's conformity, not empathy. The goal is a group where everyone feels genuinely seen, where their experience is acknowledged as real, and their perspective is treated as worth understanding even when it's inconvenient. That kind of group doesn't just feel better to be a part of. It thinks better, decides better, and performs better. And it does so because someone decided that empathy wasn't optional; it's foundational.

REMEMBER

Groups don't naturally produce empathy; they produce conformity. The social pressure to align, agree, and belong is one of the most powerful forces in human psychology, and it works directly against the kind of genuine curiosity and perspective-taking that empathy requires.

Leading with empathy in a group setting means actively resisting that pull. It means creating enough psychological safety for people to disagree, collecting real human data so your empathy is accurate and not just well-intentioned, and building processes that make genuine understanding a structural expectation rather than a personal virtue. And that only happens when a leader decides — consistently and deliberately — that empathy isn't a leadership style but is a leadership responsibility.

IN THIS CHAPTER

» Discovering and communicating with empathetic authority

» Understanding emotional clarity in leadership

» Giving feedback with empathy

» Recognizing the differences between agreement and understanding

Chapter 12
Being Empathetic and Authoritative

Let's talk about two words that most people don't put in the same sentence: empathy and authority.

On the surface, they seem like they're pulling in opposite directions. Authority feels structured, firm, and decisive. Empathy feels open, relational, and emotionally present. And if you've spent any time in traditional leadership spaces, you've probably been given the quiet impression that you need to choose — that you can be the leader people like or the leader people respect, but that trying to be both is naive at best and ineffective at worst.

I am here to tell you that is completely wrong.

Not only can you be both — you need to be both. Because authority without empathy creates compliance, not commitment. And empathy without authority creates connection without direction. Neither one alone is enough. But together? Together they create the kind of leadership that people talk about for the rest of their careers. The kind of leadership that makes people better at their jobs and more confident in themselves. The kind of leadership that builds cultures where people actually want to show up.

That is what this chapter is about. I discuss what empathetic authority actually means in practice: how to define it, how to communicate it, how to lead with emotional clarity, and how to deliver feedback in a way that makes people feel challenged and supported at the same time. By the time you finish this chapter, my hope is that you walk away knowing — in your bones — that being firm and being human are not just compatible. They are, together, the recipe for balancing empathy with authority.

Defining Empathetic Authority

Empathy is the ability to understand or share the feelings of another person. An *empath* is a person who is highly sensitive to the emotions of others and they often absorb those people's feelings as their own. It may, on the surface, seem that authority and empathy don't have much alignment. As an empathetic leader, however, you need to marry these two concepts for maximum effectiveness. I'm sure you're wondering how that works. It starts with breaking down what authority actually is in practice.

Authority has many definitions and use-cases. There is authority in the literal sense where someone is above others in a hierarchical system. There's also authority in the advisory capacity, where someone can come in and support others with their expertise as opposed to having direct control. Then there's positional authority where a person's power is derived directly from a specific job title or role.

Authority is the legitimate power or right to give orders, make decisions and enforce obedience. To have real authority, people need to respect you and view you as competent and fair. Leaders need authority to be effective because it provides structure and clarity; there's a clear chain of command and everyone knows who holds what responsibilities. Authority enables actions and pushes results; good leaders can see the roadblocks and remove them, redistribute work, and drive performance. And, maybe most importantly, good authority creates order and security.

Order and security are also important components of empathy. Both satisfy our psychological need for predictability, stability, and control. They reduce anxiety and stress, allowing people to invest all of their energy on their tasks. It creates structure which encourages a sense of normality and routine, both of which foster mental stability.

Empathy and authority are fierce allies. They both need each other to create cultures where people feel safe, can be productive, and speak with confidence about what they're thinking and feeling. With that in mind, let's give empathetic authority a definition that covers its extensive reach.

REMEMBER

Empathetic authority is:

- **The ability to lead with both a firm hand and an open heart.** It's the practice of being someone people trust enough to follow and respect enough to listen to.
- **The leadership posture of holding high expectations while genuinely honoring the humanity of the people you hold them for.** You make hard decisions, deliver difficult truths, and maintain clear direction — all while making the people around you feel seen and respected in the process.
- **Emotional intelligence in action.** It's the ability to read a room, honor what you find there, and still lead it somewhere meaningful. It's knowing what your team feels, understanding why they feel it, and using that understanding to lead more effectively rather than more cautiously.
- **The kind of leadership that earns the right to be direct because it has already proven it cares.** It does not need to be asserted because it has already been felt in the way the leader listens, responds, decides, and shows up.

REMEMBER

Empathy earns trust. Authority sustains it. Empathetic authority doesn't say "Because I said so;" it says, "Here's why, and here's how I can help you get there."

Communicating with Empathetic Authority

Chapter 10 details the ins and outs of communicating with empathy. It explores what your mindset needs to be before you speak so that, when you do start speaking, you are doing so in a manner to reinforce that empathy. To communicate with empathetic authority is to approach that same process but from a slightly different perspective.

You will have times as a leader when you need to be on equal footing for your team as a whole or for an individual needing some one-on-one support. Those moments — such as when someone is struggling in the office because of things outside of it and just need a few moments to talk — are relationship-building junctures. Those are the times when you establish your empathy; in the moments you have to flex your authority, then, you are able to do so with the trust of your team. You've proven who you are, so your firmness won't be taken as coldness.

TIP

However, sometimes the situation is a bit murky. You need to be authoritative, but you still need to show a considerable amount of empathy to maintain your team's morale. Here are a few things to keep in mind when you have to communicate with empathetic authority:

- **Acknowledge difficulties without abandoning expectation.** The first outward step of empathy is to acknowledge the situation as a whole. Addressing it directly helps stave off potential conflicts, prevent misunderstandings, and foster trust. When you're communicating with empathetic authority, however, your next step needs to always be holding the listener accountable. This shouldn't be done in an accusatory manner; it should be delivered as a matter of simple fact.

  Acknowledging a difficult situation is as simple and quick as saying "I know this is hard." It's a direct, non-judgmental way of legitimizing someone's feelings. To maintain the standards you set, follow that up with "And I know you'll find a way through it." You want to communicate to your team that they are still required to do their job, but also that you believe that they are capable of doing that work. This is an encouraging directive.

- **Avoid hedging your authority with excessive apologies.** Raise your hand if you somehow find yourself responding to things with the sentence "I'm sorry," even if nothing requires an apology. It's a habitual, subconscious response to manage social discomfort, reduce anxiety, or appease others. Avoid excessive hedging your authority with excessive apologies.

- **Be firm but warm.** Your words can be direct and your tone can still signal respect while also displaying the genuine empathy that you are pursuing. Remember all of the nonverbal cues that communicate louder than words. Your body language, eye contact, and tone of voice carry as much authority — and warmth — as your words themselves. Non verbal cues are discussed in Chapter 10. Being empathetic is a whole-body experience, and it is especially important when you are also being authoritative.

- **Listen before you speak.** When done correctly — when listening to learn, not just respond (see Chapter 10) — this builds trust by creating an environment where team members feel respected. This respect shifts how your team views you from a transactional leader to a transformative influence in their work experience (see Chapter 2). Listening also resolves conflict because everyone has a wider perspective, and it enhances decision-making by putting the focus on more than just the words. People pay more attention to the context and emotions surrounding those words, allowing for more comprehensive information gathering. Listening is a key empathy behavior, an authoritative skill, and it should be approached as an active part of every conversation.

REMEMBER

You are your team's leader — you are guiding them, you are teaching them, and you are enabling them. To be the leader that they will walk through fire for, authority is required. And empathetic authority is about direction, not domination.

Leading with Emotional Clarity

It took me a very long time to figure this out, but for most of my life I believed that the strongest people were the ones who had it the most together. The ones who didn't cry in public. Who never seemed rattled. Who walked into hard situations and walked out looking like nothing had touched them.

And then I started paying closer attention. Not to what those people look like on the outside, but to how they made the people around them feel. What I noticed was that the leaders who kept everything locked away — who performed composure instead of actually feeling it — left people feeling alone. Their teams were never quite sure where they stood. And that uncertainty quietly chips away at everything.

The leaders who stayed with me — the ones I trusted most — were the ones willing to feel things out loud. And willing to be honest, even when honesty felt risky. They named what was happening without being consumed by it. They shared what their teams needed to know without oversharing. They were present emotionally and honest intentionally. That is *emotional clarity*. This section delves into exactly what it takes to lead from that place.

Comparing stoicism and strength

I'm deeply fascinated by the people who have "never met a stranger." And I'm sure you know at least a few people in your life who are like this. They can walk into any room with any demographic and immediately have the most interesting conversations. They don't need small talk, social lubricants, or even a buffer person to get energy from; they can just pick up a conversation with anyone and have the best time.

I see these people at conferences often. It seems as if they just naturally know how to work a room, and they make it look easy. When I walk into a room, however, I immediately feel anxiety. I lean toward introversion, so being in larger group settings is a bit overwhelming for me. I naturally have a much harder time navigating conversations with more than two or three people who I'm unacquainted with, so I spend most of interaction actively listening and silently engaging (head to Chapter 10 for more about communicating with empathy). And, of course, being a person who stutters makes all of this harder. There are days when I'm just not comfortable speaking, so adding on the group element to that is an almost insurmountable proposition.

What I've learned from the people who are natural networkers isn't necessarily that they are the best conversationalists. It's not that they are more confident, though they may have an unnatural knack for chatting people up and genuinely enjoy the company of others. What I see consistently from this group of people is that have a very interesting combination of fearlessness and curiosity. It's where those two qualities meet that, in my opinion, true strength runs free. And do you know what's rarely there? Stoicism. *Stoicism* means navigating life's chaos by separating what you can control from what you cannot (see the nearby sidebar).

REMEMBER

Leading with empathy means choosing strength over stoicism. Now, I know that traditional leadership models have celebrated leaders who are indomitable yet detached. That type of authority thrives in an old-school hierarchical structure, where those further down the career ladder rarely speak up around those who are higher than them. But what teams need now are leaders who are as present emotionally as they are professionally.

WARNING

If you struggle to show emotion, to be vulnerable, and feel more comfortable having an unshakeable exterior, you're not alone. I do, however, want you to consider how stoicism could be impacting your ability to lead well. Here are a few things to consider:

- **Strength is soft. Stoicism is hard.** When I say that strength is soft, I mean it's pliable. Think of it like a sponge. Sponges are flexible and porous; they easily absorb what is poured into them, growing and shrinking as their environment changes, while maintaining their form through it all. True strength is the same; it's squishy and able to handle a squeeze every now and again. Those who possess true strength know that it thrives when it's challenged, because that's when growth happens.

  Stoicism, on the other hand, is rigid. It's similar to concrete. It's rock solid and seems impossible to break through. It can support heavy loads like roads, buildings, or columns. And it's dense, greatly reducing the risk of external damage. But with time it shrinks, which causes cracking that — if not managed properly — can result in great damage. It also slowly deforms over time under constant pressure from the heavy loads it bears.

  The squishiness — the softness — of strength means that you are capable of absorbing situations. You are able to engulf whatever emotions arise, be productive and effective in that moment, and then — once the situation has passed — you are able to morph back into who you were before. Stoicism doesn't allow that.

- **Strength is vulnerable. Stoicism is guarded.** Strong people are as strong as they are because they are willing to be vulnerable. That strength comes from their choice to be authentic, open, and emotionally exposed. Remember the person who "never met a stranger?" They are strong enough to put themselves out there, more so than other people. And that results in deeper connections with others as well as more inclusive environment.

  Stoicism is guarded because it is invulnerable, and this isn't entirely the fault of the person who is stoic. But this, unfortunately, is what others take away from this behavior. Stoic leaders unwittingly create emotional distances between them and their teams, and that slowly erodes trust.

- **Strength is active. Stoicism is passive.** Think about the strongest people you know. What is it about their strength that you admire so much? At the root of it, it's probably that they continued to show up. They might not have shown up *great* every single time, but they never stopped moving toward whatever goal they set. Strength is a choice that — once you make it — requires direction, precision, and focus.

  This is where it really differs from stoicism; real strength is feeling the weight of a situation, acknowledging it honestly, and still moving forward with intention. By contrast, stoicism doesn't engage. It looks at the situation from a distance and doesn't get involved.

TIP

Let me ask you something: Did anything you just read about choosing strength over stoicism make you think that doing so would diminish your authority? If you are leaning toward "yes," I urge you to examine your definition of strength. Look at the mentors and managers you've recently interacted with; consider the teachers and professors who modeled intelligence and thoughtfulness in your formative years; and think about the important adult role models you trusted during your earlier childhood. What about those people did you consider strong? What did you respect about them? And why did you respect it? I'm willing to bet that they all balanced their authority with empathy.

TECHNICAL STUFF

STOICISM

Greek philosopher Zeno of Citium was always modest; in fact, the wealthy merchant lived so simply that many of those around him assumed he was poor. When he lost everything in a shipwreck, however, he decided against rebuilding his wealth and instead focused on his real passion: learning from great thinkers. It was through his curiosity about philosophers such as Xenophon and Socrates that he developed his own movement: *Stoicism*. He spent the rest of his life teaching the value of goodness

(continued)

(continued)

and gaining peace of mind by living in accordance with nature. After his death in 262 BCE, Stoicism evolved. In the first and second centuries CE, philosophers Seneca and Epictetus shifted Stoicism's focus to ethics and psychology: it was viewed as a survival manual for handling stress. With the surge of Christianity in the Middle Ages and Renaissance eras, however, Stoicism was pushed to the wayside. Then, in the late twentieth and twenty-first centuries, modern psychology transformed Stoicism into a self-improvement framework centered around reframing intrusive thoughts: instead of catastrophizing ("this is a disaster"), you reframe logically ("this is an inconvenience, but I can handle it").

Today, stoicism (lower case, as it's far different from the school of thought it originated from) is viewed less as a philosophy and more as a mandate: be tough, feel nothing, stay unfazed, embrace the grind. And modern-day stoicism is glamorized in professional environments, military culture, sports, and even family dynamics where showing emotion is sometimes treated as a liability or weakness. When I speak of stoicism in this chapter, I'm not talking about the philosophical movement that emphasized self-discipline and moral improvement. I'm referring to what it has turned into in the present day.

Being transparent

During my childhood and teenage years, and even for quite a bit of my twenties, I wanted to know *everything*. I wanted to be in on every joke. If you had a secret, I was desperate for the details. And if I couldn't know something, I was frustrated; I felt like I was missing out on something special or interesting. I can look back on that now and see that what I really wanted was to belong.

We all want to belong somewhere, and to feel that we are enough just the way we are right now. We want to know that there are people in our lives who we can share experiences with and be comfortable enough with that we just relax.

TECHNICAL STUFF

The need for belonging is evolutionary; we as human are social creatures who are wired to connect. We used to travel in packs to ensure our survival — for protection, resource-sharing and mental well-being. We continue to do that now, though in a different way. It looks like the never-ending group chat where you all keep up with each other via text message; a troop of young scouts going camping; and a weekend dinner party with friends.

We get the most satisfaction from these interactions when we can speak freely; being with people who have seen us — in good and bad moments — and still accept and care about us brings us so much joy. That bonding creates safety, and our confidence grows because we know that being exactly who we are is okay with this group of people. This feeling of safety and belonging and confidence in group settings? That's transparency.

None of these wonderful, warm feelings are possible without removing some of our armor. But taking that armor off means you are vulnerable to judgment or shame, and doing that as a leader? It feels unstable, undermining your position as the powerful person in charge. But it is transparency that builds trust because that openness and honesty reduce uncertainty.

REMEMBER

Not all transparency is created equal. There are two types, and you can place these on either side of a spectrum:

- **Radical transparency.** Coined by Ray Dalio, the founder of investment firm Bridgewater Associates, *radical transparency* is based on extreme honesty. It's when every organizational decision — including mistakes and failures — is open; removing the barriers to information ideally results in a higher level of trust, more accountability, and better decision-making.
- **Intentional transparency.** This kind of transparency is more of a spotlight than a floodlight. *Intentional transparency* focuses on sharing the right information — usually a very specific part of a larger scheme — to address issues that could arise around decisions made. The honesty is still there; the openness is just targeted.

Some level of transparency is necessary for organizations to be successful. People need to know — at least somewhat — how their role, work, and tasks fit into the grander vision of the company. Many leaders struggle, however, to settle on the perfect amount of transparency to give to their teams. Something to keep in mind here is that empathetic leaders are constantly updating their teams about what's happening globally in the company, especially during a time of uncertainty; how often do you do this for your team? How *honest* are you with them?

Leading with emotional clarity means that honesty should be prioritized. And, interestingly enough, honesty helps form authority. I speak at a lot of tech events globally, so I've spent a good amount of time chatting it up with developers. One of them, we'll call him Pete, worked at a *Fortune* 500 financial institution. Pete, like a lot of developers, never fully understood the role of the Chief Technology Officer (CTO); developers put their ability to code at a very high level, and many CTOs (in their experience) no longer have to code. They're deeply entrenched in business outcomes and have to let go of their technical capabilities.

Pete told me about one of the all-department meetings the technology organization participated in where the CTO addressed the group of a few thousand employees. During this talk, one brave soul raised their hand and asked a simple question: "What do you do?" The CTO paused, a little stunned and a lot confused, and said that it was completely unacceptable that they all went into their offices every day and didn't know how the head of their organization was spending their professional time. So, the CTO stopped the talk and calmly explained what exactly their role entailed.

Many leaders would be horrified to field that kind of question. They might take it as offensive and see their direct report as overstepping and being disrespectful. But this CTO understood the value of honesty, and how that honesty leads to a team that trusts you, views you as credible, and wants to be more loyal.

They also had enough emotional clarity to know what this moment required. Their entire staff was there, and — it was obvious — very few of them understood how this CTO championed and empowered their work. This is what strength looks like; this is where transparency builds community; and this is why emotional clarity is one of the most successful ways to be authoritative. Emotional clarity isn't about having all the answers; it's about being honest about where you stand. The goal is not to eliminate emotion from leadership but to understand it well enough that it informs rather than controls your decisions.

REMEMBER

Transparency is not about sharing everything. It's about sharing what people need to know, when they need to know it, and why it matters to them.

Delivering Feedback with Empathy

As a keynote speaker, my career really hinges on feedback. As a person who stutters, that feedback can sometimes be difficult to take. But when it's given the right way, it has shifted how I approach my work. A fellow speaker early in my career gave me feedback that I still think about. Not because it was harsh or because it was extremely detailed or technically precise; I think about it because of how it made me feel.

He pulled me aside during an event we were both attending, looked me directly in the eye and said, "I really liked your talk, and I think you have the ability to be a really good speaker, but I see something in you that I don't think you see in yourself yet." And then, he told me the truth: He told me my content was excellent on a surface level, but it was lacking the depth necessary to really move people to change their behaviors. He then told me specific spots in my talk where I could delve further into the topic and add information to inspire change.

I left that conversation *immensely* grateful, because no one had ever given me constructive criticism in such a productive way. That is what empathetic feedback does. You see, empathy doesn't soften feedback; it makes feedback land more effectively. It doesn't just identify whatever gap is there, it makes the person on the other side of the table believe they are capable of closing it.

Feedback is one of the most powerful tools a leader has. And like any powerful tool, the outcome depends entirely on how you use it. When feedback is delivered with empathy — with timing, intention, and genuine care for the person receiving it — it becomes an essential tool for your team. Here's how to do it well:

- **Address the behavior, not their identity.** It's incredibly easy to take negative feedback as a knock against your character. When you work diligently and consistently at something — especially at the job where you spend so much time — hearing people you respect say it wasn't well done is crushing. That's why when you do have to deliver feedback that isn't necessarily glowing, focus on what they did and not who they are. Separating those two things softens the blow and keeps the conversation on exactly what matters: improvement.

  TIP

  To address the behavior instead of the person's identity, use words that focus on what they did without marrying them to who they are as people. Instead of "You're not good at this," say something like "That approach didn't work."

- **Focus on the future, not failure.** Empathetic feedback spends less time dissecting what went wrong and more time building a clear path forward. The goal is growth, not a verdict — so make sure the conversation ends with a direction. What can they do today to change course? What does success look like a week from now? Or in a month or next quarter? Focusing on the future over failure means having a plan in place so they can start running immediately.

- **Keep the context in mind.** Before giving feedback, take a step back and look at the situation from a broader perspective. The point of empathy is to understand how others see the world; it's through that added vision that you can better grasp why they made their decision. What pressures are they under? What do they care about? What might make this hard to hear?

  TIP

  Remembering the context when giving feedback means leading with curiosity, not with the conclusion already mapped out. And if you're lacking context (hint: you probably are!), ask questions to understand the full picture. Assuming you have context before you've listened to what they have to say is a bullet train toward making someone feel misjudged rather than supported.

» **Name the impact.** Helping the person understand not just what they did, but how it affected the team, the project, or the culture gives them a fuller picture of how they need to shift their behaviors. When people understand the ripple effect of their actions, feedback becomes meaningful rather than just critical.

» **Regulate yourself before you start the conversation.** Timing is everything. *When* you speak to someone is as important as *how* you speak to them. If you are frustrated, reactive, or emotionally charged going into a feedback conversation, it will show — and it will undermine everything you say. Empathetic feedback requires you to be grounded first, so the other person feels safe enough to actually hear you.

WARNING

Feedback is an act of belief. You believe enough in this person's abilities to tell them how to improve. When you give them that feedback thoughtfully, honestly, and with empathy, you are telling them you believe they are capable of more. That belief — when communicated with care — is a very powerful and generous gift from every leader.

Separating Agreement from Understanding

Let me clear something up, because I think it causes a lot of empathetic leaders to second-guess themselves more than they should.

REMEMBER

Empathy is not agreement. It never was. And the moment you start treating it like it is, you stop leading and start people-pleasing — and those two things could not be more different.

Here is where this gets tricky for naturally empathetic people: When someone comes to you frustrated, or pushes back on a decision, or shares a perspective that is genuinely different from yours, empathy kicks in immediately. You feel what they feel. You understand where they are coming from. And because you are a caring person, your instinct is to find some way to give them what they need in that moment — even if what they need and what is right for the team are two very different things.

But empathetic leadership is not about making people feel comfortable. It is about making people feel capable. And sometimes that requires a completely different response from you.

Separating understanding from agreement means you can look someone in the eye and say "I completely understand why you feel that way," — and mean it — and then follow up with "and here is why we are moving forward differently." That is not a contradiction. That is empathetic authority in its clearest form. You are honoring the person while upholding the standard. You are validating the feeling while maintaining the direction.

What your team needs to know is that their voice matters, even when it doesn't change the outcome. And that is only possible if you have done the work of actually listening — not performing listening, not waiting for your turn to speak, but genuinely taking in what they are sharing and letting them see that you did. When people feel truly heard, disagreement becomes something they can accept. It's being dismissed that they can't get over.

IN THIS CHAPTER

» Understanding why empathic leadership can break down

» Finding patterns in failures of empathy

» Leading your team when things go wrong

» Keeping spirits high in times of struggle

Chapter 13
Handling Failure When Leading with Empathy

Not enough people talk openly about failure. The books and the keynotes and the online posts are full of advice on how to lead with empathy — how to listen better, communicate more effectively, and show up for your people in the ways that matter. And that guidance is valuable. But there is a conversation that happens far less often, and it's the one about what you do when you get it wrong. Because you will get it wrong. Not because you're a bad leader, and not because empathy isn't something you genuinely value — but because you're human, and humans operating under pressure, distraction, stress, and the relentless pace of modern leadership are going to miss the mark sometimes. That is not a character flaw. It is a condition.

What separates the leaders worth following isn't a perfect record of empathetic communication. It's what they do when that record has a crack in it. It's whether they look at the failure honestly or explain it away. Whether they get curious about the pattern or convince themselves it was a one-time thing. Whether they repair the relationship or quietly hope time does that work for them. The response to failure is where leadership character actually reveals itself — and it is one of the most watched things you will ever do in front of your team.

This chapter is about that. It's about understanding why empathy breaks down even when you care deeply and are actively trying. It's about learning to identify your specific patterns — the conditions, the triggers, the root causes underneath the behavior you keep repeating. It's about what it looks like to encourage your team through failure, including your own. And it's about staying positive — not in the toxic, pretend-everything-is-fine way, but in the grounded, this-is-hard-and-we-are-still-moving-forward way that people actually need from a leader when things go sideways.

Getting empathy right is the goal. Learning how to handle it when you don't is the work.

Understanding Why Empathy Failures Happen

Empathy failures rarely happen because a leader stopped caring. They happen because something got in the way — and most of the time, that something is invisible to the person it's happening to. You don't usually know your empathy has failed in the moment. You find out later, in the silence of someone who stopped being honest with you, in the team that stopped pushing back, in the relationship that slowly went from warm to cordial without you being able to pinpoint exactly when or why.

That's what makes this worth understanding at a deeper level. If empathy failures were obvious — if they announced themselves clearly in the moment — leaders would course-correct in real time. But they don't. They tend to reveal themselves in hindsight, if they reveal themselves at all. And by then, the damage has already done some of its work.

What follows are some of the most common reasons empathy breaks down in leadership. Understanding them doesn't excuse the failures. But it does give you something more useful than guilt — it gives you a map showing you exactly how you got to this point of failure, and how to retrace your steps to get back to safety.

Stressing the significance of stress

Empathy requires bandwidth — both cognitive and emotional. To lead with empathy, your body needs to be prepared to handle whatever is being thrown at it.

Unfortunately, you're human; and that bandwidth is finite. Your body can only take so much physical stress until it gives out; we've all seen those athletes collapse at the finish of a race because they gave it everything they had. There's an equivalent effect consistently happening in the brain, and the consequences are drastic.

TECHNICAL STUFF

Chronic stress is harmful to your health. But a little bit of stress? The kind that lets you know that something isn't right? That's actually necessary for your survival. Stress signals to your body that you're in an undesirable situation and should take steps to remove yourself from it. This fight-or-flight response is natural and a very common function of our brains. When you see signs of danger, your *amygdala* (an area of the brain that contributes to emotional processing) activates your central stress response system. This stress response triggers the hormone cortisol; that results in a rise in glucose levels, elevated heart rate, and increased blood flow to the muscles in your arms and legs. Once that danger has passed, your body works to get your hormones back into the normal range.

Long-term stress, however, means that those levels never get back to normal. So your resting heart rate is higher, your glucose levels continue to creep upward, and you feel constant physical tension throughout your body. When you are in this state, you are mentally and physically working so much harder — much of which you are completely unaware of — that your cognitive function is compromised. Because of that, everything you do is more difficult. It's harder to focus, make decisions, and regulate emotions.

How, then, are you supposed to lead with empathy? I'm sure you know the answer: you can't. Stress both increases pressure and leads to distraction, and both of those things narrow your focus. And a narrow focus doesn't leave room for someone else's experience, meaning there's less empathy in your leadership.

TIP

The most empathetic thing you can do for the people you lead sometimes has nothing to do with them at all. It starts much earlier — in the quiet moments where you choose rest over grinding, recovery over pushing through, and self-awareness over the illusion that you are somehow above the limits of being human.

Minding the gap between intention and impact

I don't make it a practice to regret things. I try to look at every situation as a learning experience: an opportunity to assess my mindset, my behavior, and my knee-jerk reactions to reinforce the positives and identify exactly where I fell off course. Sometimes, though, when I do look back on situations where I swore I was in the right — where I was convinced I handled myself well — I can now see exactly where I went wrong. And it usually has to do with my intention versus my impact.

REMEMBER

Here are a few points to keep in mind regarding your intention versus your impact:

- **Your intentions are the starting point, not the finish line.** I'm sure you meant well; unfortunately, this is as irrelevant as it is true. It may describe what happened inside of you, but not what happened to the other person. And ultimately, all that matters is crossing that finish line. And the finish line in this instance is getting through to one another — both you and whoever you are speaking with — to get to success.

  Good intentions don't automatically produce good outcomes. In fact, those intentions can make empathy failures even harder to address because they give you a built-in defense that feels legitimate. It's actually harder to listen to someone else's perspective when you are stuck on how "wrong" they took what you said because you're too lost in the miscommunication.

  It's also worth noting here that good intentions have a ceiling: You can intend to be empathetic and then be completely convinced that the intention is indeed enough. Yes, trying is important but — just like participating in a race — what's most important is continuing to progress to the finish line.

- **You don't get to decide how your words land.** You can do everything right; you can police your tone, be aware of your body language, and use the exact words that the person needs to hear in order to receive your message. But you ultimately have to remember that as well you did, you don't get to decide how those words will land with your listener. This is because people don't hear your words in a vacuum. They hear them through their mood, their anxiety, their history with you, their stress level, and what happened to them before they started talking to you.

  A great comparison here is comedy. There are so many great comedians who you just don't think are that entertaining. I'm sure you get their jokes and understanding why other people think they are funny, but those jokes just don't land with you. And that comedian doesn't get to decide how their jokes land, but they can still try to tell them. This is what happens in many conversations; your intentions and your behaviors can be by-the-book successful, but they can still land flat.

- **Speed blurs intention.** Why? Because the faster you go, the less empathy you have. Speed ignores the time and focus needed to really understand others, so it actually widens that gap between your intention and your impact. This is actually a form of *psychic numbing*, a term coined in 1967 by psychiatrist and author Robert Jay Lifton. He surmised that individuals become emotionally desensitized and indifferent to the suffering of large numbers of people. This coping mechanism kicks in when you are overwhelmed with information, trauma, or stress; and it leads to a "cessation of feeling."

The same thing happens when you're going fast. And that's because you're not considering the nuances of a situation. Your capacity to feel empathy does not scale the faster you go; it actually shrinks. You are no longer seeing anything as unique. So when you want your impact to match your intentions, make sure you slow down and give situation the attention and awareness it deserves.

REMEMBER

Sometimes, the failure isn't a lack of empathy; it's a lack of self-awareness about how you're coming across.

Identifying Patterns in Failures of Empathy

Most leaders are good at recognizing when something went wrong. No so many leaders are good at figuring out why it keeps going wrong. That distinction matters more than you might think — because there is a significant difference between managing a moment and actually changing a pattern. One keeps you in reaction mode; the other puts you back in control.

The *3C Method* is a framework designed to put you back in control, giving you a repeatable way to move past the surface of an empathy failure and get to what's actually driving it. It's not about replaying every awkward conversation or cataloguing every misstep — it's about finding the thread that connects them. This is possible because your empathy isn't failing randomly — there is a pattern. And that pattern has an origin. And once you find that origin, you have something you can actually work with.

REMEMBER

Work through each of the three C's honestly and in order: *conditions*, *commonalities*, and *cause* (check out the sidebar, "Adding a Fourth "C": Complaints," for an extra level of analysis). The temptation will be to skip ahead — to jump straight to cause before you've really sat with the conditions or gotten specific about the commonalities. Resist that. The framework only works if you're willing to be thorough, and more importantly, if you're willing to be honest.

Let's take a look at the ordered steps of the 3C Method:

1. **Identify the conditions.** As a leader, you are probably good at identifying when things are misaligned. What's more challenging to nail down is *why* situations keep going south. On the surface, it may seem straightforward. But to really understand why you or your team are failing at empathy, you have to look at the situation — the conditions — as a whole.

   Look at the conditions surrounding the failures. These conditions aren't just the incidents; it's also the moments you fail when trying to be empathetic the most. You could be under the pressure of a strict deadline. Maybe it happens consistently in certain relationships but not in others; and this relationship is one where you already felt defensive or underappreciated. You could have just had a difficult conversation that just plain took everything out of you. Or you felt challenged, undermined, or like your authority was disrespected.

   WARNING

   These conditions are not excuses, but they are information. They are telling you exactly where your capacity for empathy gets thin. This is where you start building.

2. **Look for the commonalities.** This is where you pinpoint exactly what you do as a result of the conditions identified in Step 1. Do you withdraw when things get emotional? When a conversation gets heavy — tears, anger, frustration — you may emotionally check out. You get quieter, shorter, and more formal. You are reacting to your discomfort, but it unfortunately comes off as coldness. The failure here is that, in a moment when someone needs you the most, you withdraw instead of staying present.

   Another commonality is over-explaining instead of listening. This is most likely coming from a place of passion; you have an idea, you think it's a great one, and you really want others to get on board. So, you keep talking about it, keeping turning it over and stirring and kneading it, hopeful that someone will finally feel the excitement that you do. The issue is that you are unwilling to hear other great, passionate ideas as well. People need to feel heard, and they can't do that if you won't stop talking long enough to actually hear them.

   You may be someone who "fixes" instead of "feels." As a leader, one of your jobs is to solve problems. When they arise, then, you rush to find the solution. And those problems can present as anything: something catastrophic and damaging or something small and insignificant. Either way, your first step is going to be to correct the course. But you may be missing something critical in this process, and that is that not all problems need to be solved. When you jump straight to fix-it mode, you skip the part where you acknowledge what someone else is going through and that gloss-over communicates that the feeling is an inconvenience on the way to the solution.

3. **Determine the cause.** I will continue to hammer home how important self-awareness is when leading with empathy. It's in that pursuit of self-awareness that you uncover the core of your behaviors. This goes a step beyond just noticing what you're doing and seeing the results, because self-awareness without honesty is just self-observation. And those results? Those are the symptoms of whatever disease is plaguing you at your core.

   So, what do these causes look like? If you get cold under pressure, a lack of empathy may not be the issue. You may have discovered early on that emotions are a liability and being professional means suppressing those feelings. If you are an over-explainer, you might be afraid of being seen as incompetent. And if you are a fixer, that could be your way of coping with your discomfort surrounding others' pain.

   WARNING

   Determining your cause isn't about pathologizing yourself. Don't take this as an opportunity to turn every misstep into a therapy session, and don't view your behaviors from so far away that you can't truly connect the dots. Determining your cause is about being honest enough to say that what you are doing is a part of a pattern, and that patterns have origins and you are capable of understanding yours.

Once you've worked through the 3C Method, you're left with something most leaders never get to: a clear line from the pattern you keep repeating back to the belief that's driving it. From here, the work is choosing one small, deliberate action that runs counter to the cause you identified. Trying something like staying present for 30 extra seconds when you'd normally withdraw, or asking one question before offering a fix. And then practice it in the exact conditions where you know you're most likely to fail.

ADDING A FOURTH "C": COMPLAINTS

I thrive on the positive; my keynotes are centered around minimizing destructive behaviors to enhance productive ones. But there's one exception to this, and that's when I discuss identifying and sidestepping failures of empathy. The best way to spot a pattern is through *complaints*, which is the fourth, honorary C in this framework. If a complaint comes up more than once — from different people and in different situations — that's a pattern, not a coincidence.

Encouraging Your Team

It's interesting to watch people work through their insecurities. You can see the tension and fear at the beginning of their journey as they face something that feels insurmountable. Then you see a bit of confidence creep in as they discover more about what they're capable of, with a hint of shock at how much they might actually enjoy this new thing. And then, finally, you see them grow into the new person they are as a result of challenging their negative beliefs about themselves. Bearing witness to someone's journey of self-discovery through confronting what makes them question their abilities is something we can all find hope in, especially in chaotic or difficult times.

Early on in my speaking career, I was giving a talk at a tech conference in Vancouver, British Columbia. I was exceptionally excited for this one because it was a very visible and respected organization; I knew that speaking at an event like theirs would legitimize me, and I was thrilled they invited to take their stage. I still had a lot of hangups about my speech impediment — stuttering — and how that would impact the audience's ability to understand me. And even though I use stuttering as a teach tool in all of my talks, I was still struggling with my feelings of worth surrounding the way I sounded.

When you're speaking at conferences, you spend an inordinate amount of time talking to people. There's the tech check, the speaker dinner, the nighttime events, and of course the talk itself and the conversations happening after it with the attendees. I distinctly remember sitting at the speaker dinner and feeling very nervous. And when I get nervous, I stutter a lot more. Even though I spent the evening trying to get into my speaking groove, where I find a comfortable pace and ride that wave until the end of the event, I could never really get there. It began to get into my head.

As I was going over my slides on the morning of my talk, I had a very bad feeling about what was going to happen. It was stuck in my mind that stuttering could very well take center stage, and I tried to calm myself from the impending panic I was feeling. When I got to the venue and I watched an absolutely dynamic and energetic speaker give her talk, I lost even more confidence.

At this point, you can imagine what happened next. I got on stage, started giving my talk, and never fully found my footing. I stuttered a lot, and it was a very challenging stutter; one where I couldn't get into enough of a groove to let my personality shine. It zapped my energy, and I felt like I was coming across as afraid and unknowledgeable.

About halfway through, I just stopped. I took a deep breath. And I said to the audience "I'm having a really bad speaking day, so if I look miserable it's because I am. But I'm really so happy and honored to be here, and I hope you can see that, too." I truly don't know what I was expecting their reaction to be. I thought maybe I'd get a nervous low laugh or possibly feel an auditorium-wide sigh of relief. None of that happened. What did?

They cheered. Loudly, and for several seconds. I think they were encouraging me because I was definitely needing a boost, but honestly, I also think they were encouraged. Because it was so unexpected and my talk was so emotionally charged. We all know what it feels like to try something uncomfortable: something that maybe makes us question our worth, our abilities, or our strength. But we so often associate that with a feeling of failure.

What I did that day put on a display of a kind of failure but from the lens courage. Everyone has been there, where they try something and it doesn't go quite as planned. It can be embarrassing and hurtful, but ultimately, it's setting an example of the benefits of that courage. Of how audacity and determination inspire others to do the same. I think they all felt a little bit more seen that day.

REMEMBER

In the same way that the audience was watching me, remember that your team is always watching you. They're watching how you react when things go well and when they go wrong. They're watching to see if it's a safe space to keep showing up honestly, and your job is to confirm that it is. Here's how you can encourage them:

- **Acknowledge what's happening.** When you are encouraging your team, the first thing you need to do is acknowledge the misstep. Recognize out loud the mistake or the moment of vulnerability. Doing so elicits a feeling of relief in others; they aren't the only ones who fail or who suffer or who feel fear. It's in those moments of relief that you, as a leader, can build a real bond with your team.
- **Offer or show support.** The way you talk to and about your team shapes what they believe in themselves. So, when you uplift them, it's almost as if you are their cheerleader. That's why you cheer for your favorite sports team; you can share emotions with those around you who are rooting for the same thing. Participating in a collective reduces stress and gives you a communal experience that makes you feel like you belong. Those who are supported, especially after a failure of empathy, feel a part of a collective. That communal experience can turn a shameful moment into one of kinship.
- **Establish a plan to move forward.** Acknowledging the failure and supporting your team in that moment are two crucial steps in this process, but establishing a plan for moving forward is required to maintain your team's

trust. I talk about identifying the patterns of empathy failures (see the section earlier in this chapter "Identifying Patterns in Failures of Empathy"); you must do so both in you as an individual and for your team as a whole. But to give your team confidence that you are serious about improving the culture, you must take the information you gleaned in your pattern-discovery process and make the necessary changes.

Remaining Positive When Things Go Wrong

There's a thread that weaves through all the traits of the most successful people. Because if you really break those traits down, they have one thing in common. Yes, they have to be resilient and persistent; successful people view failures as data points, not defeat. They of course have to have passion and focus; we all need to keep our *why* in mind when the *how* gets buried. And, of course, they need to be adaptable; they are able look at what did and didn't work, make a few adjustments, and then pivot to continue progressing towards their goal.

REMEMBER

If you really look at those traits and the thread sewn through all of them — the quiet commonality among them all — successful people are positive people. Their attitude is one of "It can work." Now, the *it* may get murky as time and research and discovery and growth reveal themselves. But successful people never lose hope; they keep going and they do that because underneath the grit and discipline and focus and intelligence there is a positive attitude.

I truly believe that being positive shouldn't be considered just a trait; it should be viewed as a skill. And this is a necessary skill to have when things don't go according to plan. Empathetic leadership requires that you know how to both encourage and guide your team when even just one member is struggling to maintain an empathetic culture. That encouragement has to come from an authentic place; people will know if your positive attitude is just a show you're putting on to save face. Be authentic by:

- **Recognizing what's happening.** A dip in team morale is a very intimidating prospect for a leader. I'm sure you'll have a few knee-jerk reactions at the initial sight of discontent. You'll of course want to problem-solve; you might want to diagnose and find exactly where things started to go in a downward direction; or you may have a more negative reaction and want to start blaming the issue on others.

Empathetic leaders, however, know that the first thing to do is acknowledge that something is off. Yes, it really is that simple! Recognizing that there has been a clear decline in team spirit — and doing so in a way that isn't judgmental or accusatory — gives others a chance to be a part of the conversation.

REMEMBER

You as the leader set the tone for how problems get solved. Recognizing that there is indeed a problem gives your team a chance to be a part of the process in creating actionable solutions.

- **Reframing failure as feedback.** Start viewing success on a spectrum, because it doesn't look the same in every situation or for every person. And when the traditional view of success is not achieved, it would be really beneficial to all of us to not beat ourselves up but instead see where we can learn and grow and succeed in the future.

  To do this, stop looking at failure as some sort of moral bankruptcy. Instead, and especially when addressing missteps in empathy, you as a leader have to position "failure" as an opportunity for feedback.

  TIP

  The next time you find yourself worried about a perceived failure, reframe it as feedback. Here's a good place to start: Ask yourself what the situation taught you about what your team actually needs instead of asking why it didn't work.

- **Resisting the urge to downplay.** I am a generally positive person. When I say that everything will be fine, I actually believe that. And that is my personal way of encouraging others when they are having a hard time. The issue is that being positive when people aren't feeling their best can be read as dismissive. The person you are trying to encourage may feel that your positivity is invalidating their feelings and is your way of getting them to just move on.

  TIP

  If you — like me — struggle with *toxic positivity* (the act of dismissing negative emotions and forcing an unrealistically cheerful facade), try instead to practice *grounded optimism* (the practice of maintaining unwavering faith in your eventual success while directly confronting the current realities of your situation). Instead of saying "Everything will be fine!" try saying "This is hard, and we will get through it." This simple vocabulary shift still honors your positive nature — which is so necessary when you lead teams — but doesn't downplay the situation at hand.

- **Revisiting the *why*.** Chapter 7 discusses defining your goals in being an empathetic leader and also dissecting your *why*. Your *why* is what's going to keep you going when things head in the wrong direction. Revisiting your mission when morale sinks — and reminding your team of their *why* — is a powerful motivator when the *how* gets messy. Staying positive, especially when things seem to be falling apart all around you, means always going back to your *why*.

Remaining positive when things go wrong isn't about pretending everything is fine. It's about genuinely believing that things can get better and then doing the work to make sure they do. When you lead from that place, your team doesn't just see a leader who is holding it together. They see someone worth following, even when the road gets rough.

REMEMBER

Ultimately, positivity is not a performance. It's a practice. And like any practice, it gets stronger the more intentional you are about it. You're never too lost. You can get back to where you wanted to be — where you want your team to be — by practicing your positively like it is a skill. Because it is. The leaders who remain positive through failure aren't the ones who never feel discouraged; they're the ones who feel discouraged but keep going anyway by analyzing what's happening and making changes as they go. So, always remember that you are never too lost to be found.

4

Measuring Your Empathetic Leadership Skills

IN THIS PART . . .

Pinpoint where you fall short as an empathetic leader and develop a plan to close those gaps.

Understand how to be an empathetic leader while keeping your team accountable.

Align what you do with what you think you do.

Identify a team of empathy mentors to assist you in your practice.

Create a review system that shows your empathetic leadership progress.

IN THIS CHAPTER

» Exploring empathy gaps

» Understanding why empathy gaps happen

» Spotting where gaps commonly occur

» Determining and resolving your own gaps

Chapter 14
Identifying Your Gaps as an Empathetic Leader

Caring about your team — and every person on it — is the beginning of empathetic leadership, not the end. Most leaders who struggle with empathy aren't indifferent; they're unaware. Everyone has gaps: places where your intentions and your impact quietly diverge, where what you think you're communicating and what's actually being received are two entirely different things.

The good news is that gaps, unlike character flaws, can be closed once you can see them clearly. This chapter gives you the framework to do exactly that: to define your gaps, understand why they formed, and build a plan for closing them.

Defining Empathy Gaps

Before you can close a gap, you have to know what you are actually dealing with. Not what you fear it means about you, not the worst-case interpretation of what it says about your character, but what it actually is. Precisely, specifically, and without the weight of a verdict attached to it. The way most leaders think about their empathy gaps — as evidence of something fundamentally wrong with them — is exactly what keeps those gaps open. This section is designed to give you clarity rather than a reason to be hard on yourself.

Knowing what empathy gaps are

I used to dwell a lot. I'd look back and go over what I could have or should have done. I'd chastise myself for doing what I actually did. And I'd convince myself that the other people involved were still judging me harshly for what happened, even if it was a minor interaction that took place years ago. One day, I realized that most people stop thinking about me once our time together is over. This isn't out of malice or being dismissive; they just have their own issues and problems and lives they are navigating. They're too busy being themselves to give me more than a passing thought. Now when I look back on those less-than-perfect moments, I can more easily shrug them off and move on with my own life.

Ultimately, dwelling on the choices from the past — in my opinion — is a bit of a self-centered act. Me continuing to go over certain details, ones that probably do not matter in the grand scheme, means that I'm probably not considering the conversation as a whole or the other person's experience. I'm too busy focusing on *me*: my feelings and how I came off. And if I was expending so much energy doing that, did I have any time or energy to really engage with the other person?

This was quite a revelation for me — it helped me be less concerned with everyone else and more focused on my own passions, hobbies and goals — and I want others to feel the same way. I want the people I care about to not dwell on their mistakes or missteps. So, when someone starts to talk about something they did or said that they just can't get over, I find myself struggling to empathize with them.

Even though I understand why they experience these feelings, I find my patience during these interactions shortening. My words come out a bit quicker, and my voice gets a little flatter. I tell them that they shouldn't be so concerned about something that doesn't matter, that the other person probably will never think about again. And when they push back, I have to force myself to continue to engage.

This is by far my biggest *empathy gap*. Sometimes referred to as an *empathy bias*, the empathy gap is a breakdown or reduction in empathy where it might otherwise have occurred. For leaders, empathy gaps are the cognitive and emotional distance between what a leader believes they are communicating and what the people receiving that communication actually experience. They happen because you fail somewhere in the process of empathizing with another person, and a lot of the time you don't even know it's happening. You think you delivered honest feedback; they experienced an ambush. You think you were being appropriately direct; they experienced being dismissed. You think you created an open-door environment; they experienced a leader whose door is technically open but atmospherically closed. The gap between those two realities — your internal experience of your own leadership and their lived experience of being led by you — is the empathy gap.

REMEMBER

Empathy gaps are often invisible to the person who has it. This is why leaders with empathy gaps are not, in most cases, malicious; they're just unaware.

Knowing what empathy gaps are not

Naming something as a "gap" implies there's something missing. And for leaders who care deeply about how they show up, who genuinely want to do better by the people they lead, that implication can land harder than intended.

WARNING

Before diving into how to close empathy gaps, it's worth being precise about what having one actually means. Because what it doesn't mean matters just as much as what it does. As empathy gap is not a diagnosis. It is not a pattern, a personality, or a permanent condition. It is a moment, and moments — by definition — pass. The distinction matters because leaders who misread their gaps as something larger tend to respond in one of two equally unhelpful ways: they either spiral into self-criticism that makes them less effective, or they overcorrect into defensiveness that makes them less honest. Neither closes the gap. Both make it worse. Let's demystify something: Not everything is a gap. Sometimes, you are simply having a bad moment and you make a mistake.

Let's break down what that looks like as I do not want you to spiral every time you goof up:

- **Conscious decisions.** As much as we'd all like to, we can't control every single thing we do. There are always going to moments when our minds give way to our bodies. Maybe you're tired or stretched thin. Maybe you have run out of patience that day or you are too amped up to approach something in a measured way. You may look back on moments like these — where you lost (or couldn't find!) your cool — and think you made a bad choice. This is untrue. An empathy gap isn't a conscious decision; it's a moment of error.
- **Lack of ability.** We've all watched our favorite sportsperson miss a game-winning score. We've been the brunt of the wrath of a good person having a bad day. And we've all weirdly messed up something we've done perfectly hundreds of times before. Just because you fail at something a few times, it doesn't mean you are incapable of doing it well next time. View empathy and empathy gaps the same way.
- **Moral failures.** You are not a bad person because you struggled to have empathy in the moment. Sometimes, you react strongly or inappropriately

because you are caught off guard, are uncomfortable, didn't realize the gravity of the situation, or aren't in an ideal empathy mindset. None of these are indicative of your overall character; you are human, and sometimes you make mistakes. Empathy gaps are not moral failures; they are blind spots.

- **Solely about emotions.** Your empathy gaps are rarely just about your emotional state. Your feelings don't always align with your intentions. Sometimes, our feelings drive us into a gap — and remember, much of the time we don't realize the gap is there — and it exacerbates not-so-great behaviors. Be kind to yourself and hit the brakes on questioning your character every time you find yourself in an empathy gap scenario.
- **Traits.** Traits are specific characteristics of individuals determined by genes, environment, or a combination of both. Your traits are identifiers; they can be unchangeable — like the genetically determined ones — or they can shift as you move throughout your life. Traits are not, however, quick lapses; they stick with you for a significant period of time. Being empathetic is a trait; an empathy gap is a momentary blunder, and it doesn't define you.

Understanding Why Gaps Arise in Empathetic Leadership

Empathy gaps don't have a single cause. They're layered; they're built from cognitive shortcuts your brain takes to process information faster, cultural conditioning that shaped how you read emotions before you ever held a leadership title, and the very real way that power and pressure quietly reshape your perception over time.

TIP

To understand why your empathy breaks down, you need to look at three layers: how you naturally underestimate the emotions of others, how you naturally overestimate your own capacity to feel them, and what happens to both when you're under stress. That's exactly what this section focuses on.

Underestimating other people's emotions

Humans underestimate others' emotions. You may assume that because you feel a certain way about a specific thing, others will feel the same. What you consider a very minor issue might make another person fall down an emotional hole that they need real support to climb out of. But you struggle to help them out of it — or you don't even notice they are struggling — because you have underestimated their emotions.

WHY EMPATHETIC LEADERSHIP GAPS HIDE IN PLAIN SIGHT

Empathy operates on a spectrum; our behaviors in and approach to a conversation are determined by where our listener needs them to be in the moment. At times, as a speaker you need to be gentler in your approach, using encouraging and positive vocabulary to get them where they need to be. At other times, however, you must take more of a lead as a speaker. Your listener may want aggressive reassurance and motivating words. It's your job to figure out what exactly people need from you in that moment so everyone can move forward.

WARNING

Why does underestimation of emotions happen? Here are a few reasons:

- **Cultural factors.** Our cultures are deeply ingrained in us: our views, behaviors, perspectives, thoughts, and words. And this goes beyond our ethnic or racial cultural identities; we are a product of the cultures we spent many hours immersed in, such as the culture of our homes, religious institutions, and schools. Every consistent presence in our lives is deeply impactful to our culture perspective.

  These cultural factors are also profoundly influential in not only how we perceive others' emotions but also what is deemed an acceptable way to show emotions at all. These display rules — the cultural or social norms that dictate how, when, and to whom individuals should express specific emotions — can make it challenging to accurately discern what's happening with another person emotionally.

- **Egocentric bias.** As much as you think you know about other people, you know infinitely more about yourself. And that makes total sense; you are the main character. You have direct, continuous access to your own thoughts and emotions because you are with *you* all the time. So, you view everything in your life from the lens of *you*: your experiences, your ideas, your opinions.

  You rely heavily on your own perspective because of this egocentric bias. You underestimate others' emotions inadvertently by overestimating the extent to which others share your attitudes and behaviors. This bias doesn't come from a malicious place; it is a mental shortcut that helps you process information more effectively in real time. The problems arise when that bias gets in the way of understanding others.

- **Social conditioning.** Just as so much of who we are is because of our cultural identity, who we surround ourselves with socially is thoroughly engrained in our fabric too. The people we see and interact with every day are some of the most influential people in our orbit. If those individuals hold certain emotions in a specific regard, we will often do the same. We get comfortable with the different emotional cues they give us and are well equipped to handle them easily. Social conditioning can make it more challenging to have empathy in situations where we aren't as free to relax, such as at work.

Overestimating your own empathy

Just as it's natural to underestimate others' emotions, it's just as easy to overestimate your own capacity to feel for and understand how other people feel. It's very natural to overestimate your natural capacity for many things; we are hardwired to believe the best in ourselves. With empathy and emotions in general, though, you need to be realistic about how you are actually coming across.

TIP

The best way to be realistic about your own empathic feelings is to understand why you overestimate your empathy in the first place. Here are two common reasons why people overestimate their empathy:

- **Egocentric anchoring.** Similar to egocentric bias (detailed in the previous section), *egocentric anchoring* means that you are anchoring your perception of others in your own perspective, emotions, and experiences. This is a cognitive distortion — something that we rarely realize we are doing — and it can lead you to assuming that others think, feel, and react similarly to how you would. As a leader, you need to be careful of this.

  A 2026 study published in *Cognition,* an international journal of that covers cognitive science (`www.sciencedirect.com/journal/cognition`), found that when we read others' emotions, we tend to exaggerate the intensity of those emotions; we view what the other person is experiencing as more profound than it actually is, leading us to misread situations. This overestimation makes individuals feel they are being empathetic and strengthening bonds, when actually what is happening is they are misreading the situation entirely.

  Having empathy means pursuing perspective, even if it feels unnatural to how you feel the situation should be regarded. Decentering your ego means being self-aware enough to understand in every situation what the difference is between what you are feeling and what someone else feels.

- **Power dynamics.** According to a 2025 *Psychology Today* article by clinical psychologist Michael Wiederman, PhD (`www.psychologytoday.com/us/blog/mindful-professional-development/202511/how-power-creates-an-empathy-blind-spot`), having power impairs a person's ability to have empathy. And what's worse is that the overwhelming majority of people are entirely unaware of this tendency. As you go up in the leadership ladder — experiencing increased power in the process — you are increasingly less aware of other people's perspective.

Think about it this way: you've "been there and done that." You most likely held, if not the exact role, a similar role to every single person on your team. So, in your mind, you know exactly what they are experiencing. Added to that, you are also dealing with the increased stress of not only managing a team but also handling additional, more intricate or stressful work. You may not even realize it, but you could be viewing your burden more significantly to the organization's big picture. And so, you may think you are being empathetic toward your team, but you might be missing the mark. Chapter 13 discusses how to navigate empathy failures.

TIP

You can be deeply invested in what the people in your team are experiencing, but can still come across as disinterested or indifferent to their opinions. Be keenly aware of how you respond to the concerns of people on your team. Remember that they do not see the picture as completely as you do, so respond to their ideas and concerns with that in mind.

Experiencing decline under pressure

I'm generally a pretty calm person, and that is almost entirely due to my philosophy about life. I don't see the point in holding on to anger for any significant period of time. In my opinion, holding on to anger and bad blood only hurts one person in the long run: me. And that's no way to live. So I have a very long fuse; unfortunately, however, when it blows, it *blows*. This happens rarely, but it is quite impactful. I have a difficult time completing simple tasks because I lose focus; the things I do, I do them poorly or with little thought; and my thoughts are so jumbled and messy that I can hardly choose my words well, let alone think about what another person may be experiencing right now.

Fortunately, I have a good grasp on how to deal with this loss of empathy but I still have weak moments. And I'm sure that you do as well. We all suffer from declining empathy when we are under pressure. People fall behind on projects, someone says something obviously offensive that you just can't get past, or one of your direct reports doing the exact opposite of what you asked them to do. It's genuinely difficult to choose empathy when — let's be honest — you have every right to do anything but understand another point of view.

REMEMBER

As a leader, however, you won't always be given grace. Although it is completely natural to suffer from a decline in empathy under pressure, you still need a plan on what to do to both avoid and come back from it when it happens. To do that, you first need to know at what step in the process you lost empathy and for that you need to consider the different types of empathy:

- **Cognitive empathy.** This is baseline facts; it's understanding how someone else thinks — their perspective, reasoning, and mental framework. It's intellectual rather than emotional. If you're a more analytical person, you probably excel at this one. But be careful, because this can feel cold to others if you never step further than this.
- **Emotional empathy.** This is where you attempt to actually *feel* what someone else feels. Emotional empathy creates a deep connection, but beware: it can lead to burnout, over-identification, or difficulty holding accountability.
- **Compassionate empathy.** Action-oriented and steeped in sincere connection, this type of empathy combines both cognitive and emotional empathy and adds a response. This is the most relevant to leadership because it is action-oriented, and it is where you will want to spend most of your time in your empathetic leadership practice.

It's very important you identify which type of empathy you missed because these can also be considered as sequential phases. The first phase, cognitive, is understanding the facts. The second, emotional, is understanding the feelings. The third, compassionate, is acting on the facts and feelings presented to further or remedy the situation. Figuring out where you mis-stepped informs you if you misheard the facts, misunderstood feelings, or didn't take the correct action.

Next, you need to identify the specific *empathy competency* that tripped you up the most. Here is a non-exhaustive list of those to keep in mind:

- **Active listening.** The actual act of listening, this is where you give full attention, focus on understanding and listen without judgment.
- **Compassion.** Compassion is acting on the feelings another person expressed.
- **Emotional regulation.** This is both recognizing your own emotions — as well as the emotions of others — and managing your emotional reactions.
- **Non verbal communication.** Body language comes in here, and this includes everything from your tone of voice, facial expressions, and gestures. Words are important, but much communication happens non verbally.
- **Perspective-taking.** This is the ability to understand another person's viewpoint, thoughts, and world, even if you disagree.

» **Self-compassion.** This means being kind to yourself to better enable extending empathy to others.

» **Validation.** You are acknowledging the validity of another's experiences and feelings. Acknowledging one without the other is *not* validation.

Most of these are very straight forward and are discussed in more detail in Parts 1 and 2. If you want to understand someone's point of view, you listen to them. If someone is feeling ignored, you validate their feelings without judging them. If someone begins to turn away from you, that is a signal that they are either uncomfortable or the conversation is ending. And so forth.

REMEMBER

How you feel drives how you think. And how you think determines how you speak. When you are dealing with a decline in empathy during a stressful situation, two things generally happen:

» **The empathy competency you struggle with the most is the one that will immediately go out of the window.** And it's the one that will be the most noticeable to others in the moment. In other words, the gap between engaging empathy and not doing so gets bigger.

» **You are at risk of losing some of the self-compassion required to forgive yourself and move on.** In this case the gap between what you feel and what you say is all but gone.

TIP

So how do you recover from this empathy decline? You need to address the gaps you widened, and you need to do it head on. Name where and how you failed — not a generic apology but a true reflection of your actions — and then re-engage the conversation so you can correct your course. You also need to address the gap between what you feel and what you say. This is where self-compassion does its actual work; it's not about excusing what happened, it's about giving yourself the same grace you'd extend to someone else who had a bad moment under pressure.

Identifying Core Empathy Gaps in Leadership

You've been here before. The employee who reminds you of yourself who always seems to get the benefit of the doubt. The direct report who says everything is fine, until it isn't. The week where you were physically present in every one-on-one but emotionally absent for all of them. These aren't just random bad days; they're gaps: specific, nameable empathy gaps that show in leadership over and over again.

You wouldn't be reading this book if you didn't care about your people. But caring isn't the same as connecting, and your good intentions won't close the gaps that quietly form between you and those who you lead. This section breaks down what the common empathy gaps are in leadership.

TIP

Once you've read about the different gaps detailed in this section, ask yourself these three questions:

- Which gap have I been living in the longest without naming it?
- Who on my team has likely felt the effects of that gap?
- What's one thing I could do differently starting this week?

You don't need all the answers right now. You just need to be open enough, self-aware enough, and honest enough to ask them.

The proximity gap

We love seeing ourselves in the world around us, and we more easily see ourselves in specific parts of the outside world as we get continued exposure to those specific things. This is because of the *mere-exposure effect*, a cognitive bias where you show a preference for things you're more familiar with. The more you encounter something, the more you tend to prefer it based solely on familiarity. And, even if you're unsure of what exactly the answer is, you move through problems with more decisiveness when you have an idea of where approximately you are going.

WARNING

This same concept can actually work against you. When you aren't exposed to something as much — when you can't see yourself in what's happening around you — you struggle to identify with it. This is the *proximity gap*; you have more empathy for people who look like you, live like you, or remind you of yourself.

TECHNICAL STUFF

You might view the proximity gap as a character flaw, but it's not; it's actually just neuroscience. *Mirror neurons* — brain cells that react both when a particular action is performed and when it is only observed — fire harder when you are engaging in something familiar. This is why you feel immediate ease in certain situations that you have navigated before and tension in unfamiliar ones where the result is unknown.

For you as a leader, the proximity gap might expose itself as you playing favorites. You may favor those who you identify on a personal level; you might have the same racial or ethnic background, are alums of the same university, or from the same hometown. This is why it's always important for you to identify and address your potential biases for and against others. If you know what you're up against, you have a better chance of not falling prey to the proximity gap.

TIP

Just because you become a leader, it doesn't mean you stop being human. And being biased is a very natural part of our humanity. To combat the proximity gap, ask yourself two questions: Who do you naturally defend and who do you have to consciously remind yourself to consider?

The power gap

I used to get very nervous around "important" people. The CEO or my boss' boss. My friend's very popular or exceptionally gorgeous friend. My parent's coworkers. I'd feel inadequate or unworthy, so I'd speak less, make myself smaller, and go out of my way to defer to others. And if they asked me a direct question? I was terrified and not at all myself; I'd scrounge together whatever words I could say fluently — one of the most difficult things about being a person who stutters is that stuttering gets more pronounced when you're nervous — and try to move the conversation away from me as quickly as possible.

As it turns out, a lot of people struggle with being around those they perceive as more powerful than them and that includes you: their leader. When the boss comes around, everyone changes. People perform around their boss. They don't tell you what's really hard. They filter. Why? Because you are important, and they need you to know that they can hang. Your empathy, therefore, can be genuine and still be working from bad data because your position distorts what you receive.

WARNING

This is why the higher up you go in an organization, the harder it is to accurately read what those below you in the organizational structure are actually experiencing. The *power gap* is one of the most underdiagnosed leadership gaps; leaders think they're empathetic because they care, not realizing the information ecosystem around them has been quietly sanitized.

TIP

The power gap is a lack of information problem; you may not realize it, but you've forgotten how it feels to be that position. To close the gap, invest time in your younger staff. Listen to their experiences and views. Specifically, shift your conversations from *telling* to *asking*. The power gap widens every time a leader walks into the conversation with all the answers. Replace certainty with curiosity: "What am I missing?" or "What would you do differently?"

The fatigue gap

I love to push myself physically; and by that, I mean that my workouts generally consist of some general strength component and about 15 to 30 minutes of high-intensity training. I do these kinds of workouts because I like to push myself to failure; so much of my days are spent creating content of some sort that doing this kind of workout gives me a break from the "thought" work.

My fitness goal is simple: get stronger. Strength wise, that means gradually being able to lift heavier weights while also maintaining good form. But for my more cardio-focused work, the goal is to push my point of fatigue. Because we all get to a point where we just can go no further: where our bodies (or, in the case of empathy, our brains) have hit a wall and we cannot take one more step. In my workouts, it's when my legs refuse to do another lunge or my "sprint" looks more like a jog. When it comes to leading with empathy, it looks like irritability, performing rather than feeling, dreading one-one-ones, or giving advice instead of listening.

WARNING

Perhaps you were empathetic, then something happened — a brutal quarter, personal stress, cumulative exposure to people's problems — and your capacity quietly shrank. Maybe you're still going through the empathetic motions, but you're running on fumes. The *fatigue gap* is real and almost nobody names it in themselves until they've already caused harm. This fatigue can look differently for everyone, so you need to identify what you do — for example, rushing through conversations, giving short-tempered replies, or tuning someone out midsentence — when the weariness is beginning to overtake you so you can combat it.

The assumption gap

There's a pride that comes after certain experiences. You see life differently after big birthdays, life-changing international trips, or adding to your family. And with that experience comes knowledge; you did something that stretched you in numerous ways and you changed as a result. You learned and you expanded. You feel like you know more about the world now and — in your mind — about other people in it.

WARNING

Sure, you may be more aware of new cultures or ideas, but that doesn't mean you have any added insight in another person's actual lived experience. You do not have context on what is going on in another person's life, but unfortunately you won't always remember that fact. This is your *assumption gap*. You think you know what someone is going through, so you stop asking. You've obviously (in your mind) been through something similar. You *think* you have context. All of that context, however, becomes the enemy of actually listening.

You know what one of the least empathetic sentences you can say is? "I know how you feel." Quite simply, you don't. You have no idea what is going on in someone's life. Sure, you may have experienced something similar but you are not playing with the exact same deck of cards as anyone else. What another person encounters is always going to be different to what you do. The assumption gap shows up as finishing sentences, jumping to solutions, or saying "I know how you feel." All three of those moves, especially that last one, close the door on the person you're supposedly empathizing with.

The discomfort gap

I always loved going to the park as a kid; like most kids, I loved the swings and climbing around the jungle gym and playing with the others doing the same. But I had a nemesis: the monkey bars. I was always so impressed with people who could go from rung to rung, easily swinging across the bars with little effort getting to the other side. Me, on the other hand? I struggled with monkey bars, so much so that I'd feel a sense of unease just looking at them. And if a bunch of us were taking turns on them, my discomfort would turn to anxiety. I was worried about what the other kids would think of how slow I was going and judge how much I'd struggle. And that anxiety often made my performance worse.

Whenever I think about monkey bars — even now — I freeze. I feel a bit of shame and embarrassment, and I struggle to shake it. And sometimes, if I'm having a really difficult time, I begin to impose those same feelings on the current things going on in my life. There are certain emotions, experiences, or identities that you find genuinely hard to sit with. Your empathy works fine until it hits that edge, and then it deflects.

WARNING

You can change the subject, you over-fix, you minimize, or you get performatively positive. But the *discomfort gap* is still there, and it's tangibly more challenging to sincerely pursue perspective when you are struggling internally with your own feelings and opinions of yourself and the situation. Most leaders don't know where their discomfort edge is until they stumble across it in a real moment with a real person who needed them to stay present.

The consistency gap

Most people have certain situations where expressing empathy is like a walk in the park on the most perfect day. They see that someone needs an ear, a shoulder, or just a few extra seconds of grace. And they spring into action, being exactly what that person is seeking and doing so flawlessly. They know exactly what to say or when to listen, and everyone walks away from that situation feeling refreshed and heard and ready to tackle what's next.

But then there are other moments, ones where they struggle. And those moments aren't always specific situations. They could be moments when someone is triggered and they don't know why. Or it could be a moment when they don't consider empathy to be necessary.

REMEMBER

You are most likely empathetic in high-stakes moments such as a team member's crisis, a big announcement, or a visible situation. But empathy in the small moments such as the hallway conversation or the email you reply to curtly — that's where most people have their biggest gap and least awareness. This *consistency gap* is the difference between someone who performs empathy and someone who practices it.

Diagnosing and Closing Your Gaps: Your Empathy Mirror

Do you ever avoid mirrors? If so, you probably think you're doing it because you think you look bad. You're actually doing it because you're afraid that you *might* look bad. Honest self-reflection works the same way. It's not that you don't want to know where your empathy breaks down; you struggle with looking directly at it because it is uncomfortable.

To improve — to look better, to feel better, to grow — you have to eventually face the fear and look directly into the mirror. Because you cannot close a gap you haven't seen. This section is your mirror. What you do with what you see in it is entirely up to you.

Creating a framework for self-assessment

REMEMBER

Leading with empathy is a result of two key practices: *pattern recognition* (the cognitive process of identifying recurring structures, trends, or regularities in information) and *self-awareness* (the conscious ability to recognize and understand your own thoughts, emotions, strengths, weaknesses, and values). Identifying your gaps in empathy requires the same two skills; you have to know what your tendencies are and the exact moments they are likely to cause gaps to widen.

I realize that I'm asking you to diagnose something that is — for many people — considered a character flaw. Many people feel a great amount of shame around empathy failures, frustration around being misunderstood, and (for some) anger about bringing empathy into work in the first place.

With so many conflicting feelings involved, your best course of action is to look at this from an analytical perspective. This section considers three simple frameworks to inventory your gaps, understand your behaviors during those gaps, and identify how those gaps impact specific individuals on your team.

Step 1: The Gap Inventory Audit

The Gap Inventory Audit is the first step because it tackles how you think. Everything begins with how you think; it impacts your feelings, your behaviors, your communication, and how you treat other people. The goal here is to understand where your head is at when you are at baseline.

This is a simple self-assessment where you rate yourself on each of the six gaps detailed in the earlier section, "Identifying Core Empathy Gaps in Leadership." The urge will be to gives yourself numeric scores, but this is intended more as a reflective ranking than a quiz. When you consider this ranking, ask yourself these three questions about each gap:

- How often does this gap show up for me?
- Who in my life (or, more specifically, on my team) has likely felt this gap?
- How aware am I of it in the moment?

TIP

Do this with each of the six gaps. Remember not to judge yourself too harshly; there is a difference between being aware of your behaviors and being so critical of their impact that you can't get past it enough to build on it.

Step 2: The Witness Exercise

The Witness Exercise is the next step. It shows you how your gaps may be impacting your approach to conversations as a whole. Think about the last five significant conversations you've had with someone on your team. For each one, answer these questions:

- Was I fully present or partially elsewhere?
- Did I listen to understand or listen to respond?
- Did I make it about them, or did it drift toward me?

TIP

Remember you are looking for the overall, bigger patterns here. Your goal is to have a better understanding of how your empathy gaps present themselves through your thoughts, responses, and actions during your conversations.

Step 3: Thinking about who gets your best

Simple yet direct, this final exercise focuses on your behaviors toward specific individuals on your team. List the five people on your team you interact with the most. Then, answer these questions:

- Who suffers most from your impatience on your bad days?
- Who do you give the benefit of the doubt to automatically?
- Whose one-on-one do you look forward to, and whose do you quietly dread?

TIP

For the first two questions, also think of the person (or people) who gets the opposite of those as well. That's the point of this exercise — you want to see the disparities. Remember that you're not playing favorites! You are letting the exercise tell you where your natural biases lay.

Turning awareness into application

If the previous exercise was about identifying, this part is about fixing. You've diagnosed so now you see yourself a bit more clearly. The next step is to turn that self-knowledge into daily behavior. Let's jump right in!

Step 1: One gap, one shift

Look back at your rankings from the Gap Inventory Audit (see the previous section). Pick your most prominent gap and identify one behavioral shift that you can implement relatively quickly. This is not a personality overhaul; it's just one, small, repeatable change you can start working on today. Here are a few examples:

- **Proximity gap:** Intentionally schedule time with someone outside of your usual circle.
- **Power gap:** Replace one statement per meeting with a question.
- **Fatigue gap:** Name your fatigue to a trusted peer before your next one-on-one.
- **Assumption gap:** Lead with "Tell me more" before offering any perspective.
- **Discomfort gap:** Notice when you change the subject and stay in that moment instead.
- **Consistency gap:** Pick one "small moment" daily to be fully present for.

REMEMBER

Small shifts may seem insignificant, even useless. They're not. It's those small, everyday actions that lead to big changes. And people will notice.

Step 2: Before, during, and after

You've determined your small shift in the previous step, and now you're ready to tackle a conversation. The focus of this exercise is to better understand how your gaps present in a specific conversation. Here are three questions to ask yourself before, during, and after that conversation:

- **Before:** Which gap am I most likely to fall into with this specific person or situation?

- **During:** Am I still here, or have I drifted and allowed the gap to widen?
- **After:** Where did I show up well, and where did the gap open?

REMEMBER

This process is useful because it turns empathy from a feeling to a process. This is something you can actually practice rather than just hoping you can feel the change.

Step 3: Borrowing someone else's mirror

We all need outside opinions. The most honest diagnosis won't come from within. It comes from the people who interact with us daily, who understand our processes and know our intentions. For you, these are the people who can answer the difficult yet important question about how you impact them and the team. This step encourages you to ask two or three team members this direct question: "Is there ever a moment where you feel like I'm not fully with you, where something gets lost between us?"

REMEMBER

This question, asked sincerely, delivers more data than any self-assessment. Yes, I know it's uncomfortable; asking the people on the receiving end of your empathy failures what it looks and feels like is very humbling for you and potentially very awkward for them. But your blind spots are almost always visible to someone else before they are visible to you.

IN THIS CHAPTER

» Discovering that empathy and accountability are not competing forces

» Communicating to build trust and results simultaneously

» Adding structure to empathy

Chapter 15

Balancing Empathy with Accountability and Results

When empathy tips too far without accountability, teams get comfortable and performance quietly erodes. High performers disengage, poor behavior gets protected in the name of kindness, and the leader who thought they were being supportive is left wondering why results aren't following.

When accountability tips too far without empathy, something different but equally damaging happens: people comply, they hit their targets, and they show up and do the work. But they do it without investment, without honesty, and without any real trust in the person asking it of them. Neither scenario produces the team you're trying to build.

This chapter is about finding and maintaining the balance between the two.

Uniting Empathy and Accountability

I used to confuse gentleness with kindness. I thought that softening my words — rounding off the edges, leaving out the parts that might sting — was the empathetic choice. What I've discovered though, both from leading and from being led, is that the kindest thing another person can do for you is tell you the truth clearly enough that you can actually do something with it. Not harshly. Not coldly. But completely. Because a hard truth delivered with warmth gives you something to work with. A soft truth delivered with so much care that the actual point gets lost gives you nothing except, eventually, a consequence you never saw coming.

REMEMBER

Empathy is going to look a little different for everyone — how we show it, when we need it, how it's received by others — but one thing is a constant, and that is its marriage to accountability. This is why empathy and accountability are deeply intertwined. Because without accountability, empathy is insincere.

Understanding why empathy needs accountability

One of the recurring themes in this book is patterns: both identifying them in yourself and recognizing them on your team. Knowing what to look for is obviously a key element, but so is seeing the impact of them. Herein lies the true connection between empathy and accountability; it is seeing the patterns that exist in your behaviors and doing what you can to adjust them.

If you need a little inspiration to keep accountability in empathy, here are several reasons why these two ideas can only exist properly and sincerely in tandem. Accountability in empathy:

- **Balances relationships.** Relationships without accountability are doomed, and a big part of the reason is because they are unbalanced. One person carries the weight of unspoken expectations while the other operates without full information. This happens in our personal life with friendships and coupledom, but it also happens at work.

  REMEMBER

  Empathetic leaders know that the healthiest professional relationships are the ones where both parties know where they stand. For that reason, accountability delivered with empathy deepens relationships because it signals that you take the person seriously enough to be honest with them.

- **Ensures fairness and equity.** Trust is an integral part of successful leadership endeavors. One of the fastest ways to destroy trust is inconsistent accountability. When leaders apply empathy selectively — such as having more patience for some people than others — it reads as favoritism. Fairness requires that everyone is held to the same standard, even if the support offered to meet that standard looks a little different from person to person (my tip: it will!). Equity means understanding that different people face different obstacles but not using it as a reason to abandon expectations altogether.

TIP

True empathetic accountability asks, "Am I holding this person to the same standard I'd hold anyone else, and am I giving them what they need to meet it?"

- **Facilitates growth and change.** The most transformative leadership moments usually involve something hard paired with something soft, and usually it's a hard truth delivered with a soft edge. These two together — honest, direct feedback given in a way the receiver can fully embrace — encourage growth and drive change. That's because people cannot change what they cannot see clearly; empathy without accountability keeps people in the dark about where they actually stand.

WARNING

Accountability requires that whatever gap exists is named, and that gives people something concrete to work toward. Without it, empathy becomes static, accepting people as they are without investing in who they can become.

- **Maintains high standards.** Having high standards communicates that you as the leader have an intense belief in what your team is capable of. The opposite is also true; lowering the team's standards in the name of empathy is a subtle form of disrespect, especially to the high performers who are always wanting to be engaged at the top level. Empathetic leaders know this, so they both hold the standard and make sure everyone knows what support is available to meet it.

REMEMBER

The goal isn't to make the bar easier to clear; the goal is to make sure people have what they need to clear it. Always remember that empathetic leadership does not mean lowered standards.

- **Prevents enablement and poor performance.** Without accountability, empathy curdles into protection, shielding people from consequences they need to experience to grow. Real empathy means caring about someone's long-term trajectory, not just their short-term comfort.

WARNING

The instinct to "give someone more time" is an empathetic one for sure, but it becomes harmful when that pattern has no endpoint. The real price, however, is at the team's expense: When poor performance goes unaddressed, high performers notice and disengage.

Empathy and accountability are complimentary — not competing — forces. Empathy without accountability is enabling; caring about someone means caring about their growth, not just their comfort. Accountability without empathy is compliance theater; people hit targets while quietly disengaging.

Maintaining accountability within the empathy spectrum

Empathy lives on a spectrum (see Chapter 4). You'll have moments when you are more easily able to empathize with others and moments when empathy is impossible or nonexistent. Where you end up on this spectrum in any given moment is dependent on so many different factors: your mood, your morning commute, who you are talking to, who you just spoke to, or who you know you'll have to speak to in a couple of minutes.

One of the most practical ways to understand how the empathy spectrum operates in the context of accountability is to walk it through the full arc of a goal. Not just the beginning, when everyone is energized and aligned, and not just the end, when the results are in and verdicts rendered. But every stage: the planning, the pursuit, the support, and even the failure. Empathy doesn't have a single moment in the process where it belongs; it belongs in all of them. What changes is what it looks like.

TIP

The following five questions help you identify how exactly to operate with empathy in your current situation while still keeping your team accountable and results-driven. These aren't meant to be a checklist; they're a lens. Relate them to a current goal, project, or initiative on your team; make sure it's something real, something that matters, and something with stakes. The more specific you are, the more useful these questions will be. Tackle them in this order:

1. **What is the goal?** This is about more than just the deliverable. Yes, you need the project completed, the numbers hit, and the deadline met. But what is the larger goal? What does success actually mean for the team, the individuals on it, and the organization? And — this is the part that gets skipped — does everyone understand it the same way you do?

   A goal that lives fully formed in your head but only partially in your team's is already setting someone up to fall short. The most empathetic thing you can do at the goal-setting stage is to make sure the destination is as vivid for the people traveling toward it as it is for you. That means saying it out loud, inviting questions about it, and being willing to hear that your version of the goal and someone else's version of the goal aren't quite the same thing yet.

2. **What does your team need to do to succeed?** Now it's time to shift from the destination to the road. This is where leaders often discover that what they assumed was understood — who is doing what, by when, and to what standard — is actually a patchwork of interpretations.

   Get specific. Not in a micromanaging way, but in a way that removes ambiguity from the equation before it becomes an excuse. What are the specific behaviors, outputs, and standards that will move this team toward the goal? What does "good" look like at the halfway point? What does "done" actually mean?

The empathy here is precision, not softness. When people know exactly what is expected of them, they can rise to meet it. When they don't, they guess. And when they guess wrong, accountability feels unfair because the standard was never made concrete. Empathetic leaders know that vague expectations aren't kind; they're a setup. The clearer you are about what your team needs to do, the fairer your accountability will be when the time comes.

3. **What does your team need from you to succeed?** This seems straightforward, but it's easy to forget. It requires something that doesn't come naturally to many high-achieving people: genuine curiosity about what support looks like to someone other than yourself.

   What your team needs from you to succeed will vary by person, by project, and by moment. One person needs frequent check-ins and a sounding board; another needs you to get out of the way and trust the process. One team member is energized by public recognition; another finds it mortifying. One person will tell you exactly what they need if you ask; another will need you to notice before they ever say a word.

   This is the empathy spectrum doing its most important work: not just feeling for people but paying close enough attention to know what they actually need and then providing it. Even when it looks different from person to person. This is also where the proximity gap from Chapter 14 can quietly do damage. If you only know what the people closest to you need, you are only supporting a fraction of your team. The goal here is to ask widely, listen carefully, and resist the urge to assume that what works for one person works for all.

4. **How do you use empathy to help them succeed?** Now that you know where you're going, what success requires, and what your people need from you, it's time to get intentional about how you show up throughout the process. Not just at the moments that feel important, but consistently in the small ones too.

   Empathy in the pursuit of a goal looks like a lot of different things depending on the day. Some days it looks like a direct conversation about a missed milestone. Some days it looks like noticing that someone seems off and asking about it before the next deadline comes up. And some days it looks like holding firm on a standard even when it would be easier to let it slide.

   What these moments have in common is that they all require you to be paying attention. Empathy in action isn't a feeling; it's a practice of noticing and responding to what is actually happening, rather than what you assume or hope is happening. Your job throughout the pursuit of any goal is to stay curious: about your team's energy, their confidence, their roadblocks, and their relationship to the work itself. That curiosity — sustained, consistent, and genuine — is one of your most powerful tools.

5. **How can you use empathy to help your team if they fail?** This is the question that separates empathetic leaders from the ones who are simply

empathetic in good conditions. It's easy to show up for your team when things are going well. The real measure is what you do when they don't.

Failure on a team is never just a performance event. It is an emotional one. And how you respond to it will shape your team's willingness to take risks, tell the truth, and invest fully in the next goal. A team that has been through failure with a leader who handled it well becomes more resilient, more honest, and more committed. A team that has been through failure with a leader who handled it poorly becomes self-protective and guarded.

Failure, handled with empathy and accountability in equal measure, is one of the most powerful growth accelerators available to a team. The goal isn't to protect people from it. The goal is to make sure that when it happens, it teaches something — and that nobody has to go through it alone.

TIP

These five questions work best when they're treated as a recurring practice, not a one-time read. At the start of every new initiative, pull them back out and work through them with that specific goal, that specific team, and that specific moment in mind. The answers will be different every time and so will what accountability needs to look like. A team that has been walked through all five questions has no ambiguity about what is expected of them or what support is available. That clarity is what makes accountability fair, and fair accountability is what makes results repeatable.

Communicating Using Empathy and Accountability

WARNING

There is a version of empathetic communication that looks right but doesn't work. It's warm, it's careful, it's full of softened edges, and it leaves people confused, unaccountable, and quietly resentful. The problem isn't the intention; it's the language.

Communication that balances empathy and accountability isn't a tone; it's a discipline. It requires knowing not just what to say, but how the words you choose land differently to the ones you almost said. The difference between "You are responsible for this" and "I'm trusting you to lead this" gives the same outcome but a completely different emotional experience.

This section breaks down the six communication dimensions that determine whether a culture becomes high-trust and high-performance, or well-intentioned but stuck. For each one, there are words and phrases that move things forward, and ones that feel safe but quietly undermine everything you are trying to build. Examples of words and phrases to say and to avoid are shown in Table 15-1.

TABLE 15-1 Language That Balances Empathy and Accountability

Communication Dimension	Say	Avoid
Clarity Leaving no room for guesswork	*Can you play back what you heard?* *Let me over-explain once.* *Here's what would help the most.* *Here's the standard I'm working from.*	*More or less.* *You get the idea.* *Somewhere in that range.* *In the ballpark.* *You know what I mean.*
Collaboration United language that shares ownership throughout the entire situation	*I'm with you on this.* *How do we move forward?* *What would help right now?* *What do you need from me?*	*Just figure it out.* *That's your problem.* *I told you so.* *Not my issue.* *Handle it.*
Commitment Going from agreement to action	*Let's make this concrete.* *Who owns this next step?* *What date/time can we get this completed by?* *What does the outcome need to look like specifically?*	*Eventually.* *At some point.* *As soon as possible.* *Let's try to.*
Consequences and rewards Keeping people informed without putting them on the defensive	*The cost of inaction here is.* *This matters because.* *This touches more than just this moment.* *This is bigger than it looks.*	*You'll regret this.* *Don't push it.* *This decision has a long tail.* *I want to make sure you've thought through where this leads.*
Ownership Assigning responsibility while implying trust	*You have full authority here.* *This lives with you.* *I'm putting this in your hands.* *You have the wheel on this.*	*We dropped the ball.* *Let's all keep an eye on it.* *We'll figure out who owns it.* *It slipped through the cracks.*
Transparency Candid yet careful language	*Let me be real with you.* *I owe you honesty here.* *Can I share something with you candidly?* *Here's what I'm observing.*	*It's fine.* *Don't worry.* *I was going to mention it.* *It's probably nothing.* *I've got it handled.*

Clarity

Many people confuse empathy with being nice. They think that empathy means sparing someone's feelings at all costs, even if that means bending the truth. But lying isn't empathetic; its deceptive, and there is no understanding — no empathy — if there is iffy honesty. So, the nicest and kindest thing you can do is to be clear. Here's why: When expectations are vague, people fill the gap with anxiety. Being clear is being caring.

Many leaders fall into the trap of *kind ambiguity*. They know something is going to be challenging for an individual or the team to process, so they soften their message. But they do it so much that the actual point gets lost. You may be concerned that being clear and direct may come across as harsh. But there is a difference between being clear and being harsh; your tone and intent are what separate the two, not the directness itself.

TIP

So how do you communicate with clarity and empathy? Try this: Say it twice. Say what you mean, then confirm it was received the way you mean it. What makes sense in your heads doesn't always come out the way you intend; and even if it does, it's impact on a person isn't always what you planned. Taking a few extra seconds to make sure what you said aligned with what you meant can save you a lot of stress in the future.

Another tip? Use *pre-mortems* as a clarity tool. Before a project begins, walk the team through what failure would look like at the end of the project. This will bring any incorrect assumptions or misalignments to the surface, well before they become real problems.

REMEMBER

Clarity is a trust builder; when people know what's expected, they can succeed. To that end, when they can't succeed, they have a much harder time trusting you and anything you say.

Collaboration

Communication that is collaborative isn't about consensus; everyone doesn't need to agree with the route the team is taking. What everyone does need is a space to share their opinions as well as a clear understanding of where the road leads. This matters, especially as an empathetic leader, because you can include everyone in the process without giving everyone a veto.

REMEMBER

Something to keep in mind here is that there is a difference between *consulting* and *deciding*. Empathetic leaders make it very clear which one is happening at any given moment, because even a hint of ambiguity can breed resentment. To that end, avoid performative collaboration. Asking for input after you've already made a decision will be clocked by your team and, if you do it enough times, they will stop engaging.

Collaborative language when balancing empathy and accountability means shifting the psychological framing from prosecution to partnership. Using words such as "we" and "us" aren't soft, they're strategic. These signal that the leader has commitment to the outcome as well, and that makes accountability feel less like judgment and more like a shared standard.

WARNING

Conflict during collaboration isn't a bug; it's a feature. Teams that never disagree aren't really pushing each other to be better. They're pacifying one another to just get by, to make it to the end of the day. Your job as an empathetic leader is to create enough safety for productive friction.

Commitment

You are as committed as how you are willing to behave; by this, I mean that commitment is revealed and not declared. What you do when things get hard is the only real measure, both for you and your team. An empathetic leader's role in building commitment — rather than just demanding it — is crucial. You have to model the behavior in yourself visibly, because your team watches you. They watch if you follow through on small things just as closely as the big things. Integrity at the micro level builds credibility at the macro one.

If you do see commitment start to waver on your team, get curious before you get frustrated. Is the person in question unclear, overwhelmed, disengaged, or dealing with something personal that is impacting their behavior at work? Is there confusion about what is expected? Before you question people's commitment to you and your team, diagnose the real issue. That will change everything.

In terms of communication, commitment language exposes the difference between intent and agreement. Words such as "try," "hopefully," and "ASAP" feel collaborative but actually allow people to escape accountability. And they do this without technically breaking a promise. The result? Even more distrust.

TIP

Be sure to distinguish between commitment to the task and commitment to the team. Sometimes people check out of a project, but not the organization; catching that nuance early can save a relationship and a contributor.

Consequences and rewards

Consequences delivered without empathy feel like punishment. Empathy given without consequences feels like permission. Herein lies why this combination — of consequences and rewards together, utilized in unison — is required to create a high-trust, high-performance culture. Because consequences should never be the first time someone hears that there is a problem. And rewards have to be more than just motivation; they need to be information as well.

TIP

What does this look like in real time? It's avoiding vague praise, because "great job" is almost as unhelpful as vague criticism. Try instead "Here's exactly what you did, and here's exactly why it mattered." This changes behavior and builds confidence.

Sometimes, the most caring thing a leader — especially an empathetic one — can do is to let natural outcomes land. If you're like me, you learn best the hard way. I prefer to not be rescued from the results of my choices because when I can track exactly where I went wrong, I can more easily course correct the next time around. There will be moments when you need to allow your team to fail — with compassion, of course — because that will be the best way for them to develop. Do not, however, do this coldly, because that is abandonment.

Ownership

Giving direct reports ownership over projects can be daunting. Because ultimately, if things fail, you are the one who is held accountable. This is generally why people start to micromanage; yes, there is an aspect of control there, but there is also fear. Unfortunately, when you hover, you're implicitly communicating that you don't trust the person to deliver. That message lands even when you never say it out loud.

REMEMBER

Empathetic leaders shouldn't *assign* ownership; they should *invite* it. They know that there's a difference between telling someone they're responsible and creating the conditions where that person wants to take responsibility. In that same vein, accountability without ownership is punishment. When you hold someone accountable for an outcome they never truly owned, accountability lands as something being done *to* them rather than something they're answering *for*. On the other end, ownership without accountability is chaos. Empathetic leaders know to build both simultaneously.

The language of ownership is subtle but meaningful. Instead of "You need to fix this," consider something like "I trust you to figure out how to approach this." These two sentences have the exact same meaning, but they are completely different emotional experiences.

Transparency

The line between transparency and oversharing can seem paper thin, and that makes practicing transparency unnerving. The solution for many leaders is to withhold, but that presents a new problem: *transparency debt*. This is what accumulates when leaders withhold information for too long. When your team figures out what is happening (because they usually do), your silence can be a betrayal.

WARNING

As discussed in Chapter 7 about defining your goals, if there's no *why* behind everything that you do then it's hard to stay consistent at anything you attempt — including and especially empathy. That's why sharing the *why* behind decisions is one of the highest-leverage empathy moves available. People are very capable of handling difficult news, if you let them. Being told bad news is, for them, better than feeling like they're "managed"; it undermines their sense of autonomy, trust, and competence.

Transparent communication as it relates to accountability isn't a failure of honesty; it's a failure of omission. With that in mind, avoid phrases that come across as deferrals. Instead, try to be honest about limitations without creating information vacuums that could potentially be filled by rumors.

TIP

Never lose sight of the importance of being transparent about your mistakes. Leaders who model fallibility give their teams permission to be human, too. That is where accountability without shame becomes possible.

Constructing Compassionate Accountability Systems

Empathy without structure is just a mood. Some days it shows up strong. Some days it doesn't show up at all. If the empathy on your team depends entirely on how you're feeling on any given Tuesday, it isn't a culture; it's a personality. This section is about turning what you feel into what you build to make compassionate accountability something your team can count on, not just hope for.

Reframing empathy as infrastructure

I'm originally from Chicago, Illinois. Known for many things — deep-dish pizza, the unpredictable and extreme weather, the nightmare that is O'Hare Airport — its most famous identifier is the skyline. The biggest draw of the skyline is its originality. Chicago is known as the birthplace of the modern skyscraper, but it took quite a bit of planning, precision, and tragedy to get there. In 1871, the city was all-but destroyed by the Great Chicago Fire. That led to a rapid rebuild and eventually, with new engineering techniques and elevator technologies, architects started building *up*. Rapidly. And they did it with steel frames. The skyscraper as we know it was born.

TIP

Something that should never be lost on you is how much innovation and growth can happen after a huge setback. Chicago was able to rebuild — and do so with such fervor and fame — because people worked together. They figured out what the issues were (even if they did so the hard way by losing everything) and they pivoted. The result of that is now etched in stone in both Chicago's and the world's history. That result was possible because of infrastructure: planning, collaborating, and execution.

For empathy to be a long-term successful endeavor, you need to view it as infrastructure. Just as a company builds systems for finance, operations, and communication, you can build systems for how people are heard, how feedback flows, how conflict gets addressed, and how recognition happens. When empathy is embedded in the process, it doesn't depend on a leader's mood or capacity on any given day. This is something you, on your own, can create by consistently signaling that honesty is safe and humanity is valued.

TIP

When considering your empathy infrastructure, it's very important to remember that everyone is going to fit into that system a little differently. Think of it like a puzzle; no two pieces are the same, yet they all come together to create the perfect picture. Each single piece won't fit everywhere, but there is absolutely a place for everyone.

View empathy as more than just a feeling; it needs to be a system, and that system needs to start from day one of an employee's journey. How a person enters the organization shapes how safe they feel for years. A thoughtful onboarding process communicates "We've been waiting for you and we want you to succeed," before a single deliverable is due.

Assessing your empathy Key Performance Indicators

Measuring empathy using Key Performance Indicators (KPIs) can be tricky. Some things can easily be identified as *high empathy behaviors* (actions that demonstrate empathy in practice — such as active listening, asking open questions, and acknowledging someone's emotions) or *low empathy behaviors* (actions that signal a disregard for another person's experience — such as interrupting, dismissing feelings, or responding to a problem before fully understanding it). A lot of what you'll be looking for, however, will be a vibe. You'll feel a shift, but it'll be difficult to really pinpoint exactly what has changed.

As a lot of what you're tracking will be more of a feeling than a hard number, it helps to have a few concrete places to look. The indicators below give something tangible to watch for when the vibe alone isn't enough to go on:

- **Equity of voice across the team.** Who speaks in meetings? Who doesn't? Who gets credited for their ideas, and who gets talked over? Empathy is more than just an interpersonal skill; it's a structural one. If the same few people are always doing the talking while everyone else goes unheard, your empathy infrastructure isn't solid.

  Notice whose voice is absent. Whose ideas get picked up by someone else and attributed differently. Who waits to be called on versus who takes up space without invitation. This isn't about engineering false equity; it's about recognizing that some people have been conditioned by experience, culture, or temperament to make themselves smaller. This is why being an empathetic leader is so valuable, because it creates the conditions for those voices to exist fully.

- **Manager-initiated check-in frequency.** You probably schedule check-ins that are in the calendar and treated as a formality. I'm not talking about those. These check-ins are the actual, human, non-performative check-ins initiated by you: the leader. In these moments, you are asking "How are you doing?" in a way that makes clear that you have time for the actual answer.

  This is about who is carrying the burden of connection. If the only time you know how someone is doing is when they bring it to you, you are a *reactive leader*. Empathetic leaders are *proactive;* they go toward their people, especially when things are hard or if there's nothing specific to address. Why does this matter? Because we are all constantly navigating ambient levels of personal stress that have no clean separation from our professional lives. You, as the fearless (empathetic) leader, can't pretend that the outside world just disappears when people start working. Check in with your team because you are both having very human experiences in this very chaotic world. It is truly one of the most important things you can do.

- **Psychological safety.** How long does it take your team — or an individual on it — to recover after something goes wrong? Do people move through failure with the support they need to course-correct and move forward? Or do they stall, shut down, become defensive, or disappear into self-protection?

  Failure and innovation go hand-in-hand, and that's why your team and everyone on it needs to feel psychologically safe enough to not only take risks but also to fail. In a low-empathy culture, failure is a threat — so people hide it, minimize it, or deflect it. In a low-accountability culture, failure is absorbed without consequence — so it repeats. In a high-trust culture, failure is metabolized. It happens, it's named, it's examined, and the team moves through it together.

Watch how your team responds the moment after something goes wrong. That moment — more than any values statement or any feedback session — tells you exactly what kind of culture you have built.

- **Retention of high-trust talent.** Empathy has a retention signature. When people leave, they rarely cite workload as the primary reason — they cite feeling unseen, unheard, or undervalued. Tracking who stays and who goes, and more importantly why, is one of the most honest empathy audits available to a leader. Exit interviews are data. Patterns in those exit interviews are a verdict.

  The metric here isn't just overall attrition — it's the quality of who is walking out the door. When your highest performers leave and your most disengaged stay, that is a signal about your culture's relationship with accountability. When your most vulnerable contributors leave — the newer hires, the quieter voices, the ones who never quite found their footing — that is a signal about your culture's relationship with empathy.

LEADING AS A BALANCING ACT

Leadership is a tricky balance because so many people require so many different parts of you at any given moment. One person might need a sign-off on a finished presentation; at the same time another needs some encouragement after a bad client interaction; a third person needs clarification on a project they've lagged behind on after taking some unexpected time off. And this doesn't even consider the needs of your direct-line managers.

The problem many leaders face — especially in moments of crisis, failure, or stress — is that they lose empathy. In fact, empathy is one of the first casualties of *cognitive bandwidth depletion* (the exhaustion of the brain's working memory and executive functioning, resulting in slower decision-making, fragmented focus, and high emotional reactivity). When you're running low, the nuance disappears. You hear words but miss tone; you respond but don't connect; you show up physically but check out emotionally. And your team feels that absence even if they can't name it.

So, let's take a moment here and discuss *compassion fatigue* in leadership. This is the mental and physical exhaustion generated by exposure to trauma and distress while helping others. In leadership, it is the emotional exhaustion and diminished empathy that can happen after consistent exposure to employee, team, or client stress and trauma. There is confusion around compassion fatigue because of how it looks in real time. It often exposes itself through increased cynicism, apathy, and decreased productivity. And it manifests as irritability with colleagues, emotional numbness and bottling them up entirely, and decreased ability to feel joy at work. You may think that all of these of symptoms of not caring, but that is far from accurate. Compassion fatigue means you've been caring without adequate support or recovery. The treatment isn't caring less; it's building a more sustainable infrastructure around how you care.

This is why empathetic leadership is a true balancing act. You cannot lead from empty. The cultural glorification of exhaustion in leadership — wearing busyness as a badge and equating sacrifice with effectiveness — is one of the most destructive myths in professional life. I'm not here to tell you that you can combat this entirely; sometimes, you will absolutely feel overwhelmed with the weight of your emotional responsibility. However, you need to learn when to prioritize energy management over time management.

You can't manufacture more hours, but you can be strategic about what drains you and what restores you. And you can design your schedule accordingly. For example, knowing that back-to-back difficult conversations wipe you out should influence how you structure your week.

Leadership is not a straight line between empathy and results. It's a constant, dynamic negotiation between competing legitimate needs: the individual and the team, the short term and the long term, the heart and the bottom line. The leader who thinks they've found a permanent balance isn't leading; they're coasting.

To be successful as an empathetic leader, you need to recognize that the balancing act is the job. New leaders often think the goal is to find equilibrium and stay there. Experienced ones know that the moment you find your footing, something shifts. The skill isn't balance; it's the ability to rebalance quickly, repeatedly, and without losing yourself in the process.

Identify the specific things that replenish you and establish the discipline to protect them. This is deeply personal. For some leaders it's physical exercise, solitude, creative work, or time in nature. The point isn't what that thing is; it's that you identify it, you treat it as a non-negotiable, and you don't apologize for it.

IN THIS CHAPTER

» Developing self-awareness and self-understanding

» Being flexible yet strong

» Developing emotional boundaries

Chapter 16
Assessing Your Empathetic Leadership Style

Most leaders spend their careers looking outward: at their teams, at their results, and at their goals. The ones who lead with empathy know that the most important direction to look first is inward. Before you can genuinely understand anyone else, you have to do the harder, quieter work of understanding yourself: What drives you, what limits you, and what effect you actually have on the people around you.

This chapter is about building that foundation. It helps you assess your empathetic leadership style not as a fixed trail but as a living practice that requires honest self-reflection, the flexibility to adapt without losing your footing, and the boundaries that make sustained empathy possible without burning you out in the process.

Recognizing, Analyzing, and Categorizing Yourself

Are you a mirror leader or a window one? Some leaders only look at themselves as if they are looking in a mirror. They examine their behaviors in the most critical way, going deep into how they acted in every moment and how they can improve themselves from a personal lens. Others are window leaders. They judge their leadership abilities by what their team is or is not doing, and success is only categorized by everyone else's achievements, not their own.

TIP

Empathetic leaders look at themselves in both ways — in a mirror and through a window — to do their jobs well. It's why they invest a great deal of energy building their self-awareness muscle. If you want to be empathetic, you must recognize, analyze, and categorize yourself — your skills, your habits, your strengths and weaknesses, and your behaviors — before you can truly lead with empathy.

This section breaks down how you can do that.

Considering empathy and self-awareness

Few things can be more uncomfortable than sitting in silence. It feels uncertain and unsteady. What is the other person thinking? Are they bored? Are they judging you? Are they wondering if you're disinterested? Sitting in silence breaks social norms; so many of us see constant conversation as necessary for building rapport, so silence is a lack of rapport. Beyond just that, silence is the absence of outward stimulation; and in the world we live in — where things are constantly being thrown at us from every direction — silence can feel like a void.

For me, silence can sometimes feel like a ticking time bomb. As a person who stutters, silence means that someone will eventually start talking. And they might start talking to me. They might say something to me that I won't be comfortable physically saying, so I will stutter more. And then I will be embarrassed and ashamed, and I'll worry that the person will think less of me. So I tried to take control of the silence by always having something to say. I'd search my mind for an open-ended question I could ask so the others around me would talk more.

I approached silence and conversations this way for most of my life, until I started pursing keynote speaking seriously as a career. I reached out to people in my network to get advice and clarity on the path forward, and I eventually connected with one incredible woman named Christine. She'd built a leadership consulting firm and was an expert at finding business. She was kind and interested and encouraging. She discussed how she got to where she was, the ups and downs of her own entrepreneurial journey, and what she would have done differently. I was in total awe of her story, but also terribly anxious; I *knew* I was going to have to talk. And I was nervous because I wasn't having the best speaking day. So, when she asked me about what I wanted my career to look like, my words were slow and clunky. I eventually said something to get her to start talking again. She smiled, completely relaxed and unbothered by my speech, and said "I've got plenty of time."

This was a cannon event in my relationship with stuttering for two reasons. I realized that no one that mattered would care how my words came out; all they cared about was the message. The other thing I learned was that I spent *a lot* of time thinking about myself. How I felt. How I sounded. How I might feel if I stuttered too much. What the other person thought of me. Would the other person understand me. What words I would say. Would I stutter on those words. How I looked when I stuttered. I. I. I. Me. Me. Me. It's incredible I had any bandwidth left to actually listen to other people!

I walked away from that conversation with Christine more aware of my own habits than ever before. My insecurities around my speech had shaped how I approached conversations for such a long time that I had stopped being self-aware. Sure, I was always engaged in the conversations, but my internal dialogue was self-centered. As a result, I missed a lot of opportunities to find out more about people, to really hear about their true experiences, and to sincerely understand them at more than surface level.

Being empathetic goes beyond just understanding others; it's being honest about your limitations, beliefs, and habits. Self-awareness is a core component of empathy, but it's also a necessity in leadership. You can't truly understand anyone if you don't first know yourself. Empathetic leaders make it a point to always check in with themselves: their habits, their behaviors, their intentions, and their results.

REMEMBER

Empathy and self-awareness go hand-in-hand because each drives the other. A higher self-awareness tends to produce greater empathy; understanding your own emotions gives you a richer vocabulary and framework for understanding someone else's. And developing empathy can also deepen self-awareness; genuinely trying to understand another person's perspective often reveals assumptions and blind spots you didn't know you had.

Knowing you are what you do . . . and what you do impacts your team

Fewer things in this world keep you more honest than young children. They have little to no filter, have endless energy, and are deeply curious creatures. For these reasons, children used to terrify me. And I'm not being dramatic here when I say this; any time I had to be around small children, I would get genuinely nervous. Because what would they think of me? What would they say to me? What would they ask me? And what if I didn't know how to respond?

Now that I'm older, there are so many delightful children in my life and I'm a lot more comfortable. I've come to really enjoy the conversations I have with them, and I'm considerably more at ease during them than I once was. With some reflection, I finally figured out why I had reservations around children for so long: the probing. They want to know *everything*, and they won't stop asking about whatever part of *everything* they're currently fixated on until you provide a satisfactory answer. But I usually leave these conversations realizing that I may not actually have all of the answers, and I have to consider what I actually think; rethink what I thought I believed; and then come to a completely different conclusion. Because I'm forced to break things down in a way uncommon when speaking to adults, I challenge my own beliefs. And I discover more about myself in the process.

TIP

This is the level of questioning and awareness to have when considering your true impact on your team. You need to be actively engaged in the empathy behaviors you're practicing and deeply curious about how those behaviors are actually coming off. And you also need to be okay with a few things: realizing that you may not be doing this the best way for your team, rethinking how your intentions align with your impact, and concluding something about yourself — specifically, who you are and what you do — that you never thought you would.

REMEMBER

The gap between your self-image and your actual behaviors is where leadership development lives, and most leaders never go there. Being self-aware enough to know the difference between those two things goes a long way in assessing your actual impact in terms of both leadership and empathy.

Here are a few reflections to consider as you search for answers within yourself:

- **Align what you do with what you *think* you do.** Would you believe me if I told you that you've been using filters on yourself long before social media apps made them popular? Don't worry; we all have! We edit ourselves constantly, always trying to put our best faces forward.

  TECHNICAL STUFF

  This goes back to mirror-window analogy that kicked off this section. When you look through a window, you are a third-party viewer. You see things as they happen with little bias. Viewing your behaviors this way means you need to look at them through the eyes of others — third-party viewers through a window — as often as possible. Where the mirror comes into play is seeing what looks good and what needs to be fixed. The window gives others the opportunities to show you who you are; the mirror is there to help you align what you do with you what you *think* you do.

» **Consistency is its own form of empathy.** You constantly communicate with others; you tell them how to speak to you, listen to you, and behave around you. Every time you walk in the room, you are either confirming what people believe to be true about you or you are beginning to rewrite their ideas. Consistency, therefore, is imperative to creating the results you want on your team.

Consistency can reinforce what people believe to be true about you both as a leader and as a person. Consistently engaging in pro-empathy behaviors — as well as encouraging it within your team — makes people feel psychologically safe, reduces overall team anxiety, and it shows them what you actually value.

REMEMBER

People generally view empathy as reactive; it is noticing how someone feels in a given moment and responding to it with care. While that is real and important, it is only half the picture. That's why the most empathetic thing you can do — the quiet, more structural form of empathy not in individual moments but across time — is to be consistent. Consistency requires sustained intention rather than a moment of emotional attunement. It is empathy as a practice rather than empathy as a feeling.

» **What you tolerate, you teach.** A big part of you is what you do; and what you do deeply impacts your team. You can say all of the right words with the perfect inflection and positive tone, but if those words don't match your actions, they don't matter.

WARNING

Your team sees what you are allowing to happen. Any time you let a bad behavior go unchecked, they are making a mental note of it. They're learning what they can and can't get away with, and you are actively teaching them that. This is why you must be very aware of *empathy theatre* where you are performing empathy but not practicing it. Your team will absolutely tell the difference, and they'll see it immediately.

Creating a framework for self-understanding

REMEMBER

Empathy without self-understanding is instinct. With self-understanding, empathy becomes a practice. Before you can consistently show up for others, you need a clear picture of what drives you, what derails you, and what effect you actually have on the people around you. That starts by building a framework based on your values, your triggers, and your impact:

» **Your values.** What do you stand for? What are your core principles? What do you deeply believe in? Is it integrity? Compassion? Achievement? Open-mindedness? Your behaviors need to be shaped by your values. If you haven't identified what your core values are just yet, now is a great time to figure out what you stand for. To do that, look back on your work and think about what has mattered to you the most as an individual contributor, a member of a team, and now as a leader. You're reading this book, so I know that something involving empathy is valuable in your work; what is that? What specifically about empathy drives you to weave it deeply into your compass? Write that down. Knowing what is important to you — and by that, I mean what is actually important, not what people say should be important — is the only way forward in developing a self-understanding framework.

» **Your triggers.** What derails your empathy? Think about specific behaviors, situations, emotional states, and work stresses. Write down everything that knocks you off your game, even a little. Now, ask yourself: Why do these things bother you? What is it about these specific situations that make it more difficult for you to understand and share the feelings of another person? And then, when you've identified what those triggers are, think about how they externalize themselves in your behavior? Do you get short with others? Do you minimize feelings? Do you cut people off? Knowing your triggers reveals what lays beneath. You see your unhealed wounds, get more insight into your core values, and unpack your outdated belief systems that drive your negative reactions.

» **Your impact.** What do others say, feel, and do when you are around? Feeling empathetic is one thing, but does your team speak up? Do they feel safe enough to bring problems directly to you? Your impact is where you consider some of the indirect measures of your empathetic leadership. How is your employee retention rate? How much candor is happening on your team? Are your direct reports engaging in creative risk-taking? Your impact tells the whole story; it shows you who you are as a leader through how your team responds to you.

Being Adaptable without Losing Yourself

I'm generally a pretty positive person. Not necessarily because I have a naturally sunny outlook, but because I choose to be positive to help me stay rooted when the world feels heavy or chaotic. I know how the heaviness and chaos can impact my ability to be productive and present, so I work very hard at being positive even when it seems futile.

That doesn't mean I don't *feel*. Because I absolutely do; I feel and absorb and squirm and sit with the sadness, frustration, worry, or pain. Just because I am feeling those feelings, though, doesn't mean that any of them have to change my constitution. A yoga teacher once told me that emotions are like clouds; they hang out for a while but are in constant motion, slowly floating away.

REMEMBER

This is the attitude to focus on when striving to be adaptable. As well as knowing your triggers, you also need to know how far you can be pushed. Bamboo is a great metaphor for being rooted while staying flexible (see the nearby sidebar, "Being Rooted and Staying Flexible"), and you need both of these qualities to truly lead with empathy. As an empathetic leader, you need to marry firmness to elasticity. And you need to be unyielding in your destination but pliable in how the path looks on the journey. Here's how that adaptability looks:

- **Curiosity.** Curiosity is the desire to learn, explore, and understand. It's driven by an inquisitive nature to investigate the unknown. Curious people are naturally adaptable because the act of seeking new information means they'll be better able to adjust to the unexpected as opposed to hanging on to what is now obsolete.

  As a leader, you have to be willing to experiment. That experimentation is rooted in knowing that there are several ways to be successful. Think of it like driving, where there are several ways to get to where you want to go. Not every way is going to be the fastest or make sense to everyone. You may be driving a different type of car to another person, so one way suits your trip based on your vehicle. You will both also be dealing with varying traffic patterns and have to contend with the highway versus side streets; and maybe you'll have to make a stop along the way before you get to where you want to go. Curiosity is sometimes taking that different route and not because it's the fastest, more direct, or easiest way to go. It's because you want everyone to get from point A to point B in the way that will push them or teach them or suit them best at that moment. Empathetic leaders are willing to experiment.

- **Foresight.** In a way, we can see the future; not because we are psychic but because we can recognize the patterns of the past. And it's in those patterns that you can more accurately predict what the future will look like. Of course, we all love to be right. That's not, however, the reason you should want to look into the future. Foresight encourages flexibility. A part of an empathetic leader means having a handle of your reactions; you are able to walk through every situation — no matter how tense or uncomfortable or absurd — with emotional regulation. This is the only way you can truly engage in empathy behaviors to help you understand others, if you have enough emotional control to actually listen to them.

  Here's where flexibility comes into play. If you have an inkling of what could happen, being emotionally regulated means that, no matter how far you are bent, you will not break. Empathetic leaders know that they must think ahead and be proactive over being reactive.

- **Positive outlook.** As mentioned earlier, I work hard at being positive. I do this a few ways. I remind myself that there is always a solution; it may not be the one that I want, but it will get the job done and push the situation forward. I also stopped viewing things in a linear "win or lose" sense and started looking at everything as an opportunity to learn. And finally, I always have someone in my life who can offer an outside perspective; whatever I'm concerned about may not be going how I planned, but that doesn't mean it's a total failure and sometimes it takes a non-invested party to point that out.

  Positive thinking physically changes the brain. It boosts serotonin and dopamine, lowers cortisol, and activates the prefrontal cortex. That means less stress and more cognitive flexibility. The result is increased mental alertness, better problem-solving capabilities, and the ability think more creatively.

- **Resilience.** Maybe you've heard of "flow versus force" or "flow, don't force." If not, here's a quick primer. *Force* is a struggle; it's pushing and manipulation, and it implies a state of high-effort control. *Flow,* on the other hand, is alignment; you're motivated intrinsically and the focus feels effortless. A *flow state* is a result of being highly trained and deeply focused with complete absorption in a task, and that task is neither too easy (which can cause boredom) nor too hard (which can cause anxiety). The reward isn't the state itself but the work it took to get there. The long nights practicing, the many falls, the "no's" and "not now's," and pushing through the urge to quit.

  Resilience and flexibility go hand-in-hand. Resilience is the capacity to absorb difficulty and recover; flexibility is the capacity to adapt when circumstances change. Together, they produce something more powerful than either alone: the ability to bend without breaking, and to come back different rather than just come back.

REMEMBER

The bamboo mentioned earlier in this section and in the sidebar doesn't survive the storm by fighting. It survives by being so deeply rooted that bending is never a threat. As an empathetic leader, that needs to be the standard. Know what you stand for so completely that how things unfold — detours, setbacks, or the unexpected — never shakes your sense of direction. The goal isn't rigidity. It's the kind of grounding that makes flexibility possible. When you are rooted in your values, your purpose, and your people, you don't just weather difficulty, you grow through it.

BEING ROOTED AND STAYING FLEXIBLE

Bamboo is a fascinating plant. It spends the first years of its life growing minimally above ground: 1 to 5 feet maximum. Most of its growth happens in its extensive root system underground. Its modified stems, called *rhizomes*, grow horizontally just below the surface. Though it appears to be dormant, the roots are maturing and establishing a massive energy base. When it's ready, it shoots up — with some species growing as high as 90 feet in just a few weeks — creating one of the strongest natural materials on earth. Its *tensile strength* (the maximum resistance to being pulled apart before breaking) is higher than many alloys of steel, and its *compressive strength* (a material's ability to withstand pushing forces before it cracks or breaks) is similar to that of concrete.

Bamboo is hugely symbolic in Chinese culture, representing humility, harmony, and resoluteness. It is a hollow plant, and that symbolizes humility with a clear mind and an open heart free from arrogance. It embodies balance between flexibility and strength, symbolizing moral integrity, modest endurance, and adaptability to tough situations. Bamboo is considered the perfect harmony between inner humility and softness with outward toughness and flexibility.

Sound familiar? Yes, bamboo is a great metaphor for empathetic leadership. Being flexible allows you to break free from the rigid and egocentric viewpoints you may hold. That alone encourages understanding from a more authentic place; you are more open to experiences and new perspectives, which are both core activities to empathetic understanding. But bamboo is also strong, being deeply and extensively rooted in the ground below. And its stalks are rarely impacted by storms, no matter how intense and devastating those storms may be to the surrounding area. Bamboo bends, but does not break.

One of the coolest things about bamboo, though, is what happens when one of its stalks are cut. That stalk will not grow taller. But because of its robust and extensive root system, it sends up new shoots to replace the one that it lost. And often times, those stalks grow faster and are stronger than the one that was lost.

Developing Emotional Boundaries

To me, the term "self-care" has lost its luster. Many of the things people consider self-care don't actually create long-lasting peace or happiness. Sure, it feels great to take a fabulous vacation or have a lazy day binging a comfort television show on the couch. But does that actually fix stress? Does it eliminate worry? Does it help you better cope with everything else going on in your life? So let's rebrand *self-care*, not as a one-time event but as a daily practice that allows you to operate at your highest possible level as an empathetic leader. The number one task on your list to practice self-care every day? Developing emotional boundaries.

The point of emotional boundaries isn't to separate you from others, especially your direct reports on your team. You develop emotional boundaries so that when you do show up for them, you are doing so in a way that models healthy behavior and minimizes judgment. You also show up this way consistently. Boundaries create safety for you and stability for them.

Before diving into developing emotional boundaries, let's get something very clear: You can and need to have boundaries, and those boundaries can shift and evolve over time. This is something to keep in mind throughout this section because I'm going to challenge you to both establish boundaries and also investigate the capacity of those boundaries.

REMEMBER

Both of these ideas are important. Having boundaries means you understand your limits; investigating them means you — as a leader — are prepared to grow for the betterment of your team by stretching them.

Establishing your boundaries

I'm a natural empath, and I'm also an introverted observer. I pay attention to everything; I'm curious so I love learning about people and things, but I also see *a lot*. I notice when people's facial expressions change, even slightly, to something a bit sadder. I see the subtle shift in body language that is a dead giveaway for tension or discomfort. And I can literally feel the exact moment the vibe changes, and it's time to leave.

Early on when I was figuring out my own boundaries, I had to learn how to sit through the small shifts of emotional change during interactions. I spent a very long time not knowing how operate within those moments or how to address my feelings apart from everyone else's. With time, as well as trial and error, I learned those situations I could navigate with confidence — the ones I could handle, albeit shakily — and those where I needed to excuse myself. When I started my career as a speaker, I had to learn how to have deep and uncomfortable conversations quite quickly. Because of the nature of my talks, people felt comfortable sharing their own struggles with me. I created an environment where strangers felt comfortable talking to me about their deepest fears, and I had to figure out how to then navigate that as a person and as an empath.

TIP

The result of those experiences is how I developed my own emotional boundaries in a way that worked for my lifestyle. Your practice as an empathetic leader will require you to occasionally confront some heavier emotional moments, and you'll need to move through those moments with some warmth and sincerity. Here are four steps (and four questions to ask yourself) for when you are in one of those heavy moments. You need to work through them in order as the answer to the previous question impacts how you move through the ones following it:

1. **The moment: What does the moment call for?** Every challenging moment will look a little different. Therefore, every challenging moment requires something different from you. Survey what's needed — a listening ear, encouraging words, a shoulder to lean on, a moment of emotional support — in the current moment.
2. **Your capacity: What do you have to give?** Be aware of your limits. Do this by reflecting on your values and identify what behaviors you will and won't tolerate. In general, it's a bad idea to tolerate disrespect and emotional manipulation so those two things can immediately be taken off the table. If someone needs to vent, cry, or do a "walk and talk" to let off steam, it's up to you to determine what exactly you have to give in this moment.
3. **Your voice: How can you communicate your desired contribution?** This, for me, is difficult; and if you're an empath, it's probably hard for you as well. Of course, you always want to help, want them to feel seen and heard, and as a leader you want to be the support and provide the encouragement that your team needs. You're still human, so you will have moments when boundaries are necessary. It's how you communicate those boundaries that's most important as an empathetic leader. When you need to table something for whatever reason, use this three-step sentence structure: Acknowledge what's happening; use clear and simple "I" statements; and — optionally — give a reason why this is not the time. Here's an example: "I see that you are having a hard time. Right now, however, I don't have the capacity to walk through this with you."
4. **Your departure: How do you exit?** Make sure you are prepared to walk away from the situation and also have a plan to move forward. That may mean revisiting the case when emotions have calmed or when there's more time to really explore the issue.

To develop emotional boundaries, you have to be self-aware enough to know your own thoughts, feelings, and flaws while also being other-aware enough to understand the same in others. Empathy is *other-awareness* in practice; to set emotional boundaries, however, you need to identify where you are right now so you know what you are capable of giving to another person. These questions help you do that. And if you need to switch out the questions for ones that better suit you, feel free to do so.

REMEMBER

Get clear on your responsibility in these challenging moments when you feel your boundaries are being tested. Recognize that you are not responsible for the emotions of others but also acknowledge their feelings without taking them as your own.

Stretching your boundaries

Your boundaries may lay on a spectrum. They'll vary from day to day depending on many factors from something as flexible as your mood to something more fixed such as your current workload. Instead of looking at your boundaries as set in stone — immovable and immutable — begin to look at them as rubber bands.

People share with me incredibly personal things about themselves that they rarely get to talk about because they don't feel that they have the platform to do so. It is an honor to be in that position, to know that I've created a space so safe — psychologically and emotionally — that people can really let go and free themselves of the fear of judgment. The better you get at leading with empathy, the more often you will find yourself in similar situations. Therein lies the value of being a rubber band. Rubber bands can be stretched and shaped, keeping you secure and organized. Up to a point. Then, when you need to adjust the spectrum that your boundaries currently lay on, you can go to a different-sized rubber band.

TIP

Stretching your boundaries requires a good bit of emotional elasticity and a sense of adventure! Any time you are pushing yourself to do something beyond what you currently do, you are going on a journey: from who you are now to who you will be in the future. And, to keep this metaphor going, every trip you take in life changes you because you are exploring, seeing, and discovering new things. So I want you to view the process of stretching your boundaries like you would going on a trip. Here's how to plan your itinerary:

1. **Your gate: Where are you at right now?** I know that when I walk off the stage of any talk I give, I may be on the verge of an emotional conversation. I'm very lucky because I know exactly when they will happen, so I can very easily and quickly prepare myself for whatever is thrown my way. Usually in these moments, I'm on a high. It's right after a talk, so I'm both exhausted and pumped with adrenaline. Depending on how I felt the talk went, I might be in a great mood or a decent one.

   When you're in an emotionally charged moment, take stock of where you are right then. What are you feeling physically? Emotionally? Mentally? Where is your mind at? Where is your heart at? Take stock of the ground you are standing on; when you're rooted in who and where you are, it's easier to find your way.

2. **Your luggage: What do you need right now?** Speaking on stage is very different to speaking to people one-on-one. The skills required to be a good speaker have little to do with being a good conversationist. I know that the first thing I need to do when I start talking to people is to get out of "speaker" mode and get in to "talking" mode. I usually also need to grab water, take a few deep breaths and put down my bag. When I talk to people, I like to be as unencumbered and free as possible; I don't want anything physically between me and the people I speak with.

What do you need right now to handle what is about to be thrown your way? If you know you're going into a meeting that might get tense, a direct report is returning to work after bereavement leave, or you have a one-on-one that might get emotional for your coworker, what do you need to do to get in the right mindset to manage that moment with care? Identify your needs to be emotionally sound in this charged atmosphere.

3. **Your flight: Where do you want to go?** Here's where it gets fun! Being a leader means consistently putting yourself in a position for growth. You learn a lot more because you are put on the spot, you are in front a group, and you have to think about everything from a higher level. Emotional growth is about maturing; you experience more, you learn new things, you spend time around more people, and you have more perspective, so therefore you are able to handle more. Your job is to identify what you want to be able to handle. And that is the answer to the question of where you want to go.

   For me, it was going into every conversation completely open to whatever came my way. I wanted everyone to feel totally at ease, and I wanted the conversations to flow easily. I know as a result of my role, I create that experience; it is my job to allow people to engage with me in that capacity.

4. **Your destination: What will you need when you get there?** Emotions are an essential part of life; they're natural, and they help us navigate communication needs in addition to processing our lived experiences. Stretching your emotional boundaries means increasing your capacity to handle difficult emotions. I discovered that as a speaker, I needed to meet the moment beyond just the "big one" on stage. On paper, I'm there to give a talk and go home. But what I'm actually doing is creating an engaging experience for the audience, and that includes what happens after the talk. People want to have conversations, they want to share their feelings, and they want to know that what they have to say is meaningful. In order to meet that moment, I knew I needed to start stretching what I believed I was capable of.

   You know your current limits. You know how to communicate your boundaries. And you've come to the moment where you want to push them, to see how far that rubber band can stretch. To do that, you need to identify who you want to be going forward. And you need to put yourself situations that challenge you emotionally. This means seeking out uncomfortable conversations, stopping yourself from trying to fix the problems presented to you in those conversations, and sitting in those emotionally charged moments without trying to change the mood.

IN THIS CHAPTER

» Understanding what an Empathetic Leadership Council is

» Knowing who to include

» Finding your empathy mentors

» Planning your own empathetic leadership education

Chapter 17 Assembling Your Empathetic Leadership Council

You can't develop as an empathetic leader in isolation. It requires the right people around you, asking the hard questions, reflecting back what you can't see on your own, and holding you to the standard you've set for yourself. This chapter is about building that infrastructure. From the council you construct to the mentors you seek out to the education you take ownership of, everything in this chapter is about surrounding yourself with what your own growth actually requires.

Defining an Empathetic Leadership Council

Most leaders have people they turn to. A trusted colleague they debrief with after a hard meeting. A former boss they call when they need perspective. A friend who will tell them the truth when everyone else won't. These relationships are valuable; but they're informal, accidental, and usually built around whatever is most convenient rather than what is most useful. An Empathetic Leadership Council (ELC) is different. It is intentional.

REMEMBER

The ELC is a concept rooted in a simple but powerful idea: that developing as an empathetic leader is not something you can do alone, and it's not something that happens by accident. It requires feedback, challenge, and people who know you well enough to see your blind spots and care enough to name them. And crucially, it requires a range of perspectives; no single person, no matter how wise or well-intentioned, can give you a complete picture of who you are as a leader.

Think of your ELC not as a mentorship but as a board of directors for your empathy practice specifically. These aren't people who are guiding your career broadly or cheerleading your ambitions. They are strategic advisors with one purpose: to help you see yourself more clearly, hold you accountable to your values, and push you to grow in the areas that matter most to the people you lead. The distinction matters. A mentor develops you. Your ELC sharpens you.

What makes an ELC work is the same thing that makes empathy work: diversity of perspective. You need people who see you from different angles — those walking alongside you, those who've already been where you're going, those just starting out where you once were, and those with no stake in your organization at all. Each of those vantage points reveals something the others can't. Together, they give you a fuller, more honest picture of your impact than any one relationship ever could.

Before delving into who belongs in your council and how to build it, be clear on what it is and what it isn't. It isn't a group of people who make you feel good about yourself. It isn't a place to vent or be validated. It is a deliberately constructed circle of honest, invested, perspective-diverse people whose collective job is to help you become the empathetic leader your team deserves.

Working Out Who to Include in an Empathic Leadership Council

First things first: Your ELC isn't a support group or a fan club. It's a deliberate, carefully chosen group of people who will tell you the truth about yourself — from different vantage points, different levels of experience, and different relationships to the work you do. The diversity of perspective is the whole point. One person can't give you everything you need; a well-constructed council can. Here's who needs to be in the room:

» **Junior staff.** I know what it feels like to be 21; I don't, however, know what it feels like to be 21 right now; in the age of social media, 24-hour news cycles, and smart phones. Their insights into the world are valuable because the way they move, work, and engage is far different from how I did as a young adult in the early 2000s. That's why you need people on your ELC who are junior to you.

» **Peers.** There are a lot of ways to define your peers. They could be people who are the same age as you, in the same social circles, at your same career level, or people who you trust to review your work. A good method for defining your peers for your ELC is determining the people you can speak freely to without fear of judgment, shame, or misunderstanding. The point of having peers in your ELC is to have people going along this journey with you so you can learn and grow together.

» **Senior leaders.** Who do you admire in your organization? Who are your former colleagues or bosses who really exemplify empathy? These are going to be individuals who are further along in their career than you are in yours; not necessarily members of senior leadership but people who have an idea of what you are currently experiencing and can give you guidance from the other side.

WARNING

As you grow — both in your life and in your careers — you may think that because you have already been through what a junior person is experiencing you have automatic understanding. You have insights, yes, but you do not know what it is like to be doing their job in this specific moment. Having someone junior on your ELC gives you perspective on how you come across to people in their position. That information is invaluable.

» **People outside of the organization.** It's easy for us to get our goals entangled with that of the organization to which we belong. Once you are enmeshed in the culture, you can more easily see yourself moving comfortably within it. You adapt the language, include yourself in the future plans, and champion the products and services. This is why it's important to have some ELC members who are not within your organization; they instead bring with them different organizational policies and possibilities. They provide you with unbiased, fresh perspectives and diverse insights that have nothing to do with your company.

REMEMBER

Your ELC is made up of people who will give you advice and tips. They help you shape your mindset with their knowledge of you and your behaviors. Your ELC, however, are not mentors. Mentors are guides and teachers that offer you career and life development; your ELC is a group of strategic advisors whose primary goal is to guide you toward success in this one category. Choose your council with that in mind.

Identifying Empathy Mentors

We all eventually come to a point where we realize that in order to continue to move ourselves forward, we need help. Enter the mentor. *Mentors* have two primary functions. The first is career related; they provide advice to enhance your professional performance and development. The second is the psychological function; mentors act as role models and provide a support system for their mentees.

Empathy mentors take this a step further. There is a palpable emotional component with empathy naturally since the root of being empathetic is listening to and trying to understand other people's perspectives. *Empathy mentors*, therefore, provide you guidance on how to be a better empath; they'll also offer emotional support during that journey. They'll listen with both care and curiosity.

When looking for empathy mentors, you need to focus on three things: their behaviors, how they make you feel, and what their teams look like. All three of these together show you who they are as a person, as a leader, and as an empath.

What are their behaviors?

Empathy is a verb, a choice, and it is very easy to see who is making the choice to be empathetic versus those who are not. This is why you can't fake empathy for long. It shows up — or doesn't — in the smallest moments: a pause before responding, a question asked instead of advice given, a room that feels different after someone walks into it.

TIP

When you're looking for mentors to guide your empathetic leadership development, skip the résumé and watch how they act. Their behaviors tell you everything their title cannot. Here are the three main things to look for:

- **How they speak.** Empaths approach the way they speak to others with an incredibly high amount of consideration. They deeply understand the power of their voice both literally — their words, their tone, their pauses — and figuratively. Because of this, they take a beat before they speak; this gives them a chance to be measured and intentional in their response. They also use collaborative language that makes others feel supported and part of the team.

  When empathetic leaders speak, they do so with care. They accept other people's feelings, even if they disagree with them. They avoid well-meaning but harmful phrases such as "You shouldn't feel this way" or "I know exactly how you feel," switching those out with language that is more validating. They ask open-ended questions instead of offering quick advice, and they ask thoughtful questions to understand another person's perspective better.

- **How they listen.** Listening is just as active a part of any conversation as speaking. Look for mentors who take that seriously. Empaths listen to understand, not just to reply. They don't interrupt when others are speaking. And they know that dominating the conversation means not only taking away from people sharing, but also from them learning something they didn't know.

  They listen intently. Empaths read others' facial expressions, body language, and tone of voice to sense what people are feeling. And they do this constantly, even when people aren't speaking. They know that others are constantly communicating — how they feel, what they think, what is impacting them — so empaths, especially empathetic leaders, are *always* paying attention to what's going on with the people on their team.

- **How they engage.** The natural next step is what speaking and listening look like in action. Real empaths appreciate that their words only convey a part of the message. They move through their interactions knowing that most people will forget exactly what they said, but they'll always remember how they felt when they walked away. This is what people mean when they talk about *psychological safety;* empaths create a safe space for people to express themselves without fear of criticism or shame.

  When you look for your empathy mentors, always look at the flow of conversations in the team as a whole. How the individuals on the team engage with one another is a direct reflection of how the leader engaged with them.

REMEMBER

When you're looking for an empathy mentor, don't listen to what they say about themselves. Watch what they do when no one is performing. Pay attention to how they respond when someone struggles. And look at what happens to the people around them over time. Empathy leaves a trail, and that trail is always visible if you know what to look for.

How do they make you feel?

I am, what would be considered by most standards, a very sensitive person. I have always felt things deeply, rarely walking away from an exchange unmoved by what just happened. My sensitivity lends itself well to empathy; I'm so sometimes painfully aware of my own feelings that it's easier to gauge others' feelings.

I can always tell when I'm around a person of high character. They move with a quiet confidence; they operate within what seems to be an endless well of peace and safety; and they view honesty as an opportunity to enhance, not harm. On the other end of that, there are also people I encounter who I just can never relax around. I just *know* they are judging me, quietly tracking my missteps or looking down on my choices. I can rarely prove it, but eventually what they really think or feel always comes to the surface. I'd feel more vindicated in being correct if being around them wasn't such a negative experience.

Some of the most impactful people in my life have been the ones who have accepted who I was — good and bad — and didn't judge me for it. Those individuals are usually incredibly successful in some way, and it's my belief that they just don't see any value in judging me or my life. These are usually the people who end up being the most helpful and encouraging as well; they hear I'm doing something in a creative way, and they jump immediately to curiosity and advocacy.

TIP

While those individuals will always find a reason why you can succeed, there are some people who will always find reasons why you can't. Some people will have a solution for every problem, and some people will have a problem for every solution. Invest your time in the people who are going to uplift you, empower you, and offer you advice from a place of optimism and reassurance.

Empathy mentors should be people in your life who you not only respect, but also who you feel comfortable enough around to share unbridled honesty. These individuals should make you feel the way you are aiming for your team to feel when you are leading them — especially in difficult moments — because how these leaders make you feel is likely how they make their teams feel too. This matters deeply because it's real-life proof of what actually works, and it's a guide to the behaviors that you want to model on your own team.

WARNING

As important as it is to listen to your feelings, it's always imperative to identify where these feelings are originating. Is a negative feeling you get around a person as a result of their actions, or is it stemming from your own insecurity, fear, or a lack of confidence? Your feelings are valid; they can also trick you into believing something about yourself that isn't true — both in good and bad ways. Be honest about why someone makes you feel a certain way before you consider them as an empathy mentor.

What do their teams look like?

Individual actions are important, as are how people make you feel. Both of those things matter when choosing a mentor because you know that person is capable of both behaving empathetically and creating an environment where you feel safe enough to be vulnerable. What you really need to pay attention, however, is results. Because results can be seen, and they can be measured. That means that those leaders have figured out how to balance empathy with accountability and results; and their impact speaks for itself.

Teams led by empathetic leaders have several things in common, but here are two aspects to focus on when choosing an empathy mentor:

- **Their performance.** Teams led by empathetic leaders are more productive and, therefore, perform better. A 2019 study published in the *Journal of*

Leadership and Organizational Studies (https://journals.sagepub.com/loi/jlo) found that for every 10 percent increase in empathetic leadership, you can expect roughly a two percent increase in team performance. What does that two percent look like in real life? It translates to approximately $1,000 in additional annual performance value per person. Empathetic leadership also has a positive correlation with job satisfaction, which in turn influences both innovation and performance.

TIP

When choosing empathetic leader mentors, look for the leaders who validate and don't just direct. Most leaders just tell people what to do; empathetic leaders also acknowledge *how it feels* to do it. Instead of saying "Figure it out," an empathetic leader will say something like "I can see that this is frustrating — here's what I think is happening and here's how I can help." That small acknowledgment shifts the employee's mental state from defensive to engaged, and engaged employees are productive ones. Another thing to look out for is how the leaders treat people; more specifically, how they adjust their approach from person to person. Empathetic leaders know that managing everyone the same way — with the same feedback style, same expectations, same communication — is inefficient; they recognize that different people need different things. Because they actually understand their people, they can match their style to what each individual needs to perform at a high level. Finally, take notice of how empathetic leaders also create safety around failure. Most leaders, even if they don't realize it, signal that mistakes are costly. Empathetic leaders do the opposite. Why? Because they know that training in something new and failing is the path to both individual growth and everyday innovation. And empathy-driven managers know that everyday innovation is proven to be a major performance booster.

REMEMBER

Regular leaders manage the *work*. Empathetic leaders manage the *person doing the work*. And as performance ultimately comes from people — their motivation, their creativity, their willingness to go beyond the minimum — that distinction is crucial.

» **Their communication.** Good team communication shows itself in several ways and the biggies are engagement, alignment, and trust. People surface problems earlier, disagreements get raised instead of suppressed, feedback flows in both directions, and ideas get shared rather than held back. And studies show that leaders who engage in empathetic communication can alleviate feelings of isolation among employees, fostering a more connected and supportive work environment.

A good empathy mentor will have created an environment that's safe enough to speak honestly. A 2026 survey of 300 employees published in communication the workplace journal *Business and Professional Communication Quarterly* (https://journals.sagepub.com/home/bcq) found that empathy was the strongest predictor of that safety, which drives adaptive attitudes and engagement. That empathy also drives inclusion, and inclusive teams make higher-quality decisions. Research by Cloverpop (a decision intelligence start-up; www.cloverpop.com) found that teams enabled by leaders who actively listen and invite diverse perspectives make better business decisions 87 percent of the time and make them twice as fast.

TIP

What do you look for in an empathy mentor when it comes to their team communication? One of the first things I notice is when someone responds to an emotion before they respond to the content, and empathetic leaders are excellent at this. Their teams know that the leader won't just jump straight to solutions because that makes their teams feel emotionally dismissed. People who feel acknowledged become more open, more collaborative, and more willing to keep conversations going. Another tell is a team that communicates in both directions. Non-empathetic leaders are very good at broadcasting: sending information downward. Empathetic leaders are focused on receiving — actively pulling information upwards — as well. They do check ins, they invite input, and they act on what they hear. And that final point is critical: If people share something and nothing changes, they stop sharing. Empathetic leaders close the loop, and that keeps the communication flowing.

REMEMBER

The best empathetic leadership mentors will show you how to make people feel seen, safe, worthwhile, and valued through their behaviors, how they make people feel, and the impact they have on their team.

Managing Your Empathetic Leadership Education

You've built your council. You've identified your mentors. Now comes the part that is entirely on you: the ongoing, self-directed work of becoming the leader you're committed to being. No council or mentor can do this for you. They can challenge you, reflect you back to yourself, and push you when you stall — but the daily investment in your own growth? That's yours. This section considers three ways to take ownership of that.

Surrounding yourself with the right people

TECHNICAL STUFF

"You are the average of the five people you spend the most time with." This famous line is attributed to motivational speaker Jim Rohn. And in some ways, it is accurate. Studies on social contagion show that behaviors such as obesity, smoking, happiness, and even loneliness spread through social networks, and not just from direct contact but up to three degrees of separation away. And beyond feelings, other research on peer effects consistently shows that the people around you influence your ambitions, habits, income expectations, and risk tolerance too.

While the core insight of the "five people" idea holds up, it falls short in many ways as well. It doesn't consider the context of those relationships; work colleagues, family, and close friends influence different domains of your life differently. And online and cultural influences, especially with our current state of constant connectivity, many people shaping your thinking aren't always people you've physically spent time with. The "five people" idea also takes your impact on others out of the equation entirely; you influence the people around you, and you choose which influences to internalize.

TIP

Who you surround yourself with may feel quite passive. But it's not, because *you* are not. Just by existing in the world — going to work, going to the gym, having outside-the-house hobbies — you are actively choosing who you are around. Yes, even at work; you have favorites and besties, or you have colleagues who you gravitate toward for after-work drinks and lunches. Be sure to invest some time into people who are empathetic; of course, you want to be around people who seek to understand you, but you also want to learn from them to further your own empathy journey.

Getting uncomfortable

I felt an immense level of fear when I first started out as a keynote speaker. I thought every stage was too big (figuratively) or too intimidating (literally); I was convinced that no one would want to listen to what I had to say. I didn't think my message was valuable enough, thought that my words would fall flat, and that people would think I was wasting their time. Some of that was justified; I didn't have any experience as a speaker, zero connections in the industry, and a very prominent speech impediment.

Some of that was confidence and self-esteem related and, of course, the fear of being in front of a group is a common (and evolutionary) one. But something I discovered along the way was that a part of my fear was actually a signal; maybe I was so afraid of a specific thing because I wanted to try it out but I felt immense fear that it wouldn't work. I discovered that whenever I felt uncomfortable, I shouldn't immediately run away from it. I should explore it. Why does it scare me? Am I in actual danger or is this my body's way of letting me know that this is something I should investigate?

We are socialized to *fear* fear. But what if that fear is telling us it's time for a change? The opposite of complacency isn't always activity; sometimes, it's discomfort. When it comes to finding empathy mentors, one of your goals should be to search for the people who intimidate you or even freak you out. Chapter 16 touches upon this (discussing triggers), but this section delves a bit deeper. There are two kinds of people to seek out when you are dipping your toe into discomfort:

- **People who challenge your views.** I know, I know. This feels like a battle you have already lost. But being around people who challenge your views does not mean entertaining disrespect, insults, or willful ignorance. It means having a conversation with a rational, thoughtful person who has a different opinion and is willing to discuss that opinion in detail. It also means that they will want to hear what you have to say as well.

  Voluntarily engaging with people who disagree with you on some core principles may seem counterproductive. The point here is to broaden your world view, not change it. And it's also good practice for when you need to have a higher control over your emotional regulation — such as at work. You need to know how to approach these situations from an empathetic place and not immediately jump to the defensive.

  TIP

  You may worry about losing your cool in these situations. Getting worked up, so angry, so beside yourself that you lose your grip on your emotions. When you feel yourself slipping away from who you want to become, remind yourself of this: You are in control. Emotional regulation is an important part of empathy because it helps you think clearly.

- **People who don't look like you.** How diverse is your group of friends? Your neighborhood? What kind of media do you consume? Who is it created by? And how do you find that content? It's very natural for you to want to seek out and invest in others that you have things in common with. We all want to look at the people in our lives and see the best parts of ourselves reflected back. The issue with that is we end up in echo chambers; we make our worlds smaller because we refuse to widen them.

  TIP

  Spend time with people who do not look like you. Your experience is uniquely yours for several reasons, one of those being the way the world sees you. Whether you like it or not, you are constantly being judged by how you look. It's not coming from a bad place; it's human nature to gravitate toward those that we either see ourselves in or that we want to see ourselves in. However, get into the habit of having conversations with people who don't look like you. Their experience with the world will be vastly different from yours just because of how they present. Make friends with people considerably older and younger, people who are of a different race or ethnicity, and people who don't look like the ones you'd regularly gravitate toward.

REMEMBER

Playing it safe feels good because you are doing something that comes easily and naturally. But doing things the way you've always done them isn't going to broaden your mind. Putting yourself in uncomfortable situations is how empathy grows.

DOING YOUR RESEARCH

There are many great books on empathy. Look for ones that blend research with real-world application — titles such as *Dare to Lead* by Brené Brown (Random House, 2018), *Empathy* by Roman Krznaric (Penguin Books, 2014), or *The Empathy Effect* by Helen Riess (Sounds True, 2018) give you both the science and the practice. Don't just read them; work them. Underline, annotate, and return to the parts that challenge you most.

But books on empathy aren't the only way to expand your knowledge. Here are a few other topics and areas to look into:

- **Psychology and neuroscience.** Empathy isn't just a soft skill — it's a brain function and understanding how it works neurologically makes you better at using it intentionally. Reading in this space helps you understand concepts such as mirror neurons, emotional contagion, cognitive versus affective empathy, and why stress physically impairs your ability to read other people. You don't need a degree to do this; you need curiosity and a willingness to go one layer deeper than the surface.
- **Fiction.** This one surprises people but consider it for a moment. When you're reading literary fiction, you're consuming not only what people are saying and thinking but also what they're feeling and seeing. You are experiencing the world from another perspective. Reading literary fiction, then, improves your ability to understand other people's mental states — what psychologists call *theory of mind*. Fiction forces you to inhabit perspectives that are not your own, sit with moral ambiguity, and feel your way through experiences you've never lived. That is empathy training in disguise!
- **Online courses.** Platforms such as Coursera (`www.coursera.org`), LinkedIn Learning (`www.linkedin.com/learning`), and even university extensions offer structured empathy and emotional intelligence coursework that provides both accountability and credentials.
- **Documentaries and film.** Look into visual storytelling about real human experiences — poverty, illness, injustice, cultural difference — because that builds perspective in a visceral way that text just sometimes cannot match.
- **Your own journal.** I'm a writer by trade, so I've been pretty diligent about keep journals on and off throughout most of my life. Looking back on them years later has been enlightening for my own personal development, but also for how I've viewed interactions with others. Reflective writing is a tool for building self-awareness, and that's the foundation of empathy. Studying yourself is research too!

IN THIS CHAPTER

» Identifying behaviors that reveal whether empathy is genuine or performative

» Assessing your team's empathy

» Conducting an empathy audit

Chapter 18

Measuring Growth without Measuring People

You've done the personal work. You've examined your triggers, practiced your patience, worked on your perspective, and shown up differently — more deliberately, more honestly, more humanly — than you did before you picked up this book. That work matters. It is the foundation everything else is built on. Now, it's time to figure out if it's working. Not for you, but for the people you lead, the culture you are building, the team who watch how you show up and quietly decide whether it is safe to show up that way themselves.

That is what this chapter is about. Not empathy as a personal practice, but empathy as a leadership output — something that can be observed, tracked, assessed, and grown with the same intentionality you would bring to any other strategic priority. Because empathetic leaders are not just modeling the behavior; they are imprinting it. This chapter gives you the tools to measure whether the imprint is actually taking hold . . . and what to do when it isn't.

Computing Your Data

There is a moment in every leader's development when the question shifts from "How do I become more empathetic?" to "Is my team becoming more empathetic because of how I lead them?" That changes everything about how you pay attention, what you track, and what you consider a success.

It is the difference between a leader who practices empathy and a leader who imprints it, quietly and consistently, into the culture of their team. Into how people talk to each other. Into how they handle the hard moments. Into whether the room feels different, safer, and more honest than it did six months ago. Into whether the behaviors you have been working on in yourself are beginning to show up, organically and independently, in the people around you.

Measure not just your empathy, but its reach. The data is there. Let's break down how to compute it.

Reviewing Key Empathy Behaviors

Think about the last time someone was genuinely patient with you. Not performatively patient — the strained, tight-lipped composure of someone waiting for you to finish so they could respond — but actually, unhurriedly present with you and whatever you were working through. Think about the last time someone tried, visibly and sincerely, to understand where you were coming from even when it would have been easier not to. Think about the last time you felt truly connected to a colleague. And not because the project was going well or the team was hitting its numbers, but because something real passed between you.

REMEMBER

Those moments are what *Key Empathy Behaviors* look like when they are working. They are also, not coincidentally, the moments that are hardest to manufacture, hardest to mandate, and hardest to measure. But you should try to do exactly that: to take three of the most human things a leader can practice and develop a clear enough picture of each so that you can actually see them, track them, and build toward more of them.

The three Key Empathy Behaviors are:

- **Patience.** Patience at work is the ability to remain calm, focused, and composed when facing challenging situations, rather than reacting with frustration. For empathetic leaders, patience at work is managing delays when projects fall behind schedule or unexpected hurdles arise; allowing colleagues to finish speaking without interrupting and truly processing their input; and responding calmly rather than with anger.

Patience is the foundation of empathy because it encourages active listening as well as investing real time and energy into the thoughts and ideas of others. People who practice patience are true masters of emotional regulation; they are able to stay composed under pressure because they can identify their emotional triggers, assess their emotional state, and implement strategies to align their feelings with desired outcomes. When your emotions are regulated, you are much more likely to speak in a tone of voice that won't cause hurt or conflict. For more on patience, check out Chapter 8.

WARNING

The goal of patience goes beyond keeping your emotions in check: it's about getting clarity. Some researchers argue that up to 90 percent of conflicts are a result of misunderstandings. When you slow down — focusing on listening, confirming you heard correctly, and giving people a chance to fully explain themselves — you greatly minimize the chance of a minor disagreement turning into a major problem.

TIP

To practice real patience when you're at work, try this: take a beat. Before you respond, wait three seconds. Take a breath. Think about what was said to you or the situation as a whole. And then, when you do speak, summarize what's happening.

- **Perspective.** A natural step in engaging empathy, perspective-taking means actively seeking information to understand another person's view, rather than just relying on contextual clues. At the core, pursuing perspective is centering a learning mindset. People who naturally possess this mindset are curious, lifelong learners who revel in growing their knowledge. They often love reading and watching documentaries, but they also love hearing other people's stories and experiences.

  Perspective-taking when it's uncomfortable, when you disagree, or if there's a chance that things could devolve into an argument is a thought exercise. You aren't trying to *feel* what the other person is feeling; you are simply trying to understand and consider where they are coming from. This is why perspective-taking is only one part of empathy — not the whole shebang; at this point, you are just learning and not feeling.

  Part of the reason it's difficult to pursue perspective at work is because we didn't choose our coworkers; it's easier to listen to those people we choose or have some deep connection with (such as our family members and our close friends). You feel your control has been taken away, so as a result you have less control over your reactions and you may allow your feelings to supersede your better judgment. To find out more about perspective-taking, head to Chapter 9.

TIP

Here's a tip to help you practice perspective when it feels impossible: remember the *why*. You ultimately all have the same goal; you may just have differing opinions of how to achieve that goal. So, if you feel a situation is about to go off the rails, pull that *why* from your back pocket to keep everyone (including yourself) on track.

» **Connection.** We all want to be seen, heard, and understood. And even if that understanding from another person is harder to come by, we want to see that people are at least trying. Because that's what matters most to us: when people are attempting to include you — your views, your opinions, your lived experiences — in their worldview. This is where connection happens, in the sincerity of the effort.

Real connection, like empathy, is a continuous exercise. To form deep bonds and share emotional experiences requires you to keep showing up, especially when it's difficult. But that ultimately is what empathy looks like: caring about others enough to walk side by side with them in every terrain. Yes, that includes your colleagues.

WARNING

If empathy drives connection, sympathy halts it. Think for a moment about an onion and its many layers. Empathy is removing one layer of that onion at a time to keeping uncovering what lies beneath until you get to the core of the situation, of the problem, of the experience, of the person's *why*. Sympathy is cutting the onion in half, observing that it does indeed have layers, and assuming that you know everything going on between those layers because you've seen that they exist. Connection is the act of removing — with care and caution — every layer.

TIP

Real connection almost always happens in the silences, in sitting with your emotions. Why? Because you're signaling to the person sharing that their experiences and feelings are so valuable that you are willing to invest time and energy into them. So, here's a fun connection exercise you can start today: Instead of asking "How are you?" ask a deeper and more direct question. Something like "What's taking up most of your headspace today?" or "What is something you're genuinely excited about right now?"

Key Empathy Behaviors are about how your actions drive other people's behaviors. Patience calms you and comforts them. Perspective informs you and empowers them. Connection activates you and validates them.

Measuring empathy

I am a firm believer that everything is a data point. Sure, there will be times in life when you are experiencing a resounding success; you won't need to look back and take anything significant away from those moments other than an enthusiastic "Attaboy!" There are also times when you are a part of a full-blown failure, and you'll have every reason to erase everything you did to get there and start from scratch. These situations are extremes, the very edges of the bell curve. Everything in between is an opportunity to learn, pivot, grow, and experiment. Empathy is no different.

REMEMBER

To fully measure empathy, you need to identify your *scope*. This is a three-fold process, and it entails:

1. **Defining the behaviors both driving and deterring empathy on your team.**
2. **Determining how those behaviors are impacting your team: their success (productivity and project management, for example), their communication, and the overall culture.**
3. **Disclosing your findings to your team and getting their feedback through direct surveys on the situation as a whole.**

TECHNICAL STUFF

Before breaking down this process for Key Empathy Behaviors, be sure to understand the different categories of research. *Quantitative research* measures performance and tests theories through numbers, percentages, and metrics. *Qualitative research* focuses on extracting meaning through text and observation. Quantitative answers the "how many" and "how much" questions. Qualitative answers the "how" and "why" questions.

In this process of measuring empathy, your first step is quantitative; it's identifying very specific and clear behaviors that most people can easily point out. The second step is more qualitative; it goes beyond just observing the behaviors to determining how they influence the team. These first two steps are what you as the leader are seeing transpire: outwardly in meetings or conversations as well as behind the scenes in the quality of the work in the finished product. The third step is collaborative, and it's just as important as the first two steps. For people to want to change, they need to be an active participant in the process and that only happens with ownership. It doesn't need to be a lot but your team needs to feel that their experiences and input are reflected in these changes. It's time to break this down using the Key Empathy Behaviors.

Patience

Chapter 8 describes how to practice patience. Patience is one of the most misread behaviors on a team. It looks like stillness from the outside, which makes impatience easy to miss until it has already done damage: in a meeting that derailed, a relationship that quietly frayed, or a decision that got rushed past the person who needed more time to process it.

REMEMBER

Identify patience within your team in the following ways:

- **Quantitative.** How do your team members handle things like block tasks or slow feedback loops — do they escalate constructively or stall? What is the overall team response when they are under pressure — do people stay thoughtful when timelines slip or stakeholders push back? Do senior members give space for others to work through problems, or do they take over?

Key factors here include people's tone of voice, how hurried conversations and responses are, time-to-escalation on unresolved issues, interruption rates in meetings, and review turnaround time.

- **Qualitative.** What kind of things are you hearing in one-on-one conversations or in retrospective feedback? Phrases such as "I feel rushed" or "Decisions get made before I can contribute" are especially telling. How do people describe waiting periods — a general feeling of frustration or do they find productive uses of their time?
- **Direct surveys.** A few questions you can ask are: "When something is taking longer than expected, what's your typical first instinct?", "Can you describe a time you had to wait on a dependency and how you handled it?", and "How do you feel when a meeting is going off-track?"

WARNING

Patience is context-dependent. Someone who's impatient with bureaucracy might be wonderfully patient with a struggling teammate. Be sure to clarify what kind of patience matters most for your team's specific challenges.

Perspective

Perspective-taking (discussed in more detail in Chapter 9) is the empathy behavior most vulnerable to performance. It is easy to look like you are considering someone else's point of view without ever actually letting it land. What you are measuring here is not the appearance of open-mindedness — it is the evidence of it.

REMEMBER

Identify perspective within your team in the following ways:

- **Quantitative.** How often do team members reference other people's constraints or workloads when presenting a problem or a solution — or do they default to their own experience as the only relevant frame? In meetings, how frequently does someone build on another person's idea versus immediately redirecting to their own? When conflict arises, how quickly does it escalate versus resolve — and who is typically doing the work of de-escalation? Track how often decisions include documented consideration of stakeholder impact beyond the immediate team, and how frequently people ask clarifying questions before forming a position.

  Key factors here include how people frame problems — whether they lead with "I" or with "we," whether solution proposals acknowledge competing priorities, and whether feedback is delivered in terms of impact on others or only in terms of personal preference.
- **Qualitative.** In one-on-ones and team conversations, are people able to articulate why someone else might see a situation differently? And what's the

logic or experience behind that disagreement? Phrases such as "From their perspective, it probably looks like" or "I hadn't considered that they might be dealing with" are strong qualitative signals. So is the absence of those phrases.

Pay attention to how people talk about colleagues, stakeholders, and clients when those people are not in the room. That is where the unfiltered perspective-taking data lives. Also listen for how people process being wrong. Someone who can say "That's a fair point; I didn't have the full picture" is demonstrating perspective-taking in real time. Someone who immediately reframes or deflects when their position is challenged is showing you their limits.

» **Direct surveys.** A few questions you can ask are: "Tell me about a time you changed your mind as a result of a conversation with a colleague — what shifted for you?", "When you're in a disagreement at work, what's your process for trying to understand the other person's position?", and "Is there someone on this team whose perspective you find consistently hard to understand, and what do you think gets in the way?"

WARNING

Some people are great at performing perspective-taking — for example using nodding and paraphrasing — without actually letting the opposing views marinate a bit so they can actually consider them. The real signal is behavior change; if people aren't acting differently after hearing another viewpoint, it's time for a conversation.

Connection

Connection is the hardest empathy behavior to both fake over time and measure in the moment. It doesn't announce itself. It accumulates quietly in the small, consistent choices people make to treat each other as full human beings rather than functional colleagues, and it reveals itself most clearly not when things are going well but when they aren't. To dive deeper into how to connect with others, head to Chapter 10.

REMEMBER

Identify connection within your team in the following ways:

» **Quantitative.** How frequently are team members initiating non-task-related conversations with each other — not just responding to them but starting them? What is the participation distribution in team meetings — are the same two or three people carrying the conversation while others consistently remain peripheral? How often do people follow up after a colleague shares something difficult, personally or professionally? Track peer recognition patterns: who is acknowledging whom, how often, and whether that recognition flows in multiple directions or concentrates around the same individuals.

Key factors here include the ratio of transactional to relational communication on your team, response times to personal versus professional messages, and whether connection behaviors increase or decrease under pressure — because a team that connects only when things are easy hasn't actually built connection, they've built comfort.

- **Qualitative.** Connection is one of the harder things to observe directly because its most meaningful expressions are quiet. Look for the small, consistent signals: whether people remember details about each other's lives without being prompted, whether someone who is visibly struggling gets checked on by peers before it reaches you, and whether new team members are being actively brought in or left to find their own footing.

  Pay attention to the energy in the room before and after meetings. The quality of those unstructured margins — the two minutes before the agenda starts, the informal exchange at the end of a call — tells you a great deal about the relational temperature of a team. A team that goes immediately transactional the moment the meeting starts and disconnects the moment it ends is missing an element of connection.

- **Direct surveys.** A few questions you can ask are: "How well do you feel you know the people you work most closely with — not just professionally, but as people?", "When something is hard at work, is there someone on this team you would feel comfortable going to?", and "Can you describe a moment when you felt genuinely supported by a colleague — what did they do and what did it mean to you?"

Using your data

Across all three steps — the quantitative, the qualitative, and the direct survey — one principle holds: The data you collect is only as useful as the conversations it generates. Numbers without context produce conclusions. Conclusions without conversation produce compliance at best and resentment at worst.

TIP

When you bring your findings back to your team — which step three of the process requires — do not arrive with a diagnosis. Arrive with a question. Share what you observed, name what you are trying to understand, and then make space for their experience of it to be different from yours. Because it will be. And that difference is not a problem to resolve; it is the most important data in the room.

REMEMBER

The goal of measuring empathy is not to produce a perfect score. It is to produce a shared understanding — between you and your team — of where you currently are, where you want to go, and what it is going to take to close the distance. That understanding, built together, is both the measure of your empathy and the evidence of it.

Appraising Beyond the Metrics

What if the most important thing that happened on your team this quarter never made it into a report? What if the breakthrough wasn't a number, a retention rate, an engagement score, or a productivity metric but was instead a *moment?* A conversation that went differently than it would have gone before. A silence that was held instead of filled. A person who said something honest that they had spent months swallowing. A leader who listened all the way to the end before responding.

None of that shows up in the data. All of it matters.

Some progress is impossible to track in real time. You cannot see it accumulating or chart it week over week. You only recognize it when you look back — when you notice, from a distance, that something shifted. You are not who you were and the team is not what it was. That the culture has moved, quietly and without announcement, toward something better.

REMEMBER

Measuring empathy growth requires a different kind of attention. Less analysis. More observation. Less certainty about what the numbers mean. More comfort sitting with what you can feel but cannot yet fully articulate. That is not a weakness in the methodology. It is an honest acknowledgment of what growth actually looks like from the inside.

This section explores what to look for when the metrics run out.

Observing instead of measuring

Does anybody else feel their stomach tighten when someone brings up politics? Whether its current events or personal beliefs, it feels like any time politics comes up in conversation, that conversation begins to deteriorate. If we're lucky, it happens slowly enough that someone can stop the decay before it turns into dust. Usually, however, we are not lucky.

The worst of these fallouts happen within families. It's quite easy to dismiss a stranger or acquaintance in a negative light when you disagree with them. You don't think twice about second-guessing their character or questioning their intelligence. But when you are personally attached to someone who it is more difficult to just blindly write off — perhaps a parent, sibling, or another close family member — these conversations cut deeper. You can leave feeling personally assaulted when they are on the other side of the issue. And, just as difficult as it is to get past the disagreement, it's hard to go back to the relationship you had before. The one where there was a mutual respect and positive feelings.

REMEMBER

It's in these conversations where we really need to be practicing empathy, when it feels impossible to think or feel any other way than we currently do. These, however, are the hardest moments to do so. And that's why in those moments, the measurement is in the movement. What does that mean? It means that sometimes the biggest change isn't your ability to suddenly see someone else's perspective clearly; the change is in slowly inching closer to really hearing their ideas.

It took me years to learn this. Years of extremely negative feelings of disgust, confusion, disappointment, and anger toward some people I really cared about. Though I'd prefer to avoid conversations about politics entirely, sometimes that just not possible. So, my goal in these conversations is always to learn — not explain, not judge, not dismiss. In these moments, I am there to simply hear the other person out. I accept that there is a very small likelihood that I will agree with what they say. I also accept that I will have very strong feelings about it. But I don't need to allow my feelings to overtake me, because that's not empathy.

This is an observable yet difficult-to-measure change. And as an empathetic leader this is something for you to focus on. You aren't always going to be able to pinpoint every single thing that is better and more empathetic about your team. You also may not be able to see what exactly changed, but you will be able to feel a transformation. Here are a few things to look for in this process:

- **Affective responses.** You know how that first twinge of discomfort, hurt, or anger feels physically. Your body stiffens. Your breath shortens. Your face tightens. And your gestures quickly follow suit. Your hands might clench and your arms might swing a bit faster. Your eyes may lose some warmth, and your body language goes from open to closed. Your affective responses will change as you gradually lean more toward empathy in stressful situations, and so will your team's. There will be more eye contact, gentler facial expressions, and softer gestures when your overall team empathy is improving.
- **Behavioral changes.** The biggest change toward empathy you'll see in the non-measurable capacity is how people respond to each other. These behavioral changes are slight but palpable. Your team will have more genuine, other-oriented responses rather than self-focused reactions; this includes forgiveness, offering support, and helping one another.
- **Communication shifts.** Communicating with empathy (see Chapter 10) can be a very easy, direct way to see that the overall culture is heading in the right direction. You of course want to hear your team asking follow-up and clarifying questions, and that they are speaking with measured tones. But many of the communication shifts are going to be in what's not said. You'll begin to notice slightly longer pauses between responses; that's a sign of people actually listening and processing the information they just received.

TIP

Another behavior to look out for is how people respond to the experience of others, both in negative and positive situations. In positive moments especially, recognize how your team empathizes with another person's positive emotions. Because these opportunities are (hopefully) way more frequent than negative emotions, they will have more chances to really perfect this. You'll notice the differences in how long they engage in conversations, the sincerity of their tone of voice, and the warmth of their body language.

Using reflection and feedback as growth instruments

I love fitness; I've been an avid gym goer on and off for my entire adult life. I remember my first time walking around the weight filled with confusion, intimidation, and awe. There were people in there who had clearly been lifting weights for longer than I had been alive, and it showed. I wanted to be like them: strong and driven and gritty. But that intimidation got the better of me, so I stopped going to that area of the gym and stuck to cardio machines.

Over the years, I slowly got more comfortable with the gym and fitness in general. I picked up running for a while. I was really consistent with that for several years until a very scary and loud dog chased me down the block one morning. After that, the fear came back and I took a break.

A few years later, I got the itch again and joined a gym in my hometown. Social media was beginning to gain a lot of popularity around this time, and I was introduced to fitness models and competitions. They were so in shape and confident and gorgeous, and I wanted to be just like them. This was the first time I started seriously lifting weights, working mostly with dumbbells and machines but too scared to touch a barbell. When I did try to do deadlifts, I hurt my back badly and, again, I stopped going to the gym because of fear and uncertainty.

Something good did come out of this, however. I learned that the best way to keep my back pain at bay was to do core workouts. I did some research and found out about reformer Pilates. This was around 2010, and Pilates hadn't picked up in popularity yet; but I tried it, and I was hooked. My back pain disappeared, I was stronger and more flexible than ever, and I learned so much about what my body was capable of.

But, as it so often does, life happens. And I had to stop going. I took another few years off of fitness, but I never forgot how good it felt to physically work my body to failure. I'd started traveling quite extensively for work at this point, so it was really challenging to stay committed to any real fitness routine. I eventually started going to group classes with a friend of mine. And I was pretty consistent for a few years.

Unfortunately, I stopped again in 2020, as a result of the Covid-19 pandemic. And for six months, I had a chance to really take stock of what I'd want to invest my energy in to when the gyms started to open back up again. I kept going back to weightlifting, so I finally tried it in earnest at a local gym that was focused almost exclusively on heavy dumbbell workouts. I did that consistently for four years until I relocated to a different area; that's when I picked up CrossFit and functional fitness. And I've been committed to that ever since.

Now, I know what you're thinking: what does any of this have to do with measuring empathy? Well, everything.

I look back on my fitness journey — the injuries, the weight fluctuations, the fear, the discomfort, the uncertainty of my own abilities — and I only see progress. While I was in it, I saw a lot of failure. Quitting. Shame. Fear. It's hard to start something, get decent at it, and then have to stop it for whatever reason. Of course, everything looks different from the other side.

REMEMBER

The operative word here is *journey*. Progress is neither linear nor perfectly quantifiable; sometimes you feel a change before you actually see it. Often, progress is taking a few steps back. It's being knocked down or humbled. It's messing up, destroying good will, losing relationships, or feeling so defeated that all you can do is sit in silence and be angry with yourself.

It is in those moments that you pick up the pieces and start your forward progress again. Can it feel demoralizing to walk that same well-tread path in your journey two, three, or four times? Of course. But doing it again means you get to do it better because you have more data. And taking that step forward, no matter how many times your feet have touched that same ground, is growth.

REMEMBER

You will fail at empathy many times. I know I do, and I talk and write about this for a living! What I've discovered, however, is that just because you *failed once* does not mean you are *failing*.

Outlining Your Empathy ROIs

Most leaders know how to measure outputs. Revenue, retention, productivity, engagement scores: these are the familiar currencies of organizational performance and most leaders have spent years learning to speak fluently in them.

What most leaders have not been taught is how to account for the investments that don't convert cleanly into those currencies. The conversation that kept someone from leaving. The moment of transparency that rebuilt trust after a rupture.

The acknowledgment that was specific enough and timely enough that someone carried it with them for months. These are real returns. They compound over time in ways that eventually show up in the measurable metrics; but by the time they do show up, the connection back to the empathetic practice that produced them is almost impossible to trace.

Outlining your empathy *return on investments* (ROIs — the tangible outcomes that result from treating empathy as a discipline you invest in and measure, not a personality trait you either have or don't) is an attempt to trace it anyway. Not with false precision, but with the kind of honest, structured reflection that turns experience into learning. Empathy without reflection is just behavior; empathy with reflection becomes a practice. And a practice, unlike a behavior, can be refined, expanded, and — crucially — taught to others. Five lenses help you to review your empathy investment with the same rigor and honesty you would bring to any other strategic assessment:

» **What worked.** First, some leveling. You might want to look at what worked as a victory lap, a big pat on the back for your success. While this is warranted, stay measured. What worked isn't just a celebration; it's intelligence. The goal is to understand *why* something worked with enough precision that you can reproduce it intentionally.

  When assessing what worked, always consider if it worked because of the approach versus it working because of the timing, the person, or the circumstance. Did something work because of your empathy skills or because it was a Friday afternoon and everyone felt rushed to get to the weekend? Keep a tab on these types of distinctions when you are trying to replicate what worked.

  TIP

  Something to consider is the *delayed return*. Some of the most important empathetic leadership moves don't register as working until months later (when someone stays who almost left, when a team navigates a crisis with a cohesion that didn't exist a year ago, when a person takes a risk they never would have taken in a lower-trust environment, for example). Sometimes, you have to look backward — not just forward — to find evidence of what worked.

» **What failed.** Like success, failure is also a data point. Failure in empathy practice, however, is a bit different from failure in most other leadership competencies. Your instinct when you fail at empathy may be to feel shame, but empathy failures are not always an issue of questionable character or a lack of emotional intelligence (for more on empathy gaps, see Chapter 14).

  TIP

  Your urge may be to either spiral or minimize instead of analyzing what went wrong. Instead, get curious about what happened. Apply the same diagnostic rigor to empathy failures that you would to any other performance gap. Failure has different causes that require different responses. There is the failure of skill, where you didn't know how to do the thing. There is the failure of will, where you likely felt uncomfortable and didn't have the drive to do the thing even though you knew exactly what to do. And there is the failure of circumstance, where you were too depleted, too triggered, or too caught off guard to access what you actually had.

The ROI of examining empathy failures also includes actively seeking out the failures you haven't been told about. The conversation that seemed fine from your side but landed badly on theirs. The decision you made transparently that your team experienced as a betrayal. The encouragement you gave that someone heard as a dismissal. This requires the psychological safety that empathetic leadership builds. In other words, your ability to find your failures is itself a measure of your empathy progress.

» **What is easy to scale.** Empathy is more than just individual; it is organizational. *Scaling* means embedding the practice you take as an individual leader into systems, structures, and cultural norms that persist regardless of whether you are present or not.

TIP

Identify your *highest-leverage empathy practices.* These are the ones that, when consistently repeated, produced disproportionate cultural impact. Usually they're the little things. As a keynote speaker, I spend a lot of time talking about the small, everyday actions that are the true building blocks of empathy. Things such as following up to demonstrate that you remember, the public acknowledgment that models the behavior you want, or the moment of transparency that gives everyone else permission to be honest. These are easy to scale not because they are easy to do, but because they are easy to repeat and easy to teach.

Also consider what couldn't scale. Just because it worked doesn't mean it's a sustainable and scalable for the path moving forward. Many of the most empathetic behaviors are one-offs: a particular person engaging in a specific moment in a very unique relationship. The ROI of that work is real, even if it can't be measured, realized, or replicated.

REMEMBER

Knowing the difference between what to systemize and what to protect as irreducibly human is itself a mark of empathetic leadership.

» **What resonated.** Resonance is different from effectiveness. Something can be effective without resonating; it produces the desired outcome but leaves people feeling managed rather than genuinely seen. And something can resonate deeply without immediately producing a measurable outcome; it lands, it matters, it shifts something in the relationships, and the benefit comes later and indirectly.

WARNING

Resonance is akin to a pulse check; it is personal and therefore uneven. What resonates with one person on your team will land flatly with another. This isn't because one of them is wrong, but because resonance is about the intersection of your approach and their specific emotional reality. The ROI for you, as the leader, is to diversify your empathy repertoire rather than finding a one-size-fits-all approach and standardizing it across the board.

Keep in mind that there will be times when things resonate that you didn't intend. Sometimes, the thing that lands most deeply is not the prepared thing; it's the unscripted moment, the admission you almost didn't make, or the question you asked because you genuinely didn't know the answer. These accidental resonances are data, too. They tell you something about what your team actually needs versus what you planned to give them.

REMEMBER

A big part of empathy is meeting people exactly where they are. The leaders who resonate most broadly are the ones who have enough range to meet different people differently.

» **What got pushback.** Like resonance, pushback is incredibly nuanced. It's usually hushed, spoken softly or silent dissidence. There will always be pushback, even on empathy initiatives, but that isn't a sign that the work isn't worth doing. It's a sign that the work is real enough to provoke a reaction. And that reaction, handled appropriately, is itself an empathy opportunity.

Several different kinds of pushback exist. *Skeptical pushback* sounds like "I've seen this before and it didn't stick." This is a trust issue rooted in history and requires consistency over time, not a better argument. *Philosophical pushback* sounds like "I don't think this is what leadership is for." This is a values conversation and deserves to be engaged with directly rather than dismissed. *Protective pushback* sounds like "If I open here, I will be exposed." This is a safety issue and requires the leader to demonstrate, not declare, that vulnerability is not a liability in this environment. And *performative pushback* sounds like "I'm seen as tough and I need to maintain that." This is an identity issue and is often the most resistant to change because it's about optics, not empathy.

Pushback is information about where the culture currently is, not evidence that the culture cannot change. The team member who rolls their eyes at the word empathy is telling you something important about their history with leaders who used that word without meaning it. That is not cynicism for its own sake. That is self-protection built from experience. Meeting it with defensiveness closes the door. Meeting it with genuine curiosity — "Tell me more about that" — is the empathy move that begins to change the dynamic.

TIP

Sometimes, pushback is right. Sometimes the resistance to an empathy initiative was legitimate; maybe the timing was wrong, the approach was tone-deaf, or the initiative was designed without input from the people it was meant to serve. The ROI of honest pushback is the recalibration it produces when you actually listen to it. If you can say "The pushback on that taught me something, and here's what I changed," you are modeling the very thing you are trying to build.

REMEMBER

ROIs, especially when it comes to empathy, are not a final exam. There is no passing score, no threshold of empathy ROI that means you have arrived and can stop paying attention. The leaders who are most worth following are not the ones who figured it out; they are the ones who never stopped looking. Who kept returning to the same honest questions with the same genuine willingness to be changed by what they found. That is the practice. That is all it has ever been.

What worked teaches you what to repeat. What failed teaches you where to grow. What scaled tells you what your culture is ready to hold. What resonated tells you who your people actually are, underneath the professional performance of who they need to be at work. And what got pushback tells you where the real work is still waiting for you. None of these are destinations. All of them are directions.

REMEMBER

Measuring empathy is not about reducing it to a number. It is about paying a different kind of attention. It is about developing the discipline to look at your leadership honestly — at what it is producing in the people around you, in the culture you are building, in the distance between who you are as a leader on your best days and who you are on your hardest ones — and using that honesty to close the gap.

5
The Part of Tens

IN THIS PART . . .

Demystify myths about what empathetic leadership looks like in real time.

Realize the common mistakes made by empathetic leaders.

Reframe empathy struggles as moments for introspection, growth, and evolution.

IN THIS CHAPTER

» Recognizing the difference between being nice and being empathetic

» Replacing the myths about empathy that quietly limit your leadership

» Reframing empathy as a practiced skill rather than as a personality trait

Chapter 19

Ten Myths about Empathetic Leadership

Empathy has an image problem. It's often mistaken for niceness, softness, slowness, a checkbox, or a personality trait you either have or don't. Believing that any of these myths could be true is costing leaders more than they realize. This chapter takes on ten of the most common myths about empathetic leadership, one at a time, so you can stop confusing the real thing for its imitators.

Empathetic Leaders Prioritize Being Nice

Niceness is about surface comfort; empathy is about genuine understanding. For that reason, being nice can actually be unkind. It avoids the hard truths that people need to grow. Empathetic leaders know that not every honest conversation will be pleasant.

Emotional Softness Is of the Utmost Importance

Empathy is not about being emotionally pliable or easily moved; it's about emotional steadiness to further understanding. Softness in tone should be utilized as a tool — not a value — because emotional softness without boundaries is not supporting your efforts in being empathetic; it opens the door for you to be taken advantage of. The strongest empathetic leaders combine warmth with resolve.

Empathy Is Unprofessional

If you're aiming to get the best possible performance out of the people you lead — sustainably, over time, in a way that doesn't burn them out or break them down — then empathy is not unprofessional. Empathy is professionalism's highest expression. The leaders that matter the most in the years ahead are the ones who have the courage to close the gap between the two. Those leaders understand that being fully present with people they lead is not a weakness to manage; it is *the job*.

Empathy Always Leads to Harmony

Empathy can be a path to a peaceful, conflict-free team. Usually, however, people chasing harmony are actually actively avoiding conflict. This is rooted in a desire to be liked, to keep the peace, and to make sure that no one leaves a meeting or interaction upset.

REMEMBER

Empathy doesn't promise that everyone will agree or that decisions will be painless. What it does promise, however, is something more useful and honest: people will feel genuinely considered. The leaders who are chasing harmony are building sandcastles. The leaders who are building trust through empathy are building something that will hold.

Empathy Means Slowing Down

Being empathetic means being intentional. Now, does sometimes that intention mean slowing down? Sure, but speed isn't always an indicator of empathy. It is important to take a moment before you respond to fully process what people say to you. But taking a few extra seconds to get clarity before you respond can actually save time in the future; it combats misunderstandings down the line, relieving you of potential disagreements and hurt feelings.

WARNING

"Slowing down" gets a bad rap. Because modern society equates speed with productivity, performance, and value, taking a few extra moments to do anything is viewed negatively. It's often viewed as an indicator of laziness or even failure. But research suggests that slowing down allows for increased intentionality, better mental health, and higher-quality results in life in general.

Empathy Is an HR Thing, Not a Strategy Thing

Empathy and strategy are not opposing forces. For the leaders who understand this, who have stopped waiting for Human Resources (HR) to handle the human side of their business and started treating it as the core of their competitive advantage, it never was.

TIP

Stop asking whether empathy belongs in strategy. Start asking what strategy costs you when empathy is absent.

You Have to Change Who You Are to Be an Empathetic Leader

Think of your closest friends; they're all different but you care about them all. Empathy is the same; it comes in many shapes and sizes. You don't need a personality transplant. It isn't a character type; it's a skill set.

REMEMBER

Being empathetic doesn't mean changing yourself. It means evolving to a more intentional, attentive version of yourself. More willing to stay present in the moments when disengaging would be easier. If you're naturally direct, you don't need to stop being direct. You need to make sure your directness is landing with care. That's not a different person; that's a better version of the one already there.

You Either Have the Capacity for Empathy or You Don't

Unlike eye color, hair color, or your height, empathy is not fixed at birth. It is a skill that you develop, meaning it can be practiced and improved with intention over time.

TECHNICAL STUFF

Neuroscience studies have shown that the brain regions associated with empathy are responsive to experience and training. You may have a higher natural starting point but it's not a ceiling — it's only where you begin.

Women Are More Naturally Empathetic than Men

This one's nuanced. Studies suggest that differences in empathy between genders are largely explained by social conditioning, not neurological hardwiring: Women are more often rewarded for empathetic behavior and more often punished for the absence of it. Men are socialized in the opposite direction. What looks like a natural difference is frequently a trained one.

Once You're an Empathetic Leader, You've Arrived

Empathy is a practice: a journey not a destination. Leaders who think they've "figured it out" stop listening as carefully and stop questioning their assumptions. The best empathetic leaders stay curious about where they have blind spots, never confident they've eliminated them.

IN THIS CHAPTER

» **Challenging your assumptions about what empathy looks like for each person**

» **Divorcing empathy from negative emotions**

» **Receiving feedback as data rather than as criticism**

Chapter 20

Ten Mistakes for an Empathetic Leader to Avoid

Most empathy failures aren't coming from leaders who don't care. They come from leaders who care but express it in ways that quietly undercut the very thing they're trying to do. Softening a hard truth. Rushing to fix instead of witnessing. Explaining away someone's pain instead of sitting with it. None of these mistakes require bad intent, and that's exactly why they're so common, and why they deserve their own chapter.

WARNING

This entire chapter comes with a Warning icon stamped on it! It's a great catalog of what *not* to do.

Lowering Your Standards

High standards are not the enemy of empathy; they are one of its clearest expressions. When you lower the bar for someone in the name of kindness, you are not protecting them. You are communicating, without saying it, that you don't believe they are capable of more. That is not empathy. That is a quiet form of disrespect dressed up as compassion. Empathetic leaders hold people to high expectations and support them in meeting those expectations. Both, simultaneously.

Confusing Empathy with Fixing

The urge to fix someone's problems when they're sharing something hard might not be empathy; it could be your own discomfort looking for an exit. The moment you move to fix, you are signaling that their experience is a problem to be managed rather than a reality to be witnessed.

Failing to Regulate Your Own Emotions

REMEMBER

Self-regulation is not suppression. It is the ability to feel what you feel without letting it make your decisions. It is the floor every other empathy skill is built on, and without it, everything else is unstable.

Equating Emotion with Weakness

Treating your emotions — or your team's — as liabilities or inconveniences that need to be managed is not strength. The leaders who can accurately read the emotional temperature of a room, name what they see, and respond with intention are the most capable. Emotions are some of the most sophisticated pieces of data that you as a leader have access to.

Taking Feedback Personally

REMEMBER

When someone gives you feedback about your leadership, they are not attacking your character. They are giving you data about your impact. If you receive that data defensively, you send one very clear message to their team: honesty is not safe here.

Once that message lands, the honest feedback stops. What replaces it is a carefully edited version of reality designed to protect your feelings, which is exactly the version of reality that produces the worst decisions. Feedback is a gift. Empathetic leaders receive it like one.

Assuming Your Intent Is Your Impact

Good intentions do not cancel bad impact. When someone tells you that something you said or did hurt them, "That wasn't what I meant" is not a response; it is a deflection that centers your experience. And the worst part? This is the exact moment where empathy requires you to center their experience.

REMEMBER

Intent matters for understanding what happens. It does not determine whether the impact was real. It was absolutely real. That is where the conversation has to start.

Failing to Apologize Authentically

A bad apology can do more damage than no apology at all. "I'm sorry you felt that way" is not accountability; it is a reframe that quietly puts the problem back on the person you hurt. An authentic apology names what happened, owns the impact without qualification, and does not pivot immediately to self-defense or explanation. Authentic apologies cannot be performed. People know the difference between a leader who is genuinely sorry and one who is managing optics.

Not Following Up after Vulnerable Conversations

Sharing difficult emotions is an incredibly vulnerable experience. If someone opens up to you and you never mention it again, that silence has significant meaning. You held the door open for them — inviting them into a psychologically safe space — then you all but slammed it behind them.

TIP

Follow-ups don't need to be grand. It's as simple as a sentence, a check-in, or anything that proves you are still holding what they gave you. The follow-up is where empathy becomes credible.

Invalidating Emotions with Logic

Responding to someone's emotional experience with a rational explanation for why they shouldn't be feeling it is dismissive. You are not incorrect to lead with logic in an emotional moment; you are, however, incorrect about the timing. Always acknowledge what the person is feeling before you bring in logic.

Ignoring Cultural and Individual Differences

Empathy requires a broad lens because if it's only applied through a single template, it's not actually empathy; it's assumption. What reads as directness to one person lands as aggression to another. What feels like a warm check-in to you may feel like surveillance to someone whose history with authority taught them that attention meant trouble. What is considered appropriate emotional expression in one culture is considered unprofessional in another.

REMEMBER

Empathetic leaders stay curious about the specific person in front of them — their background, their preferences, their context — because meeting people where they are requires first knowing exactly where that is.

IN THIS CHAPTER

- » Recognizing the difference between empathy as a feeling and empathy as a decision
- » Acknowledging misconceptions that make empathetic leadership harder than it needs to be
- » Building your relationship with discomfort

Chapter 21
Ten Reassurances for Empathetic Leaders

Empathetic leadership will test you in ways that can feel like failure when moments of doubt show up, when frustration feels like proof you are not cut out for this, or when a boundary feels like a betrayal of the practice. This chapter presents reminders for those moments when self-doubt creeps in. And remember: You're doing things right more often than you think.

Empathy Isn't Agreement, It's Understanding

Agreement and understanding are two separate acts; one requires you to share a position, while the other only requires you to try to see how someone arrived at theirs.

REMEMBER

You can understand a perspective you fundamentally disagree with. You can hold space for someone's experience without endorsing their conclusion. You can listen all the way to the end without changing your mind. That is not a failure of empathy; that is empathy working exactly as it should.

Discomfort Is a Sign You're Growing, Not Failing

Discomfort isn't evidence that you are doing something wrong; it's proof that you are doing something real. The goal isn't to make empathy something that is not difficult. The goal is to know that it is difficult but then do it anyway.

You Don't Have to Fix Everything to Make a Difference

TIP

The pressure to solve, resolve, and restore is one of the heaviest things a leader carries, and it is largely self-imposed. Not every problem you encounter is yours to fix. Not every person who brings you something hard needs you to make it better. Sometimes the most meaningful thing you can offer is the simple, radical act of staying present without an agenda.

Everyone Is Doing the Best They Can with What They Know

There will be days when someone's best doesn't feel good enough, or when a person keeps making the same mistake. And those mistakes will test every reserve of patience you have. Remember that their behavior is coming from somewhere — from fear, from conditioning, from a previous environment — that taught them something different to what you're asking of them now. This isn't an excuse for poor performance; it's a starting point for a more useful conversation about it.

Frustration Doesn't Mean You've Lost Empathy

Feeling frustrated doesn't mean you're failing at empathy; it means you are a human being living a human experience. Your humanity is not a character flaw.

REMEMBER

Frustration and empathy are not mutually exclusive. You can feel frustrated and still choose how you respond. You can be depleted and still decide not to take it out on the people around you. The feeling is not the failure. What you do with it is what matters.

Empathy Doesn't Mean Saying "Yes"

Empathy is not a synonym for accommodation. It does not require you to agree to every request, absorb every boundary violation, or contort yourself into positions that compromise your integrity or your team's well-being in order to avoid disappointing someone. In fact, the empathetic "No" — the one that is clear, honest, and delivered with genuine care for the person receiving it — is one of the most sophisticated leadership moves available to you.

It's Okay to Disappoint Someone If You're Being Honest

You are not responsible for how someone feels about the truth. You are responsible for telling it with care. Those are two very different jobs.

Protecting Your Peace Protects Your People

Protecting your peace is maintenance, not indulgence. It is the ongoing work of making sure there is something left to give by the time your team needs it. A depleted leader at the head of a struggling team is not noble. It is two problems where there could have been just one.

Empathy Isn't about Being Liked, It's about Being Trusted

Being liked is easy to achieve and easy to lose. Being trusted is harder to build and far more durable. The empathetic leader who tells someone a hard truth, holds a standard that is uncomfortable, or delivers a "No" that disappoints may not be liked in that moment. But they are building something more valuable: the credibility that comes from being a person whose words and actions can be relied on.

You're Building Something Most People Have Never Experienced: Leadership with Heart

Most people have been led by someone who kept their distance. Who managed from behind process and policy and the performance of authority. Who treated emotion as a liability and people as resources. That is the leadership model that the majority of your team has been shaped by and it has left marks. Skepticism. Self-protection. The careful habit of giving just enough and holding the rest back.

TIP

Keep in mind that what you are building — slowly, imperfectly, through the daily practice of showing up with both accountability and genuine human care — is something many of the people you lead have genuinely never experienced before. That is not a small thing. It is, in fact, the whole thing. Keep going!

Appendix

Glossary

This appendix provides a handy list of terms you may want to refer back to quickly, all collected in one place.

Active listening. The practice of being fully present in a conversation — not just hearing the words but absorbing the meaning behind them — before you respond. It's the difference between listening to understand and listening to reply. Most people do the latter without realizing it.

Aesthetic. The visual and emotional language something signals to communicate what it values, before it says a single word.

Aesthetic empathy. The act of "feeling into" an object — projecting yourself so fully into a piece of art, architecture, or nature that you perceive the emotion as living inside the object itself, not just inside you.

Aesthetic theory. The study of how and why humans experience beauty, art, and form; specifically, what happens inside us when we encounter something that moves us. This term was coined by German philosopher Robert Vischer in 1873.

Affective concern. A genuine feeling of care and concern for another person's well-being.

Affective resonance. The psychological and sociological dynamic where an individual shares, mirrors, or experiences a corresponding emotional state in response to another person's emotions or shared environment; a shared experience between people.

Apathy. The absence of feeling; not a decision to disengage, but an inability or unwillingness to care in the first place.

Authority. The formal power that comes with a position; the organizational permission to make decisions, direct others, and be held accountable for outcomes. It is given to you by the structure you operate within, not earned from the people you lead.

Bias. A systematic tendency to favor certain people, perspectives, or conclusions over others, often without awareness, often without intention, and almost always in ways that feel like objectivity rather than preference.

Cognitive empathy. The ability to understand what someone else is thinking or feeling; not because you feel it yourself, but because you've made a deliberate, conscious effort to see the world from their perspective.

Command-and-control leadership. A top-down management style built on the premise that the person at the top has the answers, makes the decisions, and expects compliance from everyone below them. Authority flows in one direction (down) while information flows in the other direction (up) but only when asked for directly from someone higher up in the chain of command.

Compassionate empathy. The ability to understand someone's feelings and share their experience, while using those feelings to take action to help them.

Compliance. Public conformity without private agreement; you agree with the group while internally holding a different view.

Conformity. The act of aligning your attitudes, beliefs, or behaviors with social norms, group expectations, or established standards.

Conscious bias. A deliberate, explicit preference or prejudice; a judgment about a person or group that you are aware of holding and that intentionally shapes how you treat them.

Core value. A belief so fundamental to who you are that it guides your behavior even when no one is watching, even when it costs you something, and even when every other pressure in the room is pushing you in a different direction.

Culture. The living, breathing set of unwritten rules that govern how people behave in an organization; what's really valued, what's actually rewarded, what's genuinely safe to say, and what happens to people who color outside the lines. This is not a mission statement; culture is what happens when nobody important is watching.

Curiosity. The genuine desire to understand something more fully than you currently do; not to confirm what you already believe, but to discover what you might be missing.

Emotional contagion. The phenomenon of absorbing and mirroring the emotions of the people around you, often without realizing it's happening. It's the reason a room can feel heavy before anyone has said a word, or why one person's energy can shift the entire dynamic of a meeting.

Emotional empathy. The ability to physically and emotionally experience what another person is feeling; also known as *affective empathy*. This goes a step further than just understanding the other person — it is feeling what they feel.

Emotional regulation. The ability to recognize, understand, and manage your emotional responses in real time — especially under pressure — so that your reactions serve the outcome you actually want, not just the impulse you're feeling.

Empathetic leader. Someone who has made the deliberate, sustained commitment to understand the experience of the people they lead, and to let that understanding shape every decision they make, every conversation they have, and every culture they build.

Empathetic leadership. The practice of leading people through genuine understanding rather than authority alone; building relationships, cultures, and systems that make people feel seen, heard, and valued not as a byproduct of good management, but as the entire point of it.

Empathy. *Noun:* The ability to understand or share the feelings of another person. *Verb:* The act of perspective-taking to broaden your own view of the world.

Empathy gap. The distance between what you think you understand about someone else's experience and what their experience actually is; the space that your assumptions, biases, blind spots, and own perspective fill in.

Empathy spectrum. The range of human capacity for emotional understanding; from full, active empathy at one end to apathy at the other, with indifference sitting somewhere in between. Where someone falls on that spectrum at any given moment isn't fixed; it shifts based on environment, experience, leadership, and safety.

Groupthink. What happens when the desire for harmony in a group becomes more powerful than the desire for truth. It's the moment a team stops thinking collectively and starts agreeing collectively; nobody notices the difference until the damage is done.

Heyoka empath. Considered the most powerful and disruptive form of empath in Lakota Sioux tradition; a person who feels and reflects the emotions of those around them, but does so in reverse, acting as a mirror that shows people what they most need to see rather than what they most want to hear.

Humanity. The quality of being fully human; not in the biological sense, but in the rational one. It's the capacity to recognize yourself in other people, and to let that recognition change how you treat them.

Indifference. The decision to withhold feeling. An indifferent person is aware of what's happening around them; they simply don't consider it worth their emotional investment. Unlike apathy, indifference is a choice; you feel, but you've decided it doesn't matter to you.

Influence. The ability to move people — their thinking, behavior, commitment, and direction — not because you have the power to require it, but because you've built the trust and understanding that makes them want to move.

Informational influence. Conforming because you believe the group has accurate information or a better understanding of a situation. Conformity driven by genuine belief that others know better than you do.

Intergroup empathy. The ability to genuinely understand and care about the experience of people who belong to a different group to your own; whether that group is defined by department, function, culture, nationality, race, gender, or any other identity that creates an "us" and a "them."

Intragroup empathy. The ability to genuinely understand and care about the experience of the people within your own group — your immediate team, your department, your organization — recognizing that shared membership doesn't automatically produce shared understanding.

Internalization. The process of absorbing and integrating external ideas, values, or behaviors into your own character, identity, or system.

Intuitive empathy. The capacity to know what someone is feeling or needing before conscious reasoning catches up. Distinct from emotional empathy because it's less about feeling what another person feels and more about knowing their inner state through perception.

Leadership. The practice of guiding, inspiring, and creating the conditions for other people to do their best work; not through the authority of a title, but through the quality of the relationships you build and the trust you earn from the people choosing to follow you.

Limbic reasoning. The neurological capacity for sharing deep emotional states. The process of making decisions based on emotional response rather than rational analysis; letting the brain's emotional center drive conclusions before the thinking brain has had a chance to weigh in.

Manager. Someone who is responsible for the performance, output, and day-to-day functioning of a team, ensuring that the right work gets done, by the right people, in the right way, at the right time.

Mentalizing. The ongoing, dynamic process of reading and modeling other minds in real social situations; simultaneously holding various ideas in your mind: what the person knows and doesn't know, what they want and fear, what they believe about you, what they believe about themselves, and how history is shaping their current state. A form of cognitive empathy.

Narrative imagination. The cognitive ability to step outside your own immediate experiences and mentally inhabit the perspectives, stories, and lived realities of others.

Normative influence. Conforming to be accepted and liked by the group or to avoid rejection.

Performance. The act of presenting a version of yourself that you believe the environment requires, rather than the version of yourself that is actually true.

Perspective-taking. The deliberate act of stepping into another person's point of view. It's seeing the situation through their eyes, from their history, with their values and their concern; not just representing that others have perspectives but actively inhabiting them.

Psychic numbing. The tendency to feel less compassion and willingness to act as the number of victims in a negative situation increases.

Psychological safety. The shared belief within a group that it is safe to speak up, take risks, make mistakes, and be honest without fear of humiliation, punishment, or rejection.

Relationship. The living infrastructure of leadership; the human connection through which trust is built, influence is earned, culture is created, and everything else a leader is trying to accomplish either succeeds or fails.

Resonance. A phenomenon that happens when two objects' natural frequencies match and the output amplifies.

Selective empathy. Connecting more deeply with certain team members and not realizing it; this can easily happen in group situations.

Social identify theory. Our sense of self is deeply tied to the groups we belong to; we categorize people, identify with groups, and compare ourselves to others to boost our self-esteem, which often leads to intragroup favoritism and intergroup bias.

Somatic knowing. The intelligence of the body; the information your physical self-registers before your conscious mind has caught up. It's the tightness in your chest before a difficult conversation, the unease in your gut when something feels off but you can't yet explain why, and the instinctive sense that a room has shifted even though nothing visible has changed.

Theory of mind. The ability to understand that other people have their own thoughts, beliefs, desires, and perspectives that are different from your own, and to use that understanding to accurately predict and interpret their behavior.

Trust. The belief — built through repeated experience, not stated intention — that someone will do what they say they will do, that they have your best interests genuinely at heart, and that being honest with them is safe. Trust is the foundation everything else in leadership is built on.

Unconscious bias. A preference, assumption, or judgment about a person or group that operates below the level of your awareness — shaping your decisions, behavior, and perception of people without your conscious knowledge or consent.

Index

Numerics

A

B

C

D

E

F

I

J

K

L

M

N

O

P

Q

R

S

T

U

V

W

X

Z

About the Author

Sharon Steed started stuttering when she was three years old; and she spent the first 30 years of her life terrified to say her own name.

Before empathy became a corporate maxim, Sharon was learning it the hard way; she learned what it felt like when someone treated a block in her speech not as a message to be heard, but as a problem to be managed. Because of that, she developed a finely tuned radar for the gap between how people intend to make others feel and how they actually land.

Since that time, Sharon has become a subject-matter expert on empathy at work. An international keynote speaker, she's spoken on stages in 20 countries spanning five continents. She's helped organizations such as Google, Microsoft, `Booking.com`, Northwestern Mutual, and dozens of others improve performance, retain top talent, and be better communicators by teaching them how to be actively empathetic.

She is the author of several courses on LinkedIn Learning including Communicating with Empathy that, since it launched in 2017, has been translated into a dozen languages and has surpassed one million views. She has given a TEDx talk on empowering insecurities, and she's the author of the O'Reilly Media, Inc. eBook *Empathy at Work* (2019).

Stuttering put her on the receiving end of what an empathy failure looked and felt like before she ever had the language for what empathy was. She turned that education into teachable nuggets that she shares in her keynotes, courses, and writing. Drawing on her own experience as a person who stutters, Sharon brings a uniquely personal lens to the science and practice of empathetic leadership. She shows that vulnerability isn't a weakness to overcome but a skill that builds trust, loyalty, and stronger teams.

Originally from Chicago, Sharon currently lives in Philadelphia with her husband and mini goldendoodle. When she is not writing or traveling the world speaking, you can find her under a barbell at her neighborhood gym, exploring the city with friends, or watching movies with her husband.

Dedication

Much of empathy happens in silence. It's taking a moment to reflect on what just happened, listening to what someone else experienced, or questioning your own beliefs to see if they still feel true to who you are becoming. But that's when real growth happens — in the seconds and minutes when you shift how you process pain or joy or frustration in a way that's more productive for this moment. Empathy truly is what happens in the trenches, and it's often messy and uncomfortable and done without an audience.

That's why this book is dedicated to the community of people who support, encourage, and empower those with special needs and/or disabilities. I watched my mom care for my severely developmentally disabled brother with largely no help and little guidance except for those few that offered to be in community with her. And those people — the ones who choose to show up, especially when there's no fanfare — are genuine heroes to the siblings, loved ones, and parents of those with special needs and disabilities. This book is for you.

Author's Acknowledgments

Writing a book can be an incredibly solitary endeavor. You're staring at a blinking cursor on a blank page for far longer than you expected to, and it's easy to forget — as you spend hours ideating, outlining, writing, researching, deleting, adjusting, rewriting, researching more, editing, over and over again until you finally finish — that you aren't actually doing this alone. There is a community of people rooting for you, believing in you, and helping you work through ideas. Many of those people don't even realize their impact on you and how their words got you to where you currently are. That's who I want to acknowledge here: the ones who may not know just how invaluable their presence has been for me.

First, I have to thank the speech therapist I was seeing when I started my career in speaking. I don't think I would have ever even thought to try it if it wasn't for her encouragement. Stephie, none of this would have happened without you. Your humble confidence, kindness, and positivity shifted how I viewed the world. I truly cannot articulate just how grateful I am.

I have to also thank Jim Remsik, the organizer of the first-ever professional conference I spoke at. I truly believe you are a direct reflection of the community you build. Jim, your community was welcoming, patient, positive, and almost aggressively insistent that I was onto something with my work. So much of what I've been able to do this past decade can be traced directly back to your event, your community, and to you. I'm thankful that you're in my community.

I've met so many incredible people at conferences and events throughout the years, and many of them have had an immeasurable impact on my career and me as a person. To everyone I've met along the way — after a talk, in the hallway, at drinks or dinner, in the hotel, or as I was wandering in the city — these conversations were crucial in my development as a person and in my work on empathy. I've learned so much from you.

Thank you so much to everyone on the For Dummies team at Wiley especially Tracy Boggier for believing in this content and my story.

Massive thanks to the many friends and family who have been so excited and proud and encouraging throughout the years about my non-traditional path. Your kind words and enthusiasm have all meant a lot to me, especially in those moments when I wasn't sure if I should keep going. A special thank you to my parents and siblings who have been on my team since day one; thanks for being my biggest fans.

And to my husband, Wes: thanks for seeing in me what I struggled to see, especially in the beginning. No one has supported me more throughout this journey than you. I said in my wedding vows that being with you was the best decision I made in my life; those words are even more true all these years later. I'm deeply humbled that you choose me every day. I am so proud to be your wife.

Publisher's Acknowledgments

Executive Editor: Tracy Boggier
Development Editor: Dan Mersey
Managing Editor: Prathyusha PV
Production Editor: Magesh Elangovan
Cover Image: © Fotos1501gpr/Shutterstock